ROUTLEDGE LIBRARY EDITIONS: ARTIFICIAL INTELLIGENCE

Volume 8

THE SOFT MACHINE

THE SOFT MACHINE

Cybernetic Fiction

DAVID PORUSH

Routledge
Taylor & Francis Group
LONDON AND NEW YORK

First published in 1985 by Methuen, Inc.

This edition first published in 2018
by Routledge
2 Park Square, Milton Park, Abingdon, Oxon OX14 4RN

and by Routledge
711 Third Avenue, New York, NY 10017

Routledge is an imprint of the Taylor & Francis Group, an informa business

British Library Cataloguing in Publication Data
A catalogue record for this book is available from the British Library

ISBN: 978-0-8153-8566-0 (Set)
ISBN: 978-0-429-49236-5 (Set) (ebk)
ISBN: 978-0-8153-5513-7 (Volume 8) (hbk)
ISBN: 978-1-351-12968-8 (Volume 8) (ebk)

Publisher's Note
The publisher has gone to great lengths to ensure the quality of this reprint but points out that some imperfections in the original copies may be apparent.

Disclaimer
The publisher has made every effort to trace copyright holders and would welcome correspondence from those they have been unable to trace.

THE SOFT MACHINE
CYBERNETIC FICTION

DAVID PORUSH

METHUEN · NEW YORK AND LONDON

FOR SAL & VAL
AND MY PARENTS

First published in 1985 by
Methuen, Inc.
733 Third Avenue,
New York, NY 10017

Published in Great Britain by
Methuen & Co. Ltd
11 New Fetter Lane,
London EC4P 4EE

Typeset in Great Britain by
Scarborough Typesetting Services
and printed at the
University Press, Cambridge

Library of Congress Cataloging in Publication Data

Porush, David, 1952–
The soft machine.
Bibliography: p.
Includes index.
1. American fiction – 20th century – History and criticism.
2. Cybernetics in literature.
3. Artificial intelligence in literature. 4. Machinery in literature. 5. Technology in literature. 6. Science fiction, American – History and criticism.
I. Title.
PS374.C9P67 1984
813'.54'09356 84–20678

ISBN 0–416–37860–9
ISBN 0–416–37870–6 (pbk.)

British Library Cataloguing in Publication Data

Porush, David
The soft machine: cybernetic fiction.
1. American fiction – 20th century – History and criticism
I. Title
813'.54'09 PS379

ISBN 0–416–37860–9
ISBN 0–416–37870–6 pbk

CONTENTS

''The machine is always the counterfeiter's ally.''
(Hugh Kenner, *The Counterfeiters*)

PREFACE

The discussion in the following pages proceeds from three assumptions.

One is that the academic, elusive body of works generally called postmodern fiction is still an effective force in our culture. This has not always been a popular belief, even among teachers and scholars of literature. It differs from a view, now thankfully becoming obsolete, that contemporary fiction, particularly of the wilder species, has exhausted its sources, is irrelevant to the mass culture, and is possessed of a dwindling audience. Rather, the history of this difficult fiction shows that it has a habit of creating its own audience and of teaching us how to read in new ways, so that we can begin to read the world in new ways.

My second assumption is that disciplinary boundaries are comforting but illusory props, necessary as local, social enclaves of organization but dispensable in the larger epistemological scheme of things. The biases that help shape science are inexplicable without looking at the culture and personalities that breed them.

In the same way, literature is as much a product of the technological and scientific milieu as it is of the artistic one. Some of the large ideas, call them theories or metaphors – that humans are machines, that the observer affects the phenomenon observed, that information can be quantified – alter the way work is done in art. Metaphors invented by artists imply new ways of seeing, demolish mere logic, provoke alternatives, and lead to new theories in science. When techniques are the progenitors of specialties and specialties breed new techniques, specialization is taken for granted, but it leads to the atomizing of knowledge that can obscure broader unities about the shape of nature and about the effects of our observations and actions on nature.

That the disciplines are united by larger, more fundamental beliefs is not so much an article of faith that I brought with me to this investigation as it is a lesson I was taught in seeking an answer to my original question: why is the image of a soft machine – a construction part human and part machine – so prevalent in postmodern fiction? This led me to understand that the computers that now dominate our landscape – intellectual and otherwise – are the products of ideas in cybernetics. From there it became clear that cybernetics is a science originally invented by theoreticians who sought a way to recover certainty after the code of physics became "marred" by the uncertainty of quantum physics. Norbert Wiener, the father of cybernetics, felt that the doctrine of chance "infecting" the New Physics belonged more to the realm of art and romance. And yet, even before Werner Heisenberg's work, artists such as Paul Valéry and Edgar Allan Poe, and later many modernists, enacted the same struggle by attempting to free their art from the contingencies of invention, from accident, from mere chance by making their works as technically pure as any machine (a struggle Wylie Sypher explores in his excellent book *Literature and Technology*). After cybernetics offered a larger and more effective vision of the *machina mundi*, however, the postmodern reaction set in. Our contemporary era finds writers seeking some refuge from technique in the techniques of fiction. Or to borrow a medical metaphor, postmodern authors seek a way to innoculate themselves against technique by injecting its hardness into the soft body of their texts. Cybernetic fiction, the result of this dialectic, is the subject of this book.

My third assumption is not a new one either. It derives from the simple, but ultimately unprovable, assertion that all language is based on metaphor and that metaphors therefore hold the key to deciphering the code of our knowledge, to mapping the hidden vectors of our cosmologies. Along with many theorists of language, I am convinced that the structures of our beliefs are founded on the metaphors we have chosen; that is, metaphors are the traces of our fundamental wishes and pretenses. The metaphor of the machine especially fascinates me. I have followed Colin Murray Turbayne's lead in his book *The Myth of Metaphor* to come to believe that the vision of the universe as a machine is *an invention*, a fiction, a device for simplifying and summing. In the hands of Descartes and Newton and all their heirs it has become what John Barth calls "a screen" that partly obscures the truth. Yet, the metaphor has grown so irresistible that *it uses us* rather than the other way around.

Finally, I believe that many of the questions I grapple with find no satisfactory resolution here. This book portrays the see-sawing of an argument whose roots are as old as western thought and whose resolution lies in the unforseeable future. However, I believe our period in the history of that argument is a special one. The machine metaphysic has begun to find its ultimate embodiment (in the shape of computers, artificial intelligence devices, robots and other human cousins) with daring and remarkable rapidity. This proliferation has been motivated by, and is reflected in, cybernetics. The proposal of counter-metaphors has taken on its vivid form in cybernetic fiction, which is trying to tell us something. For these reasons, I feel that this moment is a special one for fiction as it mediates between art and technique, and yet I do not believe, nor do I think that the authors I discuss believe, that this special moment is likely to offer any final resolutions to the ongoing dialectic between humans and machines. Rather, cybernetic fiction simply engages the battle in a continuing war of metaphors.

This work was begun after I took on a dare by Ray Federman, whom I have been lucky enough to count as a friend as well as a teacher. It was pursued partly with the assistance of a National Endowment for the Humanities Summer Seminar Stipend in support of study under the guidance of Professor E. Fred Carlisle, who has remained a constant benefactor and advisor. My fellow seminarians at Michigan State University that summer of 1980 were also extremely supportive and engaging, willing to share and listen: to them I am very grateful.

I am especially lucky to be surrounded by generous colleagues and graduate students who read and discussed portions of the manuscript with finer and more critical judgment than mine. Professor William Benzon, Karen Burke Lefevre, Constance Ostrowski, and Steven B. Katz all reviewed portions of the manuscript in various stages of its disrepair, discussed it with me, and rescued me from much of my own nonsense. A late-night discussion with the ever incisive Professor Geoffrey Green, my friend, helped me unriddle several particularly stubborn conundrums.

Finally, none of this would have been possible without the constant support and love of Sally and Valerie, who brought their Southern warmth into my long Yankee winter and taught me how to be surprised again.

DP

Troy, New York

ONE

THE METAPHOR OF THE MACHINE

"The computing machine serves not only as a tool but as a metaphor; as a way of conceptualizing man and society. The notion that the brain is like a computer, that man is like a machine, that society is like a feed-back mechanism all reflect the impact of cybernetics on our idea of human nature. . . . Having taken deep roots and being partially unconscious it is partially invulnerable to evidence."
(Ulric Neisser, "Computers as tools and metaphors")[1]

"The metaphysics of mechanism can be dispensed with. The best way to do this is to show that it is only a metaphor; and the best way to show this is to invent a new metaphor."
(Colin Turbayne, *The Myth of Metaphor*)[2]

OUR CYBERNETIC AGE

We live not in an information age but a cybernetic one. Our lives are dominated not only by the getting and sending of information but the spin-offs from this technology. Children toddle around public places and homes clutching large-button plastic computers that speak in robotic voices and flash not pictures but "graphics." Students take programable calculators into math tests. In their off hours, their fingers play over the controls of video games and "micros," their faces lit up by the light of CRT screens, bodies moving in rhythm to a complex feedback mechanism, eyes, minds and hands locked in a looped circuit of reflex and reward with a more-than-mere-game. In the video arcade, the machines are united by a single principle: ultimately, hardware defeats exhaustible and vulnerable organs and intelligences grown in flesh and housed in bone. Next time you're there, watch the players hitched to their boxes and ask who controls what. Or what controls whom.

A spasm of punk or New Wave which swept pop music a few years ago both celebrated and warned us against these cybernetic developments. Punks affected a toneless speech, black and white clothes, hair colored in the impossible colors of plastic; they abhorred tans, preferring the paleness that announces perpetual life indoors, nearer the machines. Their dress incorporated small flashing lights and LED numbers, and they danced with the expressionless and stiff movements of robots, evolving a new machine aesthetic out of their bodies. The technological fears and dreams of an earlier generation, expressed in metaphor, prophecy and fiction, were here incarnated in the *style* of a later one. This style partly relied on its silence. One doesn't talk about hi-tech (it's too obvious to mention), one lives inside it.

Meanwhile, philosophers debate new transformations of old questions as passionately as ever: are human brains like a computer? can all knowledge be reduced to a set of algorithms, or mechanical techniques for discovering the truth, or highly rationalized systems of organizing information? is language a complex device hard-wired by genetics into the human mind? is there a significant difference between machine-generated art and human works? what sort of self-consciousness distinguishes human self-knowledge from computer consciousness? is there anything forbidden to a machine which humans can do? (We already know that there are things the machine can do that people cannot.)

These are the signs and questions of our cybernetic age. I take the word *cybernetic* to embrace not only the information sciences but a metaphor so deeply engrained in our culture, so silently driven down to the roots of our imaginations, that it achieves the status of an element in a new mythology, as Ulric Neisser suggests. I visualize certain figures in this mythology: a steely robot embraces a woman and plays a system of buttons implanted along her back, determining her responses; a young player finds his fingers have become wires that bind him to the exposed circuit of a computer game; a woman removes her face to reveal the flat-etched architecture of an integrated circuit board. In the parlance of science fiction, these are "cybernauts." They are the incarnations of a metaphor that can be stated quite simply: humans are only machines. Soft machines.

Fiction in the cybernetic age reaches a smaller audience than its counterpart in music. Yet, like the New Wave in music, cybernetic fiction announces its message in style and form as well as in words and substance. It has its own techniques corresponding to the weird and hyper-structured sounds produced by synthesizers equipped with a microprocessor. The confusing multiplication of simultaneous voices and instrumentations, the feeling of unlimited opportunity for expression, or conversely the spare minimalization of mathematically determined notes, rhythms, voices and tones also have corresponding features in cybernetic fiction. Of the two art forms, cybernetic fiction is older. The works I treat in this volume were all written before 1980. The latest, Joseph McElroy's *Plus*, was published in 1976. The others, fiction by John Barth, Donald Barthelme, Samuel Beckett, William Burroughs, Thomas Pynchon and Kurt Vonnegut, are products of the 1950s, 1960s and 1970s. That metaphor to which they respond, the simple cybernetic one, is even older.

The fear that we are only machines is a heritage of the Renaissance. As early as 1641, Descartes suggested that the human body "be considered as a kind of machine, so made up and composed of bones, nerves, muscles, veins, blood and skin, that although there were in it no mind, it would still exhibit the same motions which it at present manifests."[3] More threatening yet is the consideration that not only our bodies but also our minds are machines, a consideration that attacks us in that portion of ourselves we consider to be most free, most invulnerable to explanation and control.

These fears are apparently confirmed and multiplied with the growth of our technology. From the seventeenth to the nineteenth century, man was challenged by machines that did his manual work. But the advent of calculating machines like the one invented by Charles Babbage in the 1840s, and the growth of a science which sought to bring the entire natural cosmos under the dominion of logical algorithms – the Victorian view of a clockwork nature that is utimately expressed in the logical positivism of Russell and Whitehead early in this century – made it clear that more than our brute qualities could be duplicated by devices of our own invention.

Early in the eighteenth century, Jonathan Swift directed his satire at the mechanical simple-mindedness with which empirical methods are applied, a problem many sciences still struggle with two and a half centuries later. In one passage in *Gulliver's Travels*, Swift sought some technology fantastic enough to express the misguided logic of his contemporaries, those "natural philosophers" who believed that the young techniques of scientific method guaranteed answers. Swift knew that the new science, in its way, was as filled with blind faith as any medieval alchemy. He was partly enamored and partly distrustful of the movement by his predecessors in the Royal Academy, Bacon, Sprat, and Wilkinson to discover the grammar of knowledge, the perfect language in which nature's truth could be revealed. For those who struggled with the new structure of knowledge born with the scientific method, the most important question was whether or not there was a language that could match the rigor and orderliness that was being discovered in the world. This problem, of the "unresolved relationship of word and thing – or *res* and *verba*," was to plague the Royal Society in its search for a "scientific language."[4]

We can trace the longing for a language matched perfectly with nature to more mystical roots in medieval sources like the cabbala and sciences like alchemy, where the manipulation of matter is a question of discovering the "name in God's mind," the real sign of the thing. Locke, who inherits the question from Bacon and Sprat, concludes that this search for an Adamic language proceeds from false presumptions about how human understanding works. At the same time, Locke and his friend Robert Boyle conclude that language is an inescapable issue in the search for understanding.

Strangely enough, two centuries later these issues are resurrected in the form of a search for a universal grammar and for the mechanics of language, the former by strict structuralists and linguists such as Noam Chomsky, and the latter by artificial intelligence researchers, who seek an algorithm for language that will permit them to program a machine with human-like linguistic capabilities. Swift was parodying the attempt by Wilkins, under the aegis of the Royal Society, to describe the perfect grammar of scientific language in his *Essay towards a Real Character and a Philosophical Language* published in 1668.[5] Swift satirizes Wilkins's search for method by creating an absurd language machine, the prototype of much more sophisticated models we will encounter in the fiction of Burroughs, Barth and McElroy.

We can only imagine what his version would have looked like if he'd had Chomsky and an IBM 3033 as his object instead of Wilkins and the wooden printing press. But Swift was still able to portray with great vividness the inherent limitations of empiricism in his image of a hyper-evolved printing press. Gulliver, touring the Academy of Lagado, is ushered into the laboratory of one of their great philosophers. This scientist claims to have devised a machine that will help even the most ignorant person to "write books in Philosophy, Poetry, Politicks, Law, Mathematicks and Theology, without the least assistance from genius or study."

> He then led me to the Frame, about the Sides whereof all his Pupils stood in Ranks. It was Twenty Foot square, placed in the Middle of the Room. The Superfices were composed of several Bits of Wood, about the Bigness of a Dye, but some larger than others. They were all linked together by slender Wires. These Bits of Wood were covered on every Square with Papers pasted on them, and on these Papers were written all the Words of their Language in their several Moods, Tenses and Declensions, but without any Order. The Professor then desired me to observe, for he was going to set his Engine at work. The Pupils at his command took each of them hold of an Iron Handle, whereof there were Forty fixed round the Edge of the Frame, and giving them a sudden Turn, the whole Disposition of the Words was entirely changed. He then commanded Six and Thirty of the Lads to read the several Lines softly as they appeared upon the Frame; and where they found three or four Words together that might make Part of a Sentence, they dictated to the four remaining Boys who were Scribes. This Work was repeated three or four Times, and at every Turn the Engine was so contrived, that the Words shifted into new Places, as the square Bits of Wood moved upside down.
>
> Six Hours a-Day the young Students were employed in this Labour, and the Professor showed me several Volumes in large Folio already collected, of broken Sentences, which he intended to piece together, and out of those rich Materials to give the World a compleat Body of all Arts and Sciences. . . .

> He assured me that this Invention had employed all his thoughts from his youth, that he had emptied the whole Vocabulary into his Frame, and made the strictest computation of the general proportion there is in Books between the numbers of Particles, Nouns, and Verbs, and other parts of Speech.[6]

Though this claptrap machinery may seem primitive to us, Swift's satire is sophisticated. It is directed at that sensitive point in the scientific project – the attempt to determine how humans use language and learn – where even now, two centuries later, the richness of these human phenomena still evade coherent and consistent explanations by linguistics and psychology. Much as Swift's Lagadan machine did, the use of the modern computer to create models for human languages has even further highlighted the distance between our logical definitions and algorithms for language and the way it is naturally, fully, spontaneously and actually used by humans in everyday life. We will know we have succeeded in reducing language to formulae when we can teach the computer to chat with us. So far, that goal has been unattainable. And more than the deployment of computers that will keep us company is at stake. Whole philosophies have bet on the outcome, for in a world where computers seem to have nothing forbidden to them, the enriched, spontaneous and playful way that humans regularly and almost unthinkingly live inside their language represents the last bunker where those who fear the machine have taken their stand.

Swift's Lagadan Word Machine is one of the first literary uses of the machine as a metaphor. It is a rich one, for not only does it satirize all short cuts to true knowledge, all projects "for improving speculative Knowledge by practical and mechanical Operations," but it is also one of the first instances of automation being shown displacing humans not only as laborers but as thinkers. In part, this machine subjugates a few of the humans it was meant to serve (forty lads and the inventor crank the device six hours a day, waiting for scraps of sentences to emerge from piles of nonsense), and in part it is intended to make the work of philosophers, scholars and artists redundant. It is also a fine illustration of what has become the computer programmer's first law – "garbage in, garbage out" – here extended to the scientific method itself: the deficiencies in the Lagadan's concept of language (not to mention of the arts and sciences) create the deficiencies of his random sentence generator. In fact, the machine is an embodiment of everything Swift found deficient in human behavior, a subject he addressed in an earlier satire, "A discourse concerning the mechanical operation of the spirit" (1710). In this case, our Lagadan professor has mimicked the vain and mechanical devotion to method, an instance of the mechanical operation of *his* spirit, by actually building the impossible machine it implies.

Perhaps Swift himself was not aware of all the implications of his metaphorical machine, since some of these implications have accrued to it retrospectively, especially now as we view it from an age dominated by machines and "epistemological techniques." For the All-Knowledge-Generating Computer is also a Writing Machine, and thus a replacement – though a somewhat idiotic one – for the authorial hand. Further, it's a sort of industrial device (the center of what was later to be called a "cottage industry"), a do-it-yourself "Allwriter." Finally, the machine holds an almost hypnotic fascination in its own right for Gulliver. As an observer, a good empiricist, Gulliver describes the thing uncritically, although Swift relies upon the inanity of the device and its inventor to speak for themselves. Yet, through Gulliver, we get a sense of the wonder and the awesome qualities that mechanical complexity in its own right held for him and still holds for us. The silliness of its function is contrasted to the precision of the way it is described, that is, to the marvellousness of its form. The humans, working "softly" around the immense frame, are both reverent and irrelevant.

The power of the machine to focus attention and symbolize the blind devotion to "logical" method, recognized so early by Swift, remains more or less constant through two and a half centuries of its depiction in literature. Though the complexity of the machines that inspire our metaphors has grown, the literary uses to which these metaphors are put remain essentially the same. The machine usually represents both an invitation and a warning; it is simultaneously fascinating and threatening, both superior to and somehow inferior to the punier humans who build, operate and sometimes are subjugated by it. Machines are tangible proof of the success of our scientific techniques, and yet a testament to what is sadly diminished and insufficient in our blind faith that our techniques of discovery will tell us the whole story. While we may be ennobled by the grandiose vision we have constructed of the universe as a clockwork mechanism, there is also something inherently depressing about the vision of our own spirits acting merely as cogs in that mechanism.

To some behaviorists, logical positivists and certain researchers in artificial intelligence, the latter proposition is merely an inevitability. In their view, our minds are mechanisms, complex information processors. To others, especially artists and writers who have a natural bias toward viewing the products of their own labor as manifestations of the freedom and uniqueness of the human spirit, the same proposition is an affront, a monstrous notion. For them, the mind is in the body and the body is an extension of mind. Whatever its status as truth, however, the proposition that we are machines is so deeply embedded in our modern mythology that our everyday lives have achieved an undeniably cybernetic quality. The machine is omnipresent to the point of invisibility, comprising a technological environment so pervasive that it becomes visible only when resurrected by fear (what is it doing to us?) or by metaphor (we are machines!). Both present an invitation to fiction that many of our contemporary authors have found irresistible.

Yet, no matter how monstrous the notion that man is a machine may seem, fiction has confronted it, as it has always confronted monsters, in an attempt to neutralize and express our deepest fears. The growth in our sophistication expressed through our machines and the growth in our sophistication expressed through fiction describe histories that cannot be separated. In this mutual history, fiction has tended to approach the machine with a mixture of fascination and revulsion, with ambiguities and paradoxes that can only be resolved in images that are the stuff of art. If, as Ulric Neisser suggests, the machine has become "invulnerable to evidence," then art is one of our only remaining tactics for making the machine vulnerable again.

THE MORPHOLOGY OF THE MACHINE METAPHOR

This invulnerability of the machine can be clearly seen in the way it has been used historically in literature. I prefer to call the history of this interaction between the machine and literature a "morphology," for while the metaphor of the machine evolves, certain characteristics remain sufficiently constant to enable us to speak about it as the same species of thing. This literary morphology of the nineteenth-century image of the machine has already been documented in great depth by Herbert Sussman in *Victorians and the Machine*, John Kasson in *Civilizing the Machine*, and Leo Marx in *The Machine in the Garden*.[7] H. Bruce Franklin's excellent critical anthology, *Future Perfect*, also looks at the way the machine fascinated nineteenth-century American writers such as Hawthorne, Melville, and Poe.[8] Wylie Sypher explores the special relationship between literature in the nineteenth and early twentieth centuries and the allure of methods and techniques that tended to corrupt it or diminish its aesthetic value. His work shows that as the success of literary innovation grows into literary formula the work of art tends to become alienated from its spontaneous sources; hence his title, *Literature and Technology, the Alien Vision*.[9]

Taken together, these critical works establish the degree to which literature has found in the machine a rich invitation to create metaphor. Sussman carefully traces the evolution of the machine metaphor in English literature of the Victorian period. Although the philosophical knot of the mechanism–vitalism duality had already been anticipated by the Cartesians, the knot was to be untied and retied in literature over and over again. In general, the literary response to the machine falls along the two lines suggested by the dialectic. On the one hand there are those who aestheticize the machine, and on the other there are those who view the machine as a threat and a metaphor for a potentially dangerous impulse in civilization. In the first camp, Sussman places William Morris and Rudyard Kipling. Similarly, Kasson shows that a "machine aesthetic" was characteristic of nineteenth-century American culture and "ultimately extended far beyond characteristics of design, it was a mode of perception," as some of Whitman's poetry demonstrates.[10] Even Emerson, "for all his vigilance against impediments to the imaginative development of the individual, saw technology as offering new aesthetic potentialities as well as challenge."[11]

In the same vein, Hawthorne's story "The artist of the beautiful" embodies this aesthetic potential in a metaphorical machine, a robot butterfly devised by the frustrated genius, Owen Warland.

The butterfly is described as the embodiment of "perfect beauty." When it is crushed by the grasping fingers of an infant, its inventor looks

> placidly at what seemed the ruin of his life's labor and which was yet no ruin. He had caught a far other butterfly than this. When the artist rose high enough to achieve the beautiful, the symbol by which he made it perceptible to mortal sense became of little value in his eyes, while his spirit possessed itself in the enjoyment of the reality.[12]

Similarly, Carlyle wrote about "the aesthetic pleasure" to be found in contemplation of "the technological landscape," of "the technological sublime," and of "spiritualizing the machine."

This emphasis on the aesthetic potentials of the machine, to the point that it is used as a metaphor for ways of perceiving the world, became for the Symbolists a literary method. Following the manifestos for the application of rational method proposed by Poe and translated and popularized in France by Baudelaire, the Symbolists saw the poem as a field for the application of technique. Baudelaire, Mallarmé, and especially Valéry make of the poem, as the latter was to remark, "a kind of machine for producing the poetic state of mind by means of words."[13] Valéry also stressed that method was indispensable to success; in Sypher's terms, "an efficient method reduces the hazards of enterprise." This vision led to Valéry's failed "Le coup de dé," what Sypher calls

> a desperate venture in writing a pure poem by calculating everything, by ruling out the surprises of Chance – the throw of the dice, which is the aesthetic threat, the symbolists surrendered prose to the realm of chance; but the Poem (the Book) should be so duly controlled that the casual, the contingent, the irrelevant should be eliminated. The Symbolist poem was dedicated to a conquest by method . . . uncontaminated . . . by the disorder of life, the accidents in actuality.[14]

In the next chapter, I explore the result of taking this program to its logical extreme: the fiction of Raymond Roussel. Roussel's *Locus Solus* is not only devoid of the hazards of life but of life itself. By contrast, the cybernetic fiction I discuss in Chapters Five through Ten shows that such a project is doomed to failure by adopting that pose in order to explore the ways in which it fails, presuming that life can be found in the gap between method's reach and its grasp.

The aesthetic invitation of the machine is to culminate in modernism, and its more extreme experimental schools, vorticism and constructivism. Sypher shows that modernism too can be thought of as a movement most coherently in terms of its devotion to the "technical aspects" of producing an artistic work. These methods result in highly formalistic experiments in which the mechanisms of form for their own sake are brought to the attention of the audience. Thus, William Carlos Williams echoes Valéry when he writes, "The poem is a machine," and Sypher characterizes Joyce as "a technologist" of words.

We recognize modernism both in art and literature by its production of complex, formalistic works unified by the vision they offer of themselves as products of applied techniques. These techniques are often reflected in the work itself and imply a role for the audience: the machine of the modern work of art, as Gilles Deleuze suggests, must be operated in order to produce its meaning.[15]

In the visual arts, analogs of this mechanical theme are expressed in paintings by, for instance, Marcel Duchamp (*The Mechanical Bride*), Paul Klee (*Twittering Machine*), and Max Ernst (*1 Copper Plate 1 Zinc Plate 1 Rubber Cloth 2 Calipers 1 Drainpipe Telescope 1 Piping Man*).

There was another literary camp, however, that viewed the machine as a threat, explored by Leo Marx in *The Machine in the Garden*. Marx's work traces the image of the machine as the newest devil in a New Eden promised by the apocalyptic prophesies of the centuries preceding the Industrial Revolution. Similarly, Sypher and Sussman both remark that the Romantics in England thought of the machine as an intrusive force and therefore inappropriate for poetic discourse. The Victorians, however, found in the machine ample invitation for metaphor making, even when, as in the work of Dickens and Herman Melville (*Moby-Dick*, "The Tartarus of maids" and "The paradise of bachelors"), the machine stood for the cruelties of industrialization and the dehumanizing mercilessness of applied method. Gradgrind of *Hard Times* is described as "a galvanizing apparatus . . . charged with a grim mechanical purpose." Melville's "The Tartarus of maids'' depicts an enormous factory in which women are merely cogs or mechanical adjuncts, androids whose soft flesh and humanity are ground down by inexorable machinery. To complicate matters in his typical fashion, Melville also employs the metaphor for other purposes: precise descriptions of the factory soon make it clear that it is modelled on the anatomical parts of a woman. Thus, in this ingenious use of the mechanics of metaphor, the biological mechanism of female anatomy paradoxically serves as a model for the machinery that ultimately destroys the bodies of women laborers.

Samuel Butler's *Erewhon* is one of the first ''techtopian'' fantasies. Butler attempts to resolve the paradox of the machine as Sussman formulates it: the irreconcilable double vision that ''man demonstrates the predictable activity of machines and yet still feels that he possesses free will.''[16] H. G. Wells portrays the machine as an evolutionary extension of man, who uses the machine to cultivate a moral and intellectual garden in an amoral, anarchic nature; however, he also portrays that garden being overrun by machines meant to tend it. The Martians of *The War of the Worlds*, though they operate powerful, indestructible juggernaut machines, are themselves an effete, diminished race, weakened by their reliance on their technology.

E. M. Forster describes another techtopian fantasy in which an entire human civilization is kept in cubicles and controlled by an all-knowing, all-powerful machine directing human communication and education. This Ur-computer is now familiar to us, since so many variations on the same image have been given us by recent science fiction, but the visionary aspects of Forster's novel, *The Machine Stops*, written in 1906, are remarkable. As the title suggests, the machine stops, leaving the totally dependent race of humans to an apocalyptic end. Their civilization first goes mad, then crumbles.

Finally, Henry Adams summarizes the force of dehumanizing mechanization as he gazes upon the progress of a century that has just passed as it is reflected in the Dynamo. He realizes that history is a largely impersonal force, subject to its own laws. Not only has history evolved a culture that proliferates machines at the expense of the sensibility of the past and of love, but it has become a sort of self-perpetuating machine itself.[17] Adams thus anticipates the vision of an autonomous technology presented by

Jacques Ellul and Langdon Winner half a century later, and is a source of inspiration to the cybernetic fiction of Pynchon.[18]

However, even these ostensibly anti-tech authors do not envisage the machine as an unmitigated evil. Each saw that human self-determination has a tragic tendency to yield to the power and allure of technical means and control. Sussman, driving to the heart of this ambivalence in Butler, for instance, remarks that "by showing the dissimilar in the similar, the mechanical in the organic, and the organic in the mechanical, Butler is illustrating rather than explicating the paradox" of the machine.[19] I would generalize this paradox not only to all the Victorians, but to all the authors who use the machine as a metaphor: the machine represents the paradoxes of our very existence as thinking, rational, civilized beings capable of expression. On the one hand it is a sign of determinism, of the sheer predictability of mechanism, including the mechanism of the models we employ to describe our world and selves that we have grown from empirical evidence. On the other hand it is an expression of our inventiveness and freedom. Even at its most far-extrapolated point, in the technological dystopia portrayed by Forster where machines control humans, we know sadly that it was humans who first invented and controlled the machines. Butler's attitude toward the machine is paradigmatic of all these nineteenth-century authors, and even those Symbolists and modernists who viewed the perfect text as an artefact of technique: as Sussman remarks, it is an attitude filled with "unresolved antitheses," "ambivalences," and "paradoxical positions."

Those authors who seem most enthralled by the aesthetic potential of the text as a machine find, as Raymond Roussel did, that they can be enslaved by their own method. On the other hand, those authors who fear in their worst moments of paranoia that the machines are out to get them, find, as William Burroughs does, that their identities are inextricably tied up in machinery – that the softness and the machinery of invention are wedded. Inevitably, they discover that their resistance to a so-called "autonomous technology" involves the invention of some counter-method, some guerrilla counter-technique, which itself is mechanical. Wylie Sypher describes this interplay between the freedom of experimental counter-techniques and their petrification into artistic programs: "The arrest [of artistic experimentation] occurs at the instant when the experiment is worked through to a solution that can be formulated into an official method, a program, a style."[20] Thus, method and counter-method, machine and art, create a dynamic equilibrium of statement and counter-statement about mutual concerns. As the machine becomes more sophisticated, it becomes more invulnerable to explication. As literature attempts either to protect what is vital and human by resisting this ever more sophisticated machine, or somehow to appropriate its invulnerability through the application of technique, it becomes more sophisticated, more abstract, more formalistic, more hypertrophic, and apparently less human. This is the revolutionary point of departure for cybernetic fiction: what should literature look like in an age when machines are capable of outstripping certain human mental operations by unimaginable distances and whose limitations are unknown, perhaps nonexistent?

THE MACHINE AS ICON

In *The Myth of Metaphor* Colin Murray Turbayne argues that the mechanical vision of the universe is an invention, a metaphor primarily sponsored by Descartes and Newton, who are ultimately "victimized" by their own metaphor.[21] Unfortunately, as Turbayne argues, the metaphor is so powerful it has given rise to a "metaphysics." Though extraordinarily attractive as a means of perceiving the world, it is founded on a pretense; to treat the universe as a machine is an act of faith. This "metaphysics of mechanism," writes Turbayne, "can be dispensed with."[22]

The progress of technology is a measure of the extent to which value-giving aspects of our own culture have been conquered by method. In other words, the advance of technology is a measure of the extent to which the metaphors we use to define ourselves give way to mechanistic ones, a sort of myth conversion or exchange of metaphors. For example, cybernetic fiction mirrors two developments related to this advancing vision: the proposition by formalists that language is a machine and the proposition by cyberneticists that human consciousness and the operations of the brain are mechanisms. From this perspective, it is only a short step to view the production of literary texts as the necessary consequence of the actions of elaborate brain biochemistry and grammars. If we follow the implications of the work of structuralists, we are brought to view language and the literary text as "an organized network," "a system of units and functions."[23] Jakobsen suggests that a methodological application of linguistics to the study of meaning-making

> presents an algorithm for exhaustive and unbiased descriptions of a text . . . and this algorithm . . . constitutes a discovery procedure for poetic patterns in that if followed correctly it will yield an account of the patterns which are objectively present in the text.[24]

These advances in the image of the machine in our culture – to the point that we see our own consciousness reflected in it – hint that the machine has the status of something even more powerful than a metaphor. Neisser, who is quoted in the epigraph to this chapter, suggests that it constitutes "a Jungian archetype." I would go further and propose that the machine – especially as it occurs in literature – is an icon. As a figure, it is capable of crystallizing, reflecting and embodying not only a complex system of meanings (determinism, logic, order, system) but the act of making meanings itself. Umberto Eco defines the icon as "a model of relationships."[25] Wolfgang Iser, building on Eco, defines literary icons as those signs that "constitute an organization of signifiers which do not serve to designate a signified object but instead designate instructions for the production of the signified."[26]

In other words, the icon is a sort of machine, in so far as we understand machines as the incarnation or illustration of a systematic set of rules. William Barrett's definition of a machine is useful here: he suggests that we think of machines not only as those gleaming metallic objects that are designed to do work in the material world, but as the manifestation of logical systems of thought, or in his words, "embodied decision procedures."[27] The icon, if we accept Barrett's view, is a kind of machine: it is the embodiment of a procedure for the production of sense; it has dynamic properties which in turn imply an operator and an inventor. The icon is invented by an author and then "operated" by a reader who, no matter what his biases are, will "read" the icon as intended.

Therefore the machine icon is a self-referential icon; it not only *acts* as an icon, but also reflects the very properties of *being* an icon. If the icon is a sign that "designates instructions for the production of the signified," then the machine icon designates instructions for the production of a complex of ideas about mechanism. Particularly, the machine icon almost universally stands for the various deterministic and mechanistic descriptions of experience and the world that our culture has invented.

Another way of saying this is that *the icon is a special kind of metaphor in which the vehicle changes but the tenor remains the same.* Thus, in this case of the machine icon, there is an infinite variety of machines used figuratively by fiction, but only one thing that they signify: determinism. Swift's All-Knowledge machine signifies the deterministic reduction of knowledge to an accumulation of random phrases. Dickens's description of Gradgrind signifies the determinism (as well as determination) of his pedagogical method. Butler and Forster describe society itself as a machine. Henry Adams sees the machine as a metaphor for history's deterministic process. The structuralists use the machine as a metaphor for the determinism of language's structures of signification. The cyberneticists use the machine as a metaphor for the determination of human communication and mechanisms of the brain, and then proceed to translate their metaphors into hardware. When this icon is made to stand for the literary text as well as the determinism it always carries with it, an even more invulnerable paradox (can there be different orders of paradox as there are different orders of infinity?) results. Cybernetic fiction responds to the invitation to use the machine icon as a metaphor for authorship, a metaphor combining the strict structuralist view of the text as a "code" (whose "objectively present" meanings can be derived from an algorithm for reading) with the cybernetic view of the author as a machine.

THE CREATIVE DIALECTIC: CYBERNETICS/FICTION

When confronted by a poem composed by a computer, or a drawing executed by a graphics machine, or a computer that play-acts the role of a psychological therapist by flashing neutral but provocative questions on its screen (as a clever program named

ELIZA, devised by Joseph Weizenbaum, has done[28]) – then we are compelled to pose some tough questions about the distinction between what is human and what mechanical. Still, at least when it comes to language, we know certain conditions must obtain before we are satisfied that a machine has spoken to us: the machine must *invent* within the language and it must *intend* what it says. At least these requirements push the locus of speech back into that quality intimately identified with our specialness, our unique capacity to create and to be aware of ourselves, our self-consciousness. On the other hand, the devil's advocate responds, what do you mean by "invention" and "intention"? don't computers invent when they rearrange elements? don't they intend when they follow instructions in their program? how are these different from human activities? As the devil's advocate's questions suggest, there are no simple resolutions. It is this very paradoxical quality of the questions that presents an invitation to art, and especially to fiction.

In this case, fiction is privileged. Since much of the contemporary battle between the postmodern "vitalists" and cybernetic "mechanists" has occurred over the status of language, the art that is both constituted in language and capable of extended confrontation with philosophical problems, the art of fiction, has lent itself most readily to treatment of the paradoxes involved. As our machines grow ever more sophisticated and daring, our literature has been challenged to create and express in ever more daring and sophisticated ways, establishing a dialogue between creativity and technology and forming the basis for some of the most complex and compelling of our contemporary fiction, the postmodernist works that are the subject of this book.

A thorough explanation of this creative dialectic and the fiction produced by it requires definition on both sides. On the one hand there is a set of fictional works that are identifiable as members of a larger class of fiction commonly called "postmodernism." The particular sub-class of contemporary fiction which I discuss in later chapters includes novels and short stories by Kurt Vonnegut, William Burroughs, John Barth, Thomas Pynchon, Samuel Beckett, Joseph McElroy, and Donald Barthelme; they are united by at least two features. Each of them concerns some aspect of the recent explosion in communications and computer technologies called in some places "cybernetics." Either they concern robots, cybernauts or computers directly, or they confront the deeper implications of the mechanization of man on some metaphorical level. Secondly, and crucially, they are self-reflexive, illustrating in form and style their cybernetic themes.

For example, *Giles Goat-Boy* by John Barth depicts a fabulous world-university governed by an omnipotent and omniscient computer, EASCAC-WESCAC. Joseph McElroy's *Plus* concerns, at least nominally, the story of a human brain, excised from its body and fitted into the cockpit of an orbiting capsule, as it attempts to grow back into an autonomous creature after being launched into space. Part of Burroughs's paranoid fantasy, which he spins out over several works, entails the use of control machines and media technology to manipulate human behavior. Samuel Beckett's *The Lost Ones* portrays a cylinder-machine in which 200 naked bodies roam or are frozen, helplessly subjected to the slow torture and death inflicted by their mechanical prison. One of the central images of Pynchon's *Gravity's Rainbow* is the guidance system – a feedback device – used in Nazi rockets during the Second World War. *V.* is filled with images of androids. *The Crying of Lot 49* is densely organized around the metaphor of a secret communications system. Vonnegut's *Player Piano* derives its title from the image of a crude robot originally suggested by Norbert Wiener in *The Human Use of Human Beings.*[29] Vonnegut's later novel, *The Sirens of Titan*, is based on the supposition that humans are cybernetic messages controlled as part of a larger inter-galactic code. Italo Calvino's story "The night driver" in *T-Zero* is narrated by a lover driving to a tryst who describes himself in terms of a message in a communications system. In the final paragraph, the character-message calls himself "a luminous signal, the only appropriate way of being for those who wish to be identified with what they say."[30]

Were this thematic material the only distinguishing feature of this sub-class, then these fictions would belong to that much larger pulp genre of science fiction, in which technology is either glorified or blamed but always projected into some future, otherworldly, or purely imaginary realm. However, these postmodernist works are also distinguished by the elements uniting them with much of the avant-garde in literature: they are self-reflexive and draw attention to the materials and forms of their own construction. As Calvino implies, the view that the text about messages is a message, too "is the only appropriate way of being for those [fictions] that want to be identified with what they say." Therefore, not only do these authors confront technology – and in particular cybernetics – thematically, they also focus on the *machinery or technology of their fiction*, remaining uniquely conscious that their texts are constructed of words, that words are part of the larger machinery of language, and that language is shaped by the still larger machinery of their own consciousness and experience. Yet paradoxically, each of these texts calls attention to itself not merely as a machine but as a fictional work. That is, either through the direct intrusion of the authorial voice or by some more complicated arrangement of formal structures, these texts signal to the reader that they are artefacts of human creation. Because both the theme and form of this sub-class derive from cybernetics, I call it *cybernetic fiction*.[31]

Language is vulnerable. Our sciences have not yet succeeded in completely reducing the human use of language to purely formal terms. Artificial intelligence experts have not found a complex enough arrangement of algorithms to provide digital computers with the simulacra of speech. On the other hand, as the Russian formalists such as Viktor Shklovsky and later structuralists have succeeded in showing, the provisional view of language as having mechanical or algorithmic properties is fruitful, since, to a certain extent language can be reduced to patterns and codes and decision procedures, that is, to a formal syntax. Without such a deeply embedded prior structure, what Noam Chomsky has characterized as a transformational and generative grammar, communication would be impossible.[32] Therefore, language can be viewed as a sort of vulnerable machine, simultaneously rigid and pliable. Like the human body it has skeleton, muscle, tendons and fat, soft organs which change daily and bony structures which alter only slowly, if at all. That is, language is a sort of soft machine. This volume explores the way that cybernetic fiction reveals the soft machinery not only of itself but of human language and thought. Cybernetic fiction presents itself as a machine, but only ironically, for underneath the mask lies the softness, vulnerability and instability of our humanness.

On the technological side of the creative dialectic between cybernetics and fiction lies cybernetics itself. Most generally, cybernetics is defined as the science of control and communication in animal and machine. Humans are meant, I suppose, to belong to either category. In any case, it makes no difference, since in the view of cyberneticists, both are governed by the same laws.[33] Cybernetics has given us such terms as "feedback" and "entropy" (the latter term borrowed from thermodynamics), and has promoted the use of the brain as a model for the computer and the computer as a metaphor for the functioning of the brain.[34]

At the heart of cybernetics lie the notions of a *governor* – whose Greek root *kybernos* was used by Norbert Wiener to name the science he helped invent – of *information*, and of *feedback*. The *governor* is understood as any central device – including a message – which acts within a system or on parts of a system to alter its "state" or behavior. *Information* is quantified by cyberneticists in a formula that is, through no accident, analogous to the formula given by Gibbs for thermodynamic entropy. Because of the centrality of the concept of information, cybernetics is known somewhat less poetically as "information theory" or "communication theory." The aim of cybernetic analysis is to define and isolate which (or how much or what kind of) information passing between parts of a system motivates which actions or alters which states in the communicants. *Feedback* is defined by Wiener as the process by which a system is "able to adjust future conduct by past performance." In its simplest form, the cybernetic system is made up of a *receptor*, accepting information as *input* from the outside. This information is then processed, and sent along to an *effector* or *sender* which responds to the initial stimulus with *output*. The output, however, alters the original conditions on the outside, thus sending new information in the form of input back into the system, establishing what is called a *feedback loop*. *Positive feedback* occurs when the signal causes the system to increase its activity towards instability. *Negative feedback* occurs when the signal causes a change in the internal state that suppresses the activity which initially gave rise to the signal, thus moving the system towards some "desired" stable state. Both negative and positive feedback end when there is no available information left in the (closed) system.

By extension, then, cybernetics is applied, both through theory and through the construction of models and machines, to the study of any communications systems, including natural and artificial languages, the relationship between brain and behavior, the organization of large, natural, human and mechanical systems, and the development of self-governing machines such as automata, computers, and artificial intelligence devices.

POSTMODERN RESOLUTIONS

At first glance, it is hard to imagine two more divergent fields for intellectual play. On the one hand there is fiction, the expression of a solitary exercise of the imagination, a private act expressing almost unlimited freedom and invoking only those laws which help the author shape his or her purpose; on the other, there is cybernetics, an ultimate science of control over communication, seeking laws governing the flow of information in any system, whether mechanical or human or something in between, a model or a metaphor. However, even from these basic versions of the two disciplines a certain, perhaps small, area of mutual concern can be envisaged. For instance, both have at their heart the notion of a governor, an author (in the case of fiction) or a feedback device which monitors the internal states of a machine with respect to its "desired" state.

If we think of the literary text as a device intended to represent "some internal state" of the author or to produce certain desired internal states in the reader, we bring fiction into cybernetic territory. Furthermore, if we grant that the simplest literary text is an act of communication between the author and himself, or the author and the structure of expectations he believes exists in his audience, and that it is a device or coded arrangement of signs, then we bring literature at least partially under the purview of a simple cybernetic analysis. The literary text becomes yet more amenable to cybernetic analysis if we view it as a model, something constructed with the materials of a systematic code (language) and with a systematic relationship among its various parts, all designed to represent the functioning of an intelligence or world view. Finally, if the text is viewed *as a model of the techniques or methods that created it*, which in turn implies a measure of self-awareness or self-reflexiveness in the text, then we can almost speak of the text as an artificial intelligence device.

The more interesting combination of the two fields occurs,

however, not when cybernetics is used as a tool to investigate fiction, but when a certain kind of fiction brings to bear its vision upon the implications of cybernetics. This is the enriched and lively juncture at which cybernetic fiction exists. It answers the threat of cybernetics with self-actuating proof of the limitations of system. At the same time, it seems to praise the attraction, complexity and dark beauty of machinery, both material and metaphorical. Cybernetic fiction is not immune to – indeed it relies heavily upon – the aesthetics of system, its symmetry, logic, and organization. However, the threat to which cybernetic fiction is a response is real. If cybernetics succeeds in its goal of explaining systematically and completely the mechanisms by which information governs behavior among human beings, it will provide a powerful philosophical weapon against the notion of free will and a powerful technique for control and manipulation of human activity.

It is the apparently natural and "blind" self-promulgation of technology, its growth in the direction of totalitarian systems and domination of human activity by techniques of control, that Jacques Ellul delineates in *The Technological Society*. Ellul defines technique as "the totality of methods rationally arrived at and having absolute efficiency . . . in every field of human activity."[35] In Ellul's view, "Technique has become autonomous; it has fashioned an omnivorous world which obeys its own laws and which has renounced all tradition."[36] His vision, however apocalyptic, was and still is powerfully persuasive. Its influence, if not his work directly, is visible in the fiction of Pynchon and Barthelme particularly, and is echoed by Barth, Vonnegut, Burroughs, Beckett and McElroy.

The extremity of cybernetic fiction's response can only be explained by the extremity of the technology creating its context: cybernetic fiction is a means for the author to present himself or his literature as a soft machine, a cybernaut-like hybrid device, combining human vulnerability and imagination with machine-like determinism. Such an imaginative formulation answers a technology which views the acts of communicating and thinking in deterministic terms – as processes of sending bytes (small units of information) down the line – and it answers the call for a literature that will rehumanize the cybernetic metaphor from inside that metaphor. Cybernetic fiction does succeed in softening the machine, in exposing (and perhaps allaying) the fear that we are only machines, communication devices for whom learning is only feedback, experience is only input, expression is only output, and meaning is only raw data. By employing the metaphor at the same time that it counters it, cybernetic fiction strikes a creative, if temporary, resolution between the vital aspects of human experience and its mechanical ones by showing that as terms of a deep paradox, they are accomplices of each other and therefore amenable to reconstruction.

TWO

ROUSSEL'S DEVICE FOR THE PERFECTION OF FICTION

"The thought of every age is reflected in its technique." (Norbert Wiener, *Cybernetics*)

"The exploitation of a medium for its own sake might be called the technical alienation of art . . . [when] the methodologist seems more concerned with the expertise of his technique than what is brought into being – which is a way of estranging art from its end."
(Wylie Sypher, *Literature and Technology, the Alien Vision*)

POSITIVISTIC LIT

A positivistic science breeds a positivistic art. The nineteenth century was committed to the conquest of truth by scientific method and was convinced of the power of scientific method to disclose truth. At the same time, it produced a literature devoted to its own method, convinced of the power of formal structures to portray natural truths. However, as Wylie Sypher has argued with great force, that art which subjugates itself to its own technique is ultimately led away from nature and into the laboratory, into a kind of "studio artifice" in which calculation and rationalization supplant experience.[1] In our postmodern, post-Heisenbergian age, the incommensurability of life with the structures we use to describe it is taken for granted, and literature is freed to encourage its own diversions, erasures, marginalia, digressions, interruptions, discontinuities and paradoxes. As Raymond Federman, a noted postmodernist, suggests, in a postmodern fiction, "it is the hazard/fatality which determines what will happen next . . . a dangerous game because everything here has a positive value."[2] By contrast, as Sypher shows, the literary positivist seeks "an efficient method" that "reduces the hazards" of art. This leads to "desperate ventures" in which the author tries to squeeze such engendering forces out of his text "by calculating everything, by ruling out the surprises of chance."[3] Sypher's work, *Literature and Technology, the Alien Vision*, exposes the corruption and pretension in a literature that mimics the precision and power of nineteenth-century science. He finds it in the "verbal archeology" of Matthew Arnold, the "artificial language" of Dante Gabriel Rossetti, in Emile Zola's experimental naturalism, in Flaubert "who sacrificed himself to technique", in the Symbolists Mallarmé, Baudelaire, Valéry, *et al.*, and in Pater, for whom "style is a methodology where aesthetic and scientific ideas of precision intersect."[4]

Curiously, though, throughout the nineteenth century, many artists still viewed machines themselves as unfit for artistic representation. The same Pre-Raphaelites, impressionists, Symbolists, and naturalists who were most likely to "technologize" their texts were least likely to address technology itself. Rather, this was left to Jules Verne, T. H. Huxley, H. G. Wells, and E. M. Forster, popularists who were less concerned with the artifices of their texts than with the artefacts of their imagination.

Yet, early in the twentieth century, there was one peculiar, rather solitary author who was sufficiently eclectic in his personal and imaginative tastes to break down the boundary between the ultra-rationalism of the literary methodologists who preceded him and the forerunners of science fiction who predicted that the future of humanity was somehow inextricably bound up with the machine. Furthermore, this author saw that the two literary modes were somehow linked, that the logic of literary technique ultimately could be extended to the subject of that art, a maneuver that would match matter to form to create a more perfect literary device. Because he blends such disparate genres into one another, Raymond Roussel is hard to fix. He seems at once to represent a culmination of the Symbolist method and at the same time stand for an extreme form of modernism. While he traced his own inspiration back to the work of Jules Verne, he is claimed by the Dadaists and anticipates the Russian constructivists. The similarity between his own aesthetic ideal and the "vorticism" of Ezra Pound and Wyndham Lewis – in which the artist views the abstraction of the work of art as an end in itself, a product of the dynamic and static forces of the imagination rather than the observation of nature – is clear. Yet there is no evidence to suggest that Roussel had heard of vorticism when he completed his most "vorticist" work, *Locus Solus*, in 1914, the year that Wyndham Lewis advanced his theory of vorticism.

What is clear in all this is that Roussel was the consummate literary positivist. He took the assumptions of the nineteenth-century literary methodologists to their most extreme end, and in the process created a series of texts that are as close as any to becoming pure machines. Because his project is artistically sterile, Roussel stands at the end of the road of literary positivism in an aesthetic cul-de-sac. And his work provides an apt contrast to the postmodernists who superseded him, especially to those authors of cybernetic fiction who also employed the machine as a reflection of their own technique but only with extreme irony, with the presumption that the machine does not work. Since he worked without the benefit of discoveries in physics that were to occur at the end of his lifetime, and without the more clearly manifested threat to the artistic imagination offered by cybernetics, such irony was not available to Roussel. Because his work is so monumental an expression of the failure of literary positivism, and because his work is so apt a counterpoint to the cybernetic fiction that was to follow, it deserves closer scrutiny here, for Roussel did not use literary technique to soften the machine so much as he used the machine to petrify literary technique.

ROUSSEL'S SOLITARY PLACE

Roussel's life, like his work, is mysterious, elusive, extreme, and filled with contradictions. He was born to wealth in Paris in 1877 and died in poverty and dissipation in Palermo in 1933. His psychoanalysis by the eminent Dr Pierre Janet revealed that Roussel's self-confidence was grandiose to the point of paranoid megalomania, and yet he had a morbid fascination for death and self-destruction that culminated in suicide. Two conflicting accounts report that he was found dead either from four self-inflicted gun wounds (according to his literary executor Michel Leiris)[5] or from having opened his arteries in a warm bath, Petronius-style (according to his nephew).[6] Both reports agree, however, that he was found in the boudoir of Mme Dufrene, his long-time mistress, at Room 226 of LeGrand Hotel et des Palmes. Along the way to this final romance, he became addicted to barbiturates and alcohol, was involved in a passionate love affair with a young boy, and resided in a Montmartre hotel famous as a perch for *les poules*. He designed an enormous de luxe caravan, *une roulotte* or house on wheels, forefather of today's trailer homes, which included a fully equipped bedroom, dining room, bath and servant's quarters.[7] The Pope once expressed an interest in Roussel's roulotte, but thought it would be unseemly to visit; since the land yacht wasn't permitted to enter the Vatican proper, the Pope sent an emissary in his place.

Roussel was friends with Proust and Mussolini. His sister married a Russian prince and became Princess of Moscow before the revolution. He learned how to play chess at the age of 30 and within three years had devised a strategy which solved a famous problem of the time. Upon his mother's death in 1914, he designed and had built into her coffin a little window so that he could gaze upon her face until the last moment. This windowed coffin, a bizarre mixture of Romantic melodramatic longing and technical inventiveness, is typical of Roussel; his intervention in the funeral ritual betrays a perverse and ironic compulsion to tinker with the symbolic. It also emphasizes the theme of entombment, of *la cache secrète* that dominates his novel published the same year, *Locus Solus*, in its way the purest example of the modernist machine.

Roussel's works include: *La Doublure* (1897), a verse novel in 6000 lines which he wrote when only 19, and the novels *Impressions d'Afrique* (1910), *Locus Solus* (1914), *L'Etoile en front* (1925), *La Poussière des soleils* (1927) and *Nouvelles Impressions d'Afrique* (1930), all published at his own expense. A posthumous collection of works and critical essays, *Comment j'ai écrit certains de mes livres* ("How I wrote some of my books") was published in 1935, and includes the important title essay by Roussel that discloses, in part, the methodology he used to assemble the machinery of his texts. Another essay included in the collection is the case history of "Martial" (clearly meant to be Roussel's pseudonym and the same first name as the hero of *Locus Solus*) written by Dr Janet, "Les caractères psychologiques de l'extase" ("The psychological characteristics of ecstasy"), which is reprinted from Janet's influential book, *De l'Angoisse à l'extase* (*From Agony to Ecstasy*, Paris, 1926). Of the newly published short fiction and verse included in *Comment j'ai écrit certains de mes livres*, one in particular has received much attention and critical commentary, "Parmi les noirs" ("Among the blacks").[8] In addition to these publications, Roussel produced, at his own expense, stage adaptations of *Locus Solus* and *Impressions d'Afrique* among other plays, all of which were received with derision, disbelief, and, in some cases, near-violent protests.

Locus Solus reflects the remarkable combination of the Romantic and the technical in Roussel's life and character. In essence, it sterilizes Romanticism by devoting itself to technique for its own sake, which was also one of the goals of vorticism. Though Roussel's fiction is very much in the literary vanguard of its time, it also contains arcane and archaic devices that echo the literary movements of previous centuries. From the Gothic novels, Roussel takes his fascination for folk-tales, dreams, fantastic creatures, imaginary kingdoms populated by princesses, dangerous dungeons, genii, talking animals, and magical objects. From the extensive travel and discovery literature of Richard Burton, Mungo Park, Charles Darwin and other explorers and naturalists we may find the source of his fascination for the exotica of Africa: arcane rituals, primitive tribes, and cannibalism. From the Symbolists, particularly those who emulated Poe – Baudelaire and, later, Valéry – he takes his philosophy of composition: "The goal of poetry is of the same nature as its principle; it should have nothing in view but itself."[9]

The hero of *Locus Solus* is Martial Canterel, a bachelor genius who has great wealth at his disposal. He lives upon a large estate outside Paris, appropriately named "Locus Solus," that he has converted into what is essentially a combined laboratory, museum and retreat.

Contrasted to Canterel is the anonymous narrator who plays chorus leader and member of a perpetually awed and faceless audience, announced by the *nous*, the "we" of the narrative.[10] The narrator is taken on a tour of Canterel's estate where he views a series of marvelous objects on display. One of these objects is a statue whose mute but tantalizing arrangement of parts begs for an explanation: in the deep niche of a large rock, a smiling naked child holds his two hands in the gesture of offering; sprouting from the middle of his left hand is a small, long-dead flower. Underneath the statue's niche engraved in three bas-relief rectangles are three elusive friezes, two of which include words. This mysterious rock inspires Canterel to a long explanation, which becomes a complex story involving imaginary kingdoms, mythical royalty, hereditary oaths, supernatural events, attempted assassinations, secret treasures, strange texts and codes, stories within stories, and happy endings; a tale, in short, worthy of Scheherazade and typical of Roussel. Another chapter is devoted to the explanation of a

> monstrous jewel, rounded into an ellipse, throwing off in the full light of day, fires so unbearably dazzling that they seemed like lightning flashes in every way! . . . [D]ivided into facets like a precious stone, [it] seemed to encase different moving objects.[11]

Upon their approach, the tourists hear faint, marvellous music coming from it, "consisting of a strange series of arpeggios or scales running up and down." They discover that the jewel is in reality a large container filled with water in which a graceful woman, dressed in a flesh-colored bathing suit, is completely immersed. She performs a tantalizing aquatic dance, apparently capable of breathing freely in the water, while the seductive music is produced by some property of her hair as it undulates in the water, each strand producing its own note.

The exhibition of wonders at "Locus Solus" is large: each is exotic, symbolic, comprised of many parts, seemingly defiant of natural laws, and requiring long explanations. The marvel that seems most quintessentially Rousselian, however, and which is most relevant to a study of the literary uses of the machine, is the fabulous paving beetle of Chapter II of *Locus Solus*.

THE PAVER-PUNNER: SECRET MECHANISMS

Canterel ushers the tourists to a large esplanade, a broad expanse open to the sun over which a device hovers. Upon closer inspection this device appears to be a "paving beetle," an instrument used to level walkways, attached by a complex metallic arrangement to a small, clear-yellow, bell-shaped balloon. Beneath the balloon lies an enormous number of human teeth of every conceivable shape, color and size: exceptionally white ones contrast with decayed, smoke-stained incisors; immense molars and monstrous canines lie next to tiny, barely visible milk teeth. Many are filled with metal that reflects the sun. Beneath the mechanism, some of the teeth have been arranged into a fantastic but unfinished mosaic, comprised entirely of the teeth. By virtue of their variety, the teeth form the individual brushstrokes of this elaborate mechanical painter.

The picture thus created shows *un reître*, a German cavalry soldier. The soldier is sleeping in a deep cave by the banks of a subterranean pool. In what looks like a puff of smoke emanating from his head – apparently representing a dream – there are "eleven young men, crouching in terror before a transparent globe floating before them." The globe casts a shadow like a dark bird's, and yet a white dove flies above it. Next to the soldier, "partially illuminated by a torch planted in the cave floor, is an ancient tome, lying closed." As the spectators watched, the balloon "rose into the air, pushed by a little breeze, flew slowly and directly fifteen or twenty feet" to a portion of the mosaic still unfinished. As they approach the machine, led by Canterel, they hear a strange ticking noise and are able to discern the particulars of the apparatus: "an automatic aluminum valve," "a small chronometer with a dial," a net woven of fine red silk attached to an aluminum gondola which in turn is riveted to an aluminum cylinder.

Roussel revels in the details of his invention, creating technical descriptions surpassing in minutiae those of his mentor, Verne (whom he elsewhere calls "the incomparable Master"). We get lost in the sheer elaboration of the mechanism:

> A long rod, also of aluminum, was attached to the side above the post, rising at an angle towards the sky, higher than the flat circle and terminating in a triple subdivision. Each of the three branches supported at its tip a largish chronometer backed by a round mirror of equal circumference. The three dials, ignoring each other, looked outwards in three different directions, whereas the three silvered-glass discs faced common middle ground and, respectively, more or less the west, the south and

> the east. Just then, the first mirror was getting the image of the sun directly and reflecting it fully into the second, which sent it to the gondola – while the third played no apparent role. Each mirror held its chronometer with four delicately-toothed horizontal rods, fixed individually atop, below, to the right and left of the back of its rim; these rods, in all three cases, ran clear through the chronometer and stuck out from the other side at the peripheral edge of its face, slightly smaller in diameter than that of the clockwork.
>
> Operated by invisible gears attached to the chronometer's mechanism, these rods were able to adjust the mirrors to any angle through a great variety of lateral movements; the front of each rod was a small metallic ball two-thirds cupped by a hollow partial sphere [in turn] attached to the back of the working mirror. This fitting made it easy to move the reflecting disc in the most diverse number of directions.[12]

This exhaustive technical description goes on for three and a half equally detailed and dense pages, mapping a magnified, machine-tooled, imaginative topography from which the human is virtually absent. ''We'' learn that the mechanism uses the sunlight to evaporate a specially prepared chemical lying in the gondola, thus adjusting its altitude and direction. It catches winds according to some elusive but incredibly complex plan and is guided to the tooth it ''wants'', grasps it by ''obeying some mysterious magnetism,'' and returns to the mosaic where the tooth is placed. The ''paver'' is sensitive as well, it seems, to the wind, the time of day, its altitude and direction. Exactly how the machine knows where to go and when to go there ''escaped [their] uninitiated eyes'' and understanding.

Furthermore, how the machine has derived an intelligence capable not only of recognizing the tooth it wants but placing it in a pictorial representation of a complex story, is beyond their imagination. Even the mural itself presents only mysteries, with its complex arrangement of dreamer and dream, elusive symbology, and in the innermost tale, a reflexive image of a balloon-like globe that mirrors in its frame the artistic globe that created it. Roussel's faceless narrator explains that

> the Master had pushed the art of predicting the weather to its ultimate possible limits. He had developed a system whereby

> the direction and strength of each breath of air, as well as its advent, and the size, opacity and potential condensation of the smallest cloud

could be predicted days in advance.

The fabulous mechanism is itself the embodiment of a series of subsidiary inventions and systems ("decision-making procedures") that Canterel has devised over the years as genius-in-residence at "Locus Solus": a method for pulling teeth painlessly through magnetism; the derivation of a chemical compound which releases quantities of hydrogen when light is focused on it; the fantastic meteorological system for predicting local winds, etc., etc. For twenty pages following the first description of the balloon, Canterel explains in details either fascinating or excruciating – depending on your temperament, taste and patience – not only the principles of the paver, but the story represented by the still-incomplete mosaic. It is this effortless glide between Canterel's explication of the mechanism and the explication of the work of art produced by that mechanism which leads us to the point where Roussel's literature parts company with cybernetic fiction of the postmodern period.

Canterel is a scientist and a technician, not an artist, as Roussel makes apparent on the first pages of *Locus Solus*. "He had consecrated his entire life to science," writes Roussel. His work is "research," which astounds "the scientific world," and his villa has been converted into "laboratories." Though Canterel is not an artist, his invention seems to be one. It is only upon clarification we discover that it is merely a programmed machine, a sort of mosaic-generating computer using solar and wind power instead of electricity, and teeth instead of rasters on a video screen. Canterel, as programmer, is the real tale-teller and muralist. In order to explain his device fully he must also regale his captive audience with a long fairy-tale about the German soldier and his dream.

Roussel seems to hint that the two roles of scientist-inventor and artist-author are not separate but complementary, perhaps congruent, identities. The *demoiselle de reître en dents* (the "paver in teeth") and the mural of *le reître* are constructions, inventions produced by the application of certain predetermined principles aimed at excluding all contingencies and accidents. Canterel did not write the story his machine illustrates, but he did design the mural. Significantly, though, his description of his own motives for choosing that particular tale stresses the subordination of the story material to the technical demands (teeth, weather, mechanism) of telling it. Roussel writes:

> For the work of art to be executed, Canterel had to choose some rather dim subject, on account of the necessary predominance of the browns and yellows among the mosaic materials; a picturesque scene from the recesses of some deep and feebly-lit cavern seemed to him most apt. He recalled a certain Scandinavian story that Ezaias Tegner entitled "Den Rytter" in his *Frithiof's Saga.*

What follows is purportedly the French translation by "Fayot-Roquensie" (a name bearing a suspicious resemblance to "Raymond Roussel") of "Den Rytter," the tale of a powerful Norwegian duke who sends a German soldier, Aag, to abduct the wife of one of his vassal barons. Aag is discovered and held captive in a dungeon, where he reads a story about the magical globe, the incarnation of an evil genie, and eleven princes who are ultimately rescued by a sister they meant to betray. This tale, inscribed in the closed volume next to the reiter depicted by the mural, is entitled "Le conte de la boule de l'eau" – "The story of the water-orb."

The subordination of the choice of subject to the constraints imposed by the medium is not uncommon in art; indeed, the limitations of the medium are often the very point of any artistic project. The artist strives to create a picture of depth and naturalistic color despite the two-dimensionality of his canvas and the artificiality of his colors. The dancer seeks to articulate a story despite the silence of her movements. But there is something odd about Canterel's inversion that goes beyond his choice of a murky tale because of the color of teeth at his disposal. It is the intervention of an elaborate mechanism between an artist and his product that seems remarkable and perhaps intolerable. If it is intolerable, it is because the machine has effaced the human author and is masquerading in his place. Canterel programs his machine ten days in advance, sets the thing out in a field, laboriously chooses each single tooth, arranges the lot of them according to a most precise method, and leaves the scene at which the creation will occur. He saunters back to it as a sort of tour guide who can play audience to his own creation. At the time, the closest analogues to Roussel's fantastic metaphor for this artistry-at-a-distance were the scripts of a playwright or the scores of a musician: both are first created in forms entirely different from the ones in which they are ultimately performed. But it was not until half a century later that technology provided a fulfilment of what now seems like Roussel's prophetic notion of machine-generated art, with the development of computers capable of being programmed for sophisticated music and visual creations, and even a crude and extremely reduced "poetry."

Anyone who has tinkered with or witnessed good (amusing, complicated, inspiring) computer-generated art knows that the initial fascination and pleasure of the performance is its apparent autonomy: the sight of an unattended computer displaying extraordinarily complex visual patterns or playing intricate mathematically derived canons.[13] However, what threatens us is the pretense that the machine is creating in the same way that human artists create, a pretense adopted by programmers eager to prove that machines rival humans. Further, both Canterel's punner and the computer art-generator obtain symbolic weight. Roussel celebrates the machine without irony; he asks us to applaud the masquerade of the machine as author in order to emphasize the identity, the unity between the two, whereas later cybernetic fiction shows the author ironically masquerading as a machine in order to confirm their differences.

CODES, PASSWORDS AND SECRET DEVICES: ROUSSEL'S *"DEVICE DE PROCÉDÉ TRÈS SPÉCIAL"*

These mysterious devices inspire awe in the audience, which in turn provokes Canterel to explain, which in turn engenders a mysterious story that in turn requires explication, and so on. The message at each turn is the same: the worker of apparent magic is really only operating a hidden mechanism, exploiting an elusive technology, or invoking a set of complex algorithms (which recalls Arthur C. Clarke's Law: "Any sufficiently advanced technology is indistinguishable from magic"[14]). Canterel's punner, at first magical, is nothing more than a hyper-advanced mechanical paintbrush. Aag the reiter (pronounced "writer") is released from his crypt by Christel the princess, who has read a secret text revealing a complex system of passageways opened by a set of hydrodynamic locks. The story Aag reads, "The water-orb," describes another apparently supernatural object, but it is commanded by a secret language. Each level contains carefully coded references to the other levels, a strategy that announces the unity of the text: the water-orb reminds us of the role of water in Aag's escape and also of the "aerostat" or Montgolfier-like balloon punner. The inventiveness of the mechanism releasing Aag from his cave reminds us of Canterel's inventions. The long and complex instructions which Christel reads, and which are painstakingly reiterated in the text of *Locus Solus*, echo the technical explanations by Canterel. There is no room in any of this for accident, spontaneity, or randomness.

Roussel is anxious to communicate his (and Canterel's) exemplary control over his medium. The series of recursions itself is a formal (literary) mechanism. In the story of the water-orb, eleven brothers are being threatened by the shadow of the orb. The only way to stop its evil magic is by "*un mot cabalistique*." (Unfortunately, they have spent a year in debauchery and have forgotten it. They are finally saved by their sister, who has been metamorphosed into a dove.) The story of the water-orb is contained in a book opened by Aag. Aag is held in a cave opened by a procedure revealed in a book read by Christel. Christel is described by the story written by Ezaias Tegner, whose work is translated by Fayot-Roquensie which in turn is translated (into mosaic form) by Canterel, a character in a text by Roussel. A similar nested arrangement is produced if we take the mechanical creator as our point of reference: the evil floating globe of water (a sort of mechanism) is shown hovering in a smoky dream-bubble coming from Aag's head (in comic book terminology, these are "balloons"); this balloon is part of a mural created by the flying paver; the paver is constructed by Canterel who is made of words comprising a text-machine constructed by Roussel.

The logic of this recursive series structuring the text invites a question: what opens the text we are reading? Or: what is the machinery of the text? To be consistent, we must conclude that there is some hidden mechanism, some secret procedure or password that underlies or will unlock the secret mechanics of Roussel's text.

This deduction based on the loop of recursions in *Locus Solus* is confirmed by Roussel's own posthumous revelation of *un procédé très spécial*. In *Comment j'ai écrit certains de mes livres* he describes a method of composition that resulted from his attempt to exert mechanistic control over language itself. Roussel attempts to do for art what cybernetics was to attempt to do for science three decades later. He tries to erase the boundary between the human and the machine by showing that one has made the other redundant, once the human imagination has devised and set in motion that machine. Further, he is even more subtly cybernetic in the sense that he attempts to exert control over art as a *code marred by contingencies*, which describes perfectly the position of science after Heisenberg as it was viewed by many mechanists, including Norbert Wiener, who was motivated by the emergence of chance in physics to invent (along with other theoreticians) cybernetics. (See the following chapter.)

Roussel's secret mechanism is a sort of primitive linguistic feedback mechanism constructed of self-reflexive levels of narration. In *Comment j'ai écrit . . .*, Roussel simply and directly reveals the secret of this process, which he calls "essentially poetic . . . improvised of phonetic combinations . . . and akin to rhyme."

> While still rather young, I had already written short stories several pages long which used this device.
>
> I had chosen two words nearly like (in thinking of metagrams). For example, *billard* and *pillard*. Then I added to them words which were similar but could be taken in two different senses, and obtained two phrases nearly identical:
>
> 1. *Les lettres du blanc sur les bandes du vieux billard.*
> 2. *Les lettres du blanc sur les bandes du vieux pillard.*
>
> In the first, *lettres* is taken in the sense of "typographical signs," *blanc* in the sense of "a cube of chalk," and *bandes* in the sense of "stripes."
>
> In the second, *lettres* is taken to mean "missives," *blanc* in the sense of "a white man," and *bandes* in the sense of a "tribe of warriors."
>
> Having discovered the two phrases, the task was then to write a story which began with the first and ended with the second.[15]

Roussel reconstructs (in a manner reminiscent of, but far more plausible than, Poe's reconstruction of his poem "The raven" in *The Philosophy of Composition*) the deductive and mechanical methods by which he chose not only his subject but the actual words of his text. The narrative is created by the linking of the first sentence with the last, along with a series of similar internal recapitulations of the punning mechanism which generated the endpoints. Further, as Roussel reveals, this technique operates in all his texts, and not just in "Parmi les noirs," the story formed by the exemplary illustration above.[16]

In the same way, the chapter about the paving beetle uses *une demoiselle* explicitly in two of its three senses and implicitly in its third: it is both "a paving beetle" and a "young girl"; these two senses give rise to the central homophonic phrases of the story: *une demoiselle à prétendant* and *une demoiselle à reître en dents*. The third, hidden meaning is "a dragonfly": both the genie incarnated as an aerial globe and the paving beetle with its various appendages have qualities in common with the dragonfly. From these initiating phrases, numerous other puns, homologues, phonetic analogues and near-rhymes arise, sometimes bilingually and even trilingually. The most significant of these is *reiter* which can be taken both as a tool used to lay and level a path (a paver) and, rather self-referentially, a "reiterator." In German, it designates the young soldier, *den Rytter* which Roussel himself translates in a footnote as *le reître*. Furthermore, the French word is a homonym of the English "writer." Finally, we would note that the British call a paving beetle a "punner"!

The careful reader finds similar deformations and isomers of sentences, phrases, words and phonemes generated by operation of the Rousselian device. Carl Lovitt, in an article which contributes a great deal to the cracking of the Rousselian code, places special emphasis on the gamesmanship and playfulness of Roussel's device. Lovitt subdivides the single Rousselian device into a series of related processes and strategies and proposes that Roussel's technique is not merely a machine for the production of puns, but rather a strategy for "semantic expansion." "The introduction of a [new] term into the text" by use of the procedure "also constitutes the introduction of the one or more descriptive systems to which the term belongs. The introduction of the descriptive system in turn gives the text access to all the other elements belonging to that system."[17] Lovitt's analysis goes beyond a linear cross-correlation of this system of semantic expansion into the mapping of an "n-dimensional space" of the textual territory of *Locus Solus*. Not only does the text use the "repetition of words as a generative process," writes Lovitt, "the text tends largely to reproduce what it already contains."[18]

In order to understand the total congruence between the operation of this device and the control it expresses, it is helpful to invoke cybernetic terms. Two phrases that are *presque identique* or even completely identical phonetically but are semantically divergent form the points of origin and closure of the ideal Rousselian text. However, in cybernetic terms, a homonym is highly uncertain, entropic, since it gives two options for interpreting a single word. Uncertainty can only be reduced by coding – that is by providing a context, more information. Roussel's strategy of "overdetermination" (both Leslie Hill and Lovitt use the term) is aimed at reducing this uncertainty, by bringing under systematic accountability the entropic potential of natural language to offer and tolerate one word having two different meanings. Thus, the incredible degree of redundancy in the text, "its tendency to use what it already contains," to "obey a double constraint of overdetermination and discursive revision" reduces entropy – proportionate to the amount of available information – by creating redundancies. This technique, in short, is used to create a system through which the uncertain can be made certain and the random aspects of language subsumed in an ordered system. Authors (and humorists) often exploit the completely arbitrary way in which the two possible meanings of a single word remain unrelated. Roussel was clearly driven to distraction by the notion, and sought a way to escape what must have appeared to him an arbitrary and uncontrollable contingency in language.

In *Locus Solus* the author is masquerading as a totalitarian computer from whose control every portion, every aspect – from the phonetic to the semantic to the formal – is under the control of a carefully-coded mechanism. As Albert Jenny remarked, Roussel's device is designed "*pour une production du sens purement livré du hasard, uniquement mécanique*" – "for the production of meaning purely free from chance, solely mechanical."[19] Roussel's project is to literature what cybernetics was to be for science: an attempt to free the text from the same taint of contingency that was to arise in physics through Heisenberg's deduction that the observer could only establish the probable position of an electron. In short, Canterel's method of permitting the deterministic mechanism of the medium to override the content it communicates is merely a reiteration of Roussel's larger strategy: story is a function of strategy; the machine-medium is the message.

It is on this point that our investigation of the Rousselian puzzle comes to rest: the strategy is not meant, as Leslie Hill implies, to call attention to the author. In part, this is demonstrated in our first view of the "punner": it seems as though the machine is the force or author that brings coherence out of incoherence, forming "local enclaves of organization" in an otherwise universal tide towards disorder. It is to the machine, despite the genius of Canterel, that our attention returns. In part this is reiterated by the invisibility of Canterel and Roussel behind the opacity of their characterless and incredibly long technical descriptions. In part, it is proven by the absent *je* merged into the *nous* of the narrative. In part, we may see it in the effect a "proper" – that is Rousselian – reading of one of Roussel's texts has on us: we are inevitably turned into Russian formalists or pure structuralists, reading machines whose vision of the text is narrowed down to elaborately clever correlations and recombinations of a series of coded elements but no further. For this implied reader, the code and the text are one.[20] We may even see this artistic position – to divert attention away from the technician towards the technique – in the fact that Roussel guarded his secret mechanism until after his death. Far from being "a posthumous literary testament" to himself,[21] his revelation of the device after death is just another operation of the device, "a sort of ultimate revelation," as Foucault called it, the disclosure of yet another decision-making procedure operating to control creation, a revelation to which "death plays the password." Like the window into the coffin Roussel built for his mother, Roussel's lingering gaze, and the gaze he extracts from his reader, are saved for finality and closure.

We may conclude then that *Locus Solus* does not imply a series of infinite regressions, which in its way is a form of irony. Rather, the text embellishes a finite, circumscribed space in which a machine retraces its message again and again, an embellishment that everywhere announces the compulsive desire to leave no space blank and no part incomplete. Roussel's patented process is designed to produce a literature that recaptures the merely haphazard elements of language within a larger structure of logic, an artistic positivism that leaves nothing to chance.[22]

Roussel leaves us with a parable of this construction of order out of apparent disorder in *Locus Solus* itself. When the spectators first come upon the tableau they note that on one side is "a still incomplete mosaic" surrounded by a variegated and enormous pile of teeth "spread around with the most complete incoherence." But, in the end, we discover that the chaotic pile is itself the more direct product of order than the neat mosaic: Canterel spent a night of "appalling labor" sorting through the teeth and arranging them according to his calculations. What appears to be casual is causal. The cosmology implied by Roussel's imagination suggests a deserted, intricate machine world in which solitary humans, if humans exist there at all, have as their sole task to be tourists, discovering the principles which operate the machine. Here, the individual intelligence is marooned in a solitary place, or else dissolved into the *nous*, the collective consciousness which bears mute witness to the machine's self-perpetuation and elaborate expression.

Dr Janet reports "Martial's" (Roussel's) own description of his philosophy of composition:

> *Il faut que l'oeuvre ne contienne rien du rêel, n'aucune observation du monde ou des esprits, rien que des combinations tout à faire imaginaire à dont déjà des idées d'une monde extra-humain.*[23]
> (The work of art must contain nothing real, not one observation of the world or the mind, none but imaginary combinations which create the impression of an alien world.)

ROUSSEL AMONG OTHER MODERNISTS

Robbe-Grillet writes of Roussel's work that

> his opacity . . . is quite as much an excessive transparency. Since there is never anything beyond the thing described, that is since no supernature is hidden in it, no symbolism (or else a symbolism immediately proclaimed, explained, destroyed) the eye is forced to rest on the very surface of things: a machine of

> ingenious and useless functioning . . . a celebration whose progress is quite mechanical . . . there is nothing behind these surfaces, no inside, no secret, no hidden motive.[24]

The limitation of Roussel's applied technique becomes apparent when it is contrasted with the work of his contemporary, Franz Kafka. The patron saint of both authors, and also of James Joyce, may be Daedalus the Engineer, the builder of labyrinths and devices for flight, but Roussel clearly prefers Daedalus's more modern incarnation in the lofty and morally detached masterminds, Canterel and Verne's Captain Nemo.

Hugh Kenner's characterization of modernism in general could serve for Roussel as well as Joyce and Kafka; for them, "attention to things as trivial as cotter pins and bicycle spokes is an intellectual mark."[25]

Kafka's "In the penal colony" was published the same year as Roussel's *Locus Solus*. It portrays what is perhaps the most well known of all fictional writing machines, and the two texts bear striking resemblances to each other on first glance. The "traveler" or "explorer" who arrives on the island of the penal colony is introduced to the new commander, who proudly takes him on a tour of the island and describes the system of justice governing it. The central tourist attraction of the island is the "sentencing machine," which receives the same awe and is shrouded with the same ritual pride as Canterel's punner.[26] J. H. Matthews compares Kafka's machine to Roussel's, noting that "the explorer can make out nothing in the blueprint but an incomprehensible accumulation of lines . . . offering no explanation for the precision with which the machine performs as it has been designed to do."[27] Here, the explorer's vision of the machine is quite important. At first he is indifferent to the apparatus, in contrast to the enthusiasm and pride of the operator who, though he is not the inventor, is "a devoted admirer of the apparatus." However (and here differences between Kafka and Roussel arise), as the explorer soon discovers, the new commander is over-zealous. The machine is not the perfected instrument or computer of *Locus Solus*, either. As the officer remarks, "Things sometimes go wrong, of course; I hope that nothing goes wrong today, but we have to allow for the possibility."[28]

The entire "colony" seems to be a post-lapsarian *locus solus* abandoned by its Canterel and left in the hands of assistants and aides who understand neither everything they need to know about the operation of its machinery nor the principles behind that operation. Instead, they have surrounded the absented commander's work with an awe proportional to their ignorance.

> Well, it isn't saying too much if I tell you that the organization of the whole penal colony is his (the first commander's) work. We knew even before he died that the organization of the colony is so perfect that his successor, even with a thousand new schemes in his head would find it impossible to alter anything.

As a result the machine is not quite broken down, but it is suffering decay. "'One of the cogwheels in the Designer is badly worn; it creaks a lot when it's working, you can hardly hear yourself speak; spare parts, unfortunately, are difficult to get here.'" A leather strap has broken and has had to be replaced by a crude chain. The penal colony is clearly a *locus solus* yielding to entropy.

Various things conspire to capture the explorer's growing interest in the Designer or torture device: the state of decay, the dawning recognition of the injustice represented by the very mechanicalness of the machine, the piteousness of the condemned man and his ignorance regarding his own fate. The officer carefully explains the mechanism in a detailed manner approaching Canterel's. He does so in French, though, knowing that the intended victim does not speak that language, even as the latter peers curiously at the machine. Though neither the explorer nor the condemned man understand its principles, its deeper significance dawns on us; as the explorer remarks, perhaps ironically, "'Now I know all about it.'" The machine is hideous and inhumane.

Similarly, the fiction invites the reader to expand interpretations beyond the literal text to some transcendental commentary on law, religion and man's relationship to God-given justice, a task essential if one is to "really read" "In the penal colony." This transcendence derives from the same linguistic points exploited by Roussel – ambiguity and the ambivalent quality of words – but this is a fulcrum used by Kafka to lever a much larger weight. Where Roussel directs our attention to the operation of the machine, Kafka asks us to peer only at the harrow, the rake-rack which inscribes its message upon the living flesh. "Imaginatively drawn to the horrible results of the machine's efficient operating we have no compelling reason to wonder how its separate parts work together in making its operation possible."[29] Indeed, Kafka invites us to "look beyond the harrow" where its only true significance lies. The explorer, as he witnesses the horrible operation, "found himself tempted [to interfere]. The injustice of the procedure and the inhumanity of the execution were undeniable."

From this point, we can trace the significance of all the other contrasts between the two modernist writing machines: Roussel's machines are filled with flourishes and embellishments that serve, if they have any purpose at all, as parts of the internal system; the script of the "Designer" is filled with ornamentation because, as the officer states,

> of course, the script cannot be a simple one . . . so there have to be lots and lots of flourishes around the actual script. The script itself runs around the body only in a narrow girdle; the rest of the body is reserved for the embellishments.

The embellishments of style prescribed by Roussel's "device" (what is called *pattes de mouche* in his short story "Parmi les noirs") exist for their own sake, pure formalisms. By contrast, Kafka metamorphoses them into elements of torture, a metaphor for the unjust arbitrariness of The Law. While Roussel's machine must function properly, or else the control of the master (and therefore the closure of the text) would be open to question, Kafka's machine *must* break down. Ultimately this writing machine is transformed from an "exquisite" instrument into, simply, a device for "plain murder." In the eyes of the explorer, the Designer's entropic writing is significant of the corruption of the principles upon which it was founded. At the climax of the story, the officer inserts himself into the machine and it breaks down, killing him.

Kafka collapses his various frames of significance: the machine breaks down, the officer dies, the corrupt system of justice reaches its final expression, the story ends. Each of these levels of signification serves to complement the meaningfulness and parable-like potential for interpretation of the story as a whole. When Roussel collapses his systems or levels of signification it is to emphasize even further the sterile perfection and unity of his machine. This difference is mirrored in the contrasting effect that reading Kafka and reading Roussel have on the reader. Kafka's fictions are invariably subjected to an enormous number of varying, sometimes conflicting interpretations, many of which seem plausible. Kafka's stories are likened to parables and fables whose universal appeal derives from their "tolerance," or "uncertainty."

Locus Solus, by contrast, can tolerate the exploration of a large number of internal correspondences, but very few, if any, external references. Roussel's texts stand in monolithic resistance to subjective interpretation, or, as Robbe-Grillet suggested, Roussel invites us to open the drawer, but "the drawer is empty."

THREE

CYBERNETICS AND LITERATURE

The events that have intervened between our postmodern age and Roussel's to make Roussel's project seem naïve are mostly scientific. What has made Roussel's inventions obsolete today are structures of seeing the world presented by the New Physics and complications in our concept of the machine offered by cybernetics.

Our century shows a remarkable intellectual unity, a vivacious dialogue between the arts and sciences that can be easily missed by a student working narrowly in a single discipline. Cybernetic fiction derives its material, method and imagery as much from the scientific developments of the twentieth century and the philosophical responses to those developments as it does from its literary predecessors. In order to understand fully the derivation of cybernetic fiction from this intellectual milieu, and in turn its contribution to what is perhaps the most important and moving debate of our age, it is first necessary to look at the philosophical and scientific roots of that debate. In the following two chapters I sketch the interplay between the scientific and philosophical movements which have created the terms on which cybernetic fiction is based.

THE ROOTS OF THE ARGUMENT

Cybernetics is one of the major scientific and intellectual movements of the postwar period. It evolved as a response to certain changes in the way physics viewed the universe that had their source in the work of John Clerk Maxwell in the 1860s. Maxwell's theories concerning thermodynamics and statistical mechanics were later refined and expanded by Ludwig Boltzmann and Willard Gibbs. These names – Maxwell, Boltzmann, Gibbs – are already familiar to readers of contemporary fiction through the work of Thomas Pynchon, especially as a result of Pynchon's fascination with entropy.[1] The power that Pynchon, for one, recognizes in the term *entropy* derives from the crucial role it played in the birth of cybernetics and in the philosophical battle waged between those twentieth-century physicists who viewed the universe as non-probabilistic, causal, and therefore mechanistic, and those who viewed our knowledge of the universe as essentially uncertain.

The power of cybernetics is that it holds out the promise of a resolution to a major ambivalence that has plagued (and inspired) western philosophy. The ambivalence, simply stated as a question, asks: "Are we machines whose functions, including mental ones, are describable by a formal, closed system of laws (algorithms), or are we transcendent (and therefore 'free') of our own mechanical descriptions of ourselves?" The cybernetic position on this question is to dismiss it, as Norbert Wiener does, "to the limbo of badly posed questions."[2] Acknowledging that we systematize what we see, we can sketch the ambivalence in slightly different terms: if the human observer is merely neutral with respect to the world he describes – essentially a device for receiving and processing information received about the world – then the universe, and humans as objects in that universe, should be amenable to description by totally deterministic logical systems. But if the human observer somehow creates or affects what he observes, then his descriptions are never free from his own paradoxical presence and the contingencies attendant upon his humanness.

These questions imply other ones concerning how humans know, to what extent the "objective" construct we call science is similar to the cultural construct we call myth, and whether the physical universe itself at all obeys the laws we use to describe it. The argument has its roots in the split between the Sophists and later Aristotelian thought, but it has especially gained popularity and pertinence in the last hundred years, during which it has played a role in science as well as philosophy. The shifting paradigms have lent credence to one side or another in this period, as classical dynamics have given way to thermodynamics, thermodynamics to statistical mechanics, statistical mechanics to quantum mechanics and the New Physics, and the New Physics to cybernetics. At the same time, the complementary philosophies and movements in the humanities – logical positivism and phenomenology, behaviorism and *Gestalt* psychology, modernism and postmodernism – have pursued the argument as well.

The Newtonian universe of classical mechanics was one in which time was reversible: since in the Newtonian view every action has an equal and opposite reaction, the amount of energy transferred from one moment in time through the actions of a system of energy and matter to another moment in time remains constant. This law of the conservation of matter and energy implied that the process could be reversed with no loss of energy, and then reversed again with the same results, *ad infinitum*. Because no essential change occurs over time, in the Newtonian view, time itself is reversible.

The trouble with this ideal or conservative view is that the world doesn't really work that way. If one pool ball strikes another, it transfers a good portion, but not all, of its energy to the second. Some of its energy is given up in the contact and to the felt surface of the table in the form of friction. No matter what its initial energy, in time the system of balls will come to rest. Although energy is still conserved, some of it is given up as unusable, randomized movement of molecules, called *entropy*. Furthermore, because the energy given up in this fashion is unrecuperable, we know that time is irreversible. In temporal and energistic terms, you can't go home again. Even on a cosmic scale, the planets in the solar system exert a sort of "drag" on each other which cannot be put back into the system to push those planets along. Rudolph Clausius gave entropy its name in 1845, and was the first to portray the universe as inevitably "running down" in the direction of maximum entropy. In the 1860s, John Clerk Maxwell proved the theorem in a more rigorous form which became known as the Second Law of Thermodynamics.

Although Newton was wrong (at least for closed systems locally), it was still held that if large numbers of systems were looked at statistically – or averaged, in a sense – Newtonian mechanics could still be applied. From this long view, groups of dynamic systems had statistically averaged energies which adhered to Newtonian predictions; at least, this was held to be true through the series of modifications made in physics through the successive work of Maxwell, Boltzmann, and Gibbs.

However, lurking uncomfortably just behind the apparent solidity of thermodynamics was Maxwell's demon – an unresolved challenge to the entire argument. Maxwell's demon is also familiar to readers of Pynchon's *The Crying of Lot 49* and "Entropy" and has been described to various extents in critical works about Pynchon. Yet, the proposition bears repetition here since it is crucial to the later philosophical debate as well as to cybernetic fictions like Pynchon's.

Maxwell proposed the following gedanken experiment: given an insulated box divided into two chambers such that there is a little doorway between the first and second chambers, imagine that sitting atop the box there is a demon. Now imagine that there is a gas divided into each chamber so that there is an equal average number of warm and cool molecules (the heat of a molecule is a function of how fast it is moving) in each chamber. The box then is in a state of maximum entropy, since the molecules in each chamber are undifferentiated and random, and there is no differential in energy across the barrier between the chambers available to do work. This demon is capable of distinguishing warmer molecules from cooler ones. Every time he sees a hot molecule heading from the first chamber to the second, or a cold molecule heading from the second chamber to the first, he opens a little door between them. Every time he sees a cold molecule heading from the first to the second or a hot molecule heading from the second to the first, he doesn't allow them to pass. If the demon is patient enough, all the faster, hotter molecules will be in chamber one and all the more sluggish, cooler ones in chamber two. This creates a temperature differential across the wall dividing them, and this differential can be used to do work. After all the available energy is used, and the system is at maximum entropy once more, the demon can repeat the process. The result is a perpetual-motion machine contravening the Second Law. Though everyone agreed the demon was impossible, he could not be conjured away by mathematics for several decades.

The solution to this paradox only became clear when the demon was treated as an agent who, at the minimum, needed information to decide which molecules had higher or lower velocities. In order to get this information – not only about their velocities but about their direction (i.e. whether they were headed toward the gate or not) – the demon had to "see" the molecules. In order to see, he had to have some channel between himself and the molecules such as light. The presence of such a channel implies that the demon had available energy, and therefore the system of which he was a part – the box-gas-demon system – *was not* in equilibrium or in a state of maximum entropy.

The exorcism of one demon conjured up another, more powerful one in the form of the Uncertainty Principle, codified by Werner Heisenberg in 1927 as an answer to the quantum mechanical view of the atom developed by Erwin Schrödinger. Schrödinger, building upon the work of Einstein, Louis de Broglie, and Wolfgang Pauli, evolved a model for the behavior of electrons in their orbits (quanta) that explained how they existed in discrete quanta as particles and yet propagated as waves, why the quanta were distinct, and why each quantum had its own invariant number of electrons. This latter proof is called "the Pauli Exclusion Principle." However, Heisenberg offered another interpretation of the same mathematical description of the behavior of electrons in the atom. He began with the empirical assumption that everything describable is knowable and observable, and vice versa. (The vice versa we might call "the positivist assumption.") Then he asked, but what and where is the electron? It cannot occupy all its possible positions in the orbit at once. How can we observe an electron from which to deduce the mechanics of the atom? Heisenberg was led to conclude, and then prove, that an observer cannot be certain of the position of the electron within the range of its possible positions; one could only establish its probable positions.[3]

One aspect of the Uncertainty Principle states that in order to determine the future position of a given body in motion – particularly an electron – one must first illuminate it or in some way receive information about it. That illumination will consequently alter either the momentum or the position of that particle. Therefore, it is impossible to predict the future position of a particle, although we have obtained from that particle all the information that should be sufficient to determine it.

This had shattering implications for the view of nature constructed by physics. For one thing, in the macroscopic world delivered to us by our senses, such a proposition is highly counter-intuitive. It does not make "sense." For instance, by looking at the direction and speed of a car, I am able to predict where it will be in a few seconds with respect to my body. I am performing a differential equation based on what I can see. (If the car is slowing down or speeding up, that calculation becomes a bit harder – a second-order differential equation – and I am likely to wait on the curb for it to pass.) On such natural judgements my life depends every day, especially when the taxicabs are out in downtown Manhattan. The amount of energy of the light needed to deliver this information to me, however, is insignificant compared to the momentum of the car, so it can hardly alter its direction. But on the sub-atomic level, from which a picture of the universe is extrapolated, such relatively small quantities matter, and certainties, as Heisenberg maintains, become impossible.

Heisenberg himself, in two later dissertations on the implications of quantum physics – *Physics and Beyond* and *Physics and Philosophy* – describes the philosophical consequences of his theory: "We can no longer talk of the behavior of a particle apart from the process of observation," he writes. That is, man no longer can rely upon empirical reality "as such."[4] As he explains,

> The conception of the objective reality of elementary particles has thus evaporated in a curious way; not into the fog of some new, obscure, not-yet-understood reality concept, but into the transparent clarity of a mathematics that no longer represents the behavior of elementary particles, but rather our knowledge of that behavior.[5]

In other words, "The thing in itself is for the atomic physicist, if he uses the concept at all, finally a mathematical structure."[6] *The observer can never know reality, he can only know his theory*, which in essence is nothing more than a structure of information the theoretician has devised, a model or a metaphor. "In science," Heisenberg states, "the object of research is no longer nature in itself, but rather nature exposed to man's questioning, and to this extent, man also meets himself."[7]

This troubled those scientists who relied upon the sense of absolute certainty and causality traditionally promised by nineteenth-century science. It echoes the spirit of scepticism that has re-emerged in western philosophy in influential (though often brief) periods from the Sophists, through Democritus to Kant. Heisenberg's position also looks forward to the version of man's relationship to his world offered by phenomenology. As Norbert Wiener explains it in his book *Cybernetics*, this development devastated the positivistic tendencies of "that still quasi-Newtonian world of Gibbs."[8] It replaced that semi-classical view of time and order "by one in which time . . . can in no way be reduced to an assembly of deterministic threads of development." Or in other words, "There is no set of observations conceivable which can give us enough information about the past of a system to give us complete information as to its future."[9]

The physics community was soon embroiled in a profound debate, an intense theoretical struggle between those who saw the power of this view of chance and uncertainty as an essential feature of the universe, and those who rejected such a notion as abhorrent. Max Planck and Einstein held to the "intuitively obvious" view of the universe as a system of causes that would ultimately be explained by a mechanistic model. Bohr's iconoclasm is understandable in the light of the fact that he proposed the anti-classical notion that the electron can move around the atom only in certain orbits. By contrast, Einstein's and Planck's conservatism is curious, considering the fact that Einstein devised the single most powerfully counter-intuitive view of the universe in his theory of relativity, and Planck proved that light existed – monstrously it then seemed – both in wave and particulate (or "quantum and corpuscular") form simultaneously. But each of these theoreticians was revolutionary in a way that preserved the mechanistic view of the cosmos and was therefore acceptable: their theories complicated our view of nature but adhered strictly to the tacit and unquestioned assumption underlying all modern sciences, that theory could predict events because they were causally linked.

Heisenberg's principle, complemented a few years later by Gödel's theorem (which proved mathematically that no logical system was both complete and consistent) seemed unacceptable. Even though incontrovertible mathematical rigor was at least for the moment on the side of Heisenberg, intuition, and even a sort of vigorous spiritual belief, the sort of metaphysics of the machine which Turbayne describes, lay with the conservative view.

In an excellent book which stresses the role of the aesthetic and emotional components of this debate among great physicists, Arthur I. Miller uncovers the intuitive imperatives that governed their views. Miller writes, "Should the search [for a refutation] fail, a dramatic change in the world view would be necessary because it could very well signal the need for statistical laws denying knowledge of the cause of phenomena: [entailing] a priori probabilities."[10] This threat inspired Einstein to one of the century's most famous snappy replies: "I cannot be convinced that God plays dice with the universe." Bohr tried to envisage a resolution or synthesis between the two opposing terms of the dialectic, but failed. Erwin Schrödinger, whose work in quantum physics complemented Heisenberg's, confessed that he was motivated to work towards a refutation simply because he felt that "a theory of knowledge for which we suppress intuitions" was philosophically insupportable when applied to the atom. He wrote: "For although there may exist things which cannot be comprehended by our forms of thought . . . from a philosophical point of view I am sure that the structure of the atom is not one of them."[11]

Heisenberg's views none the less slowly gained ground, supported by the unassailability of his proof and the growing body of physical evidence. At the same time, an interesting counter-development was also growing. In 1929, Leo Szilard suggested that if the information gained about the electron in its own right were equated to the loss in entropy (the gain in organization) in a system such as the demon's box of Maxwell's gedanken experiment, then some of the contradictions between a total explanation and uncertainty could be resolved. He further suggested what was apparent everywhere in man's culture: intelligence intervened in nature to reduce entropy, a notion echoed by Wiener and one that has only recently been given an approximate explanation on the level of physical theory by Ilya Prigogine.[12]

A few years later, in the 1930s, several theoreticians working separately but along parallel lines began to formulate a statistical equation that would be proportionate to entropy and define the amount of information in a given transmission. These researchers included Claude Shannon of Bell Laboratories, Erwin Schrödinger, and Norbert Wiener, who became most closely associated with the development of cybernetics as a result of his two books on the subject, *Cybernetics: Control and Communication in Animal and Machine* (1948) and *The Human Use of Human Beings* (1950). Wiener is most eloquent about the direct link between the New Physics and the growth of cybernetics in reaction to it. In *The Human Use of Human Beings* he wrote:

> This recognition of an element of incomplete determinism, almost an irrationality in the world, is in a certain way parallel to Freud's admission of a deep irrational component in human conduct and thought. In the present world of political as well as intellectual confusion, there is a natural tendency to class Gibbs, Freud, and the proponent of the modern theory of probability, Heisenberg, together as representatives of a single tendency; yet I do not wish to press this point. . . . Yet in recognition of a fundamental element of chance in the texture of the universe itself, these men are close to one another and close to the tradition of St Augustine. For this random element, this organic incompleteness, is one which without too violent a figure of speech we may consider evil; the negative evil which St Augustine characterizes as incompleteness.[13]

In an attempt to answer these "evil" propositions, Wiener assisted at the birth of a new science, coining the word *cybernetics* for a field of study he recognized as essentially interdisciplinary.

The actual community of theoreticians and researchers who became the intellectual godparents of cybernetics included physicists, electrical engineers, communications engineers, mathematicians, physiologists, psychologists, biophysicists, and one doctor, Jerome Lettvin, who then practiced at the Boston City Hospital. In the winter of 1943–4, a joint meeting on the subject was held at Princeton, and in 1947 Wiener, consulting his colleagues, agreed to name the entire science after the Greek word for governor, *kybernos*. The fact that only forty years later we may safely use the word *cybernetics* to include work not only in information theory and communications sciences, but artificial intelligence, computer science, certain mechanistic schools of psycho- and neuro-physiology, and those branches of psychology that view the human as a sum of stimulus-response (or input-output) mechanisms, particularly behaviorism, is a tribute to the power of the original concept.

Wiener was right in recognizing so early the essentially interdisciplinary implications of the science of information. Even before it was named, cybernetics attracted the attention of Margaret Mead and Gregory Bateson, who subsequently used the notion of the black box as a metaphor for the human brain and applied some cybernetic principles to construct a model for human behavior.[14]

Despite these outward-rippling implications, cybernetics was still at its core a direct reaction to the contingent and uncertain view of the universe promoted by the New Physics. Its primary intention was and still is to reconquer chance by subordinating it within a larger system of mathematical logic, and to bring the world described by physics into conformity with the actual conditions of the natural and social structures which are the contexts for human experience. The essence of the nonconformity between man-made and physical systems swung around the fulcrum of entropy: physics described a world doomed to ultimate degradation, but man experiences a biosphere continually evolving, specializing, growing more complex, and a social and intellectual world that outstripped even nature. The Second Law still held for the cosmos but was contradicted by the human condition, all metaphors aside. As Wiener noted, biological and social systems are local islands of increasing order surviving in the universal tide toward increasing entropy or disorder. The genetic code, the very presence of man's convoluted brain and the convoluted intellect implied thereby, the cities, sciences and advanced technology conceived among those convolutions, all could be attributed to this anomaly. The codification and quantification of uncertainty, in the form of information itself, was intended to resolve the contradiction. Further, it was meant to bring under the purview of a scientific theory all communication, human or otherwise, the very act of expression – particularly systematic expression – itself. While Heisenberg placed man, that essentially uncertain creature, at the center of his theory, Wiener *et al.* suggested a way that uncertainty itself could be resolved. All codes, all the structures of information, could be accounted for, as well as man's relationship to the universe as cosmic cryptographer.[15]

AN INTRODUCTION TO CYBERNETICS

Despite the humanistic bent Wiener shows in *The Human Use of Human Beings*, cybernetics encouraged, and in fact provided, a sort of ultimate justification for a view of the human brain as an elaborate mechanism. Ashby's and Turing's theoretical designs for ultimate "learning machines," and the convenient analogy between the all-or-nothing electrochemical action of the neurons that comprise the brain and the binary gates that formed the basis for electrical computing machines, both contributed to the cause. Even in the original document of the science, *Cybernetics*, Wiener extends his technical assertions about the nature of information transmission to include the physiological information processor in the human skull.

In turn, these suggestions added more ammunition to the argument against Uncertainty. *Cybernetics* did not provide a refutation of Heisenberg; it subsumed his theorem into a more powerful determinism. Although the observer's act of observation is an essential part of the phenomenon observed, according to this argument, the very act of observation itself, because it derives from a mechanism (the human brain), can be reduced to the terms of a mechanical model for the communication of information. Thus, the laws of cybernetics concern the telephone transceiver and the cortex of the brain, electrical pulses and brainwaves, information coding and human languages equally. Such esoterica, traditionally reserved for philosophy, the study of learning and aesthetic perception, now also were in the rightful, some might say necessary, province of mechanical descriptions or formulae.

In his reconstruction of the pedigree of cybernetics in *The Human Use of Human Beings*, Wiener carefully chose the pantheon of philosophers and scientists who (he claims) formed its intellectual ancestry. In his chapter "Computing machines and the nervous system," he notes the complementarity between Bertrand Russell's logical positivism and the Turing machine. He also contrasts the "static" theory of ideas and perceptual mechanisms proposed by the empiricists – Locke, Berkeley and Hume – with Pavlov's dynamic notion of "patterns of action."[16] At the same time, *The Human Use of Human Beings* is filled with Wiener's sincere and often striking disquisitions on the value of art, on language, philosophy, aesthetics and creativity. He even relates the growth of corrupting influences on the mores of western civilization, particularly commercialism, to a sort of social entropy. Despite these humanizing embellishments, the title of *The Human Use of Human Beings* retains a chilling ambiguity that characterizes the potential of the metaphors proposed by cybernetics to promote the techniques of human manipulation and control. There is no denying that cybernetics represents the ultimate science of technique, most successful and enlightened when it is translated into the hardware of computers, communications devices, prosthetic substitutes for human anatomy and functions (pace-makers, hearing aids, reading machines or "vocoders" for the blind, etc.), yet most threatening where it has been least demonstrably effective, in social engineering.[17] Still, the fervor of the scientific and philosophical debate over programs for human engineering arises from the extent to which the mechanization of humanity tends to entice those for whom the manipulation of people holds profit.

Information, Uncertainty, Entropy

The pivotal concept that gives cybernetics its philosophical as well as scientific power is its definition of the relationship between the triad of terms *information, uncertainty* and *entropy*. Information theory proposes an algorithm for quantifying uncertainty in terms of probabilities, thereby attacking directly the irritant: the Heisenbergian view that any statement we can make about nature is probabilistic. The formula for this quantification is an analog of the Boltzmann-Gibbs equation, implying an analogy that can be translated more plainly as follows: just as in thermodynamic systems there is an inevitable tendency for organization and usable energy to decrease in favor of randomness and unusable energy (entropy), so in information systems there is an inevitable tendency for messages between parts of the system to be degraded by disorganization.

However, the relationship between thermodynamic and informational entropy is more than an analogy. Since all systems are comprised of matter, energy and information (as the solution to the Maxwell demon puzzle implies) and every physical channel has a certain measurable capacity to transmit information (as Shannon showed) – the amount of information delivered by such a channel in a system is proportional to the amount of thermodynamic entropy that results from the transfer.

For most of us who first look at the concept of information without the aid of the calculus by which it is defined, there are several problems that it presents to our intuition. First, while the metaphorical potency of entropy in thermodynamics is negative (entropy is randomness, disorganization, an ineluctable loss that occurs with every physical reaction and which contributes to the final "heat death" of the universe), entropy in information science is more ambiguous: it designates the initial conditions of variability – the amount of uncertainty – which are the necessary preconditions out of which information arises. *Information* is simply a measure of the probability that a given signal or element will be selected from among a set of differentiated elements, a set of alternatives. Therefore, information is proportional to the amount of variety (entropy) in the original set and has an accompanying sign change; information is "negentropy." The more random the assortment of potential signs or elements in a code, the more information a choice from among those alternatives communicates. Information is maximized when all the possible signs are equiprobable (randomly distributed or varied) since this implies a state of maximum uncertainty or maximum entropy.

For this reason, the binary code on which digital computers and models of neural action in the brain are based is a simple ideal. The elements – the choice between zero and one, on and off – are equiprobable: the system favors neither one nor the other and all middles are excluded. Thus, the essential unit of information, the *bit*, is measured by the logarithm in base 2 of the selection. Abraham Moles describes this as "the binary logarithm of the number of choices necessary to define the message without ambiguity."[18]

The conditions in the natural languages, by contrast, are far from this ideal of maximum entropy, since as every amateur cryptographer knows, certain letters are much more likely to occur than others. The Scrabble game gives a neat, though crude, model for this natural condition in the way it weights certain letters. In the repertoire of all letters, E, A, I, O, U, S, T, R, for example, are much more likely to occur in a word (a condition also reflected in the fact that there are more of these letters than others in the finite set of tiles that come with the game, amounts that roughly approximate to their use under normal conditions) and therefore these letters carry less information and are worth only one point each. At the same time, letters such as J, Q, X, and Z are much less common under natural circumstances, occur much less frequently among the set of letter tiles, and thus carry more information and are weighted eight or ten points each. Similarly, in literature, we know intuitively that a pulp genre novel – a detective fiction, say – by the very degree it adheres to certain conventions of that genre, by its very predictability, communicates less information than a so-called experimental or post-modern novel. Such "generic" novels are much less rare than the latter kind, are much more available to the consumer-reader, and offer, in terms of the entire repertoire of possible novels, less variety than a novel which deviates from a norm. As we shall see, however, this analogy (it is nothing more) relies on a very reduced version of literature and reading.

Redundancy

This leads us to the third important concept in cybernetics, that of *redundancy*. The more redundant an element in a code is, and the more redundancy or duplication in the code itself, the less information it carries. The amount of information in a message is an inverse measure of the receiver's expectation that a certain element will be sent down the line. For instance, I can be almost certain that when it is my turn to select seven letters at the beginning of a Scrabble game, at least one will be an *a* or an *e*, but I would be very surprised if I selected a *z*, an *x*, and a *q* all in one turn. The difficulty of constructing words from those letters, particularly if there are few highly redundant letters to help me, reflects a corollary theorem: the message most difficult to communicate is the one with the most information.

I form my expectations on the basis of previous experience, and previous experience is brought into the present by memory, constituted in part by redundancy. If an event has occurred frequently, I infer that it is more likely to happen in the future. When it does occur, it carries with it less information.

Redundancy has two natural effects on the amount of information carried in a message: there can be a great deal of redundancy in the initial array or repertoire from which signals are selected, decreasing the potential for information; and the message itself can obtain redundancy as it is selected, reducing over time the amount of information it transmits. For example, the signal: * – † * – † * – †, though it is selected from an equiprobable repertoire of three signs, is redundant. I can be fairly certain that the next two terms will be * and –.

Wiener extrapolates the notion of redundancy into a discussion of the banality and decadence of certain works of art. "More and more," he complains, "we must accept a standardized, inoffensive and insignificant product which, like the white bread of the bakeries, is made rather for its keeping and selling properties than for its food value."[19] For Wiener, novelty is a positive good in itself, since it opposes banality, adds information to the environment, and derives directly from the will to express something new, to create. At the same time, Wiener derides the "pedantic avantgardistes" (who are presumably imitating the creativity or novelty of certain true innovators and are thus more imitative than they would be willing to admit) and a system of education "in which forms have largely superseded educational content."[20] Forms are the traces of redundancy, Wiener implies, and patterns are the fulfillment of expectations.

But Wiener has here glossed a crucial paradox in the human use of information, a paradox that leads us to an appreciation of the second difficulty encountered when trying to translate the mathematical concepts described by the calculus of information theorems into more familiar terms. This paradox can be stated simply: *information is quantified in proportion to its variety only, but humans rely upon redundancy in order to perceive meaningful patterns in their communication with the world and each other.* For this reason, all natural languages are highly redundant (approximately

80 per cent according to some calculations) not only on the level of the letter but on the increasingly complex levels of syntax, semantics, normal conversation, organizational communication, etc. Even in those most "original" codes of literary expression, the discourse between author and reader relies upon conventions – manifested redundancies – of plot, characterization, theme, structure, narrative, etc. Redundancy is a measure of organization, and for human purposes organization communicates information.

To see this, we need only examine the replication of structures in the human brain's processing of information, reflected in the replication of structures in our cities, social patterns and cultural artefacts: the all-pervasiveness of form and the ubiquity of the relationship between form and redundancy reveal this association between pattern and significance. Or we could merely examine the effect of the techniques of repetition, the paratactical devices of classical rhetoric in a hortatory speech, or meter, rhyme and epithets in poetry (what Michael Riffaterre calls "the recurrence of equivalent forms, *parallelism*"[21]), or the complex collusion between patterns of words, actions, and ideas that comprise even the simplest story. Or we could examine the traditional and instinctive equation between beauty and the structures that rely on redundancy in all the arts: symmetry, balance, harmony, unity.

Abraham Moles's work, *Information Theory and Esthetic Perception,* confronts this paradox and attempts to resolve it by distinguishing between *semantic information* and *aesthetic information.* Semantic information is that part of a message received by a human that can be systematically analyzed. It has a "universal logic, structured and articulatable, translatable into a foreign language and serves in the behaviorist conception to prepare actions." By contrast, however, Moles posits the existence of another component of human communication, aesthetic information that is

> untranslatable, refers to a repertoire of knowledge common to the particular transmitter and particular receptor. Theoretically, this information cannot be translated into any other language or system of symbols because this other language does not exist. One may liken it to the concept of personal information.[22]

This does not resolve the paradox; it merely states its terms. By so doing, it fully anticipates the counter-philosophy offered cybernetics by phenomenologists such as Edmund Husserl, Martin Heidegger, and Maurice Merleau-Ponty, and echoes – though not intentionally – Michael Polanyi's notion of "personal knowledge." (I explore the phenomenological counter-statement to cybernetics in the next chapter.) Moles is at least partly participating in the movement, or at the very least echoing the *Gestalt* psychologists and phenomenologists whose ideas were current in France, where Moles wrote in the 1950s. He even refers to Maurice Merleau-Ponty explicitly, for instance, and in nominating the term "aesthetic information" is attempting to signal his awareness that the work of art is more complex and apparently spontaneous than any calculation can account for.[23]

Yet, at the risk of quibbling over semantics, I would suggest that the term *information* itself is misleading, since it includes tacitly the sort of determinism that has been lent that word by cybernetics. I prefer the less cumbersome word *meaning* to refer to the private, profound, *Gestalt*-like component of communication that is independent of information and beyond the reach of mathematically derived formulae. Whatever we call it, it is clear that humans have a certain unquantifiable capacity to appreciate "significance" or gain enlightenment or be moved to action and emotion by messages independently of the quantity of information they receive (in cybernetic terms). We need only note the high degree of redundancy, the number of clichés, the singing of rhythms and repetitive phrases which demagogues traditionally employ to move audiences to fervor and action. The inverse is also true: messages with large amounts of information do not necessarily communicate significance to an audience nor move them to action. Texts with maximal information are often unintelligible, let alone moving. A sentence can retain its grammatical structure and correctness but lose its semantic significance. (The English translator of Moles's original French offers a typical nonsense passage from Edward Lear as an example.)

Similarly, if pushed to its natural limit, we could maximize information by completely randomizing or disorganizing, producing a situation similar to the kind of intentional chaos and potent randomizing William Burroughs performs through his cut-up method (see Chapter Five) or Donald Barthelme achieves in some of his more curious experiments. One of these, "Bone bubbles," a text I like to think of as "dissociative" (as opposed to associative), appears to offer some sense, but is nothing more than a collection of phrases and words that end by creating a striking total expressive effect but communicate no "message" in the conventional sense. Yet it has high information content. On the other hand, any meanings that accrue to it have to do with how we interpret the text as an artefact. In sum, information is related neither to sense nor to meaning, though sense and meaning are usually related.

> strange reactions scattered black satin pulp hitched up her skirts for a look but he forgot to sigh world power ambiguous orders dipstick sweating or beaded with fine amber colours disabled servant standing in the center of the frame dead tulips convulsions lasting more than three hours arrested for having no ticket hinges of the body so cough spit feel slights pains local or general heat red flags on naval vessels I gave water away married but they can't live together packing the air the souls of the sleeper was enlarged preposterously.[24]

The message which cannot be predicted beforehand and which has no visible or discernible order, communicates the most information but also seems the least human. Many Burroughs readers have felt the ordinary surprise at the novelty of his images turn to shock and outrage. But these result as much from the rate at which new elements are forced upon us as it does from the nature of the elements themselves. I conjecture that there is some invisible and indefinable threshold of "tolerance" for new information that is peculiar to each reader and interpreted in terms of pleasure and pain. That this threshold varies not only from reader to reader but from page to page of the same text demonstrates the paradoxical relationship between information and meaning.

Similarly, Pynchon tends to disorganize his message, exposing edges and levels by selecting surprising elements and combinations – shifting perspectives, voices, metaphors, etc. – and yet compels the reader to perceive the presence of deeper patterns of organization, "a plot" amid the "universal rot." This paradoxical effect makes the explicator's task extremely difficult, since it simultaneously compels and frustrates the reader's task (see Chapter Six).

On the other side of the scale are messages which have very low information content but high, even compelling, import for the human audience. Examples include parables, which adhere to relatively conventional structures, fairy-tales, and even certain phrases and words that seem to catch fire in the public imagination all at once, get repeated to death, and then become frozen permanently into the language or, exhausted from use, wander off to die in some linguistic graveyard. This sort of linguistic Darwinism can be found in the fate of lively metaphors which become petrified into clichés.

We can talk about the redundancy of a work of art increasing as it progresses (a specialized case of what information theorists call a "Markoff Process" in which past events in the message affect future ones). Names and formal elements recur. Descriptions fall into a pattern. The plot itself is a product of repetitions. In fact, the redundancy of literature and music seems to protect the integrity of their central message just as genes for similar features (phenotypes) become encoded on different chromosomes to protect the integrity of their message. In terms of organization, the form of a work functions to reduce information, but at the same time it presents a meaningful ensemble of signs, so that significance is preserved by that form like an insect in amber.

For example, consider the letters "ERT" as an ensemble. These letters, in the repertoire of all letters in English, would communicate the same amount of information in any order, but none of those orders "mean" anything in themselves: RET? TER? TRE? However, consider the following ensemble: A LOWER R TE in which the elements RTE are separated by a space (which can be considered a twenty-seventh element of the alphabet). Adding punctuation marks and the differentiation between capital and lower case, we get an alphabet as high as sixty or so. In this form, the redundancy of the message, its context, and its arrangement as elements in what we can presume is the repertoire of all words in English, indicate that R TE is probably part of the word "RATE" in which the "A" has been omitted. The more of a pattern I present, the more I protect the intended message, and the less crucial the presence of that missing "A" becomes to preventing any ambiguities. With the addition of semantic information to make the three letters part of a unit which is taken from the ensemble "All phrases in English," we get a message that is locked into a pattern by the author's experience of the language and the readers' certainty that the particular message will adhere to certain rules:

"Nor would I love at a lower rate"

a line in a poem by Andrew Marvell, "To my coy mistress." Note that as we present higher levels of organization, we also reduce our uncertainty. Note also the strong relationship between rule and redundancy. As we read more of the poem, we invoke more rules and systems, which in turn create redundancies. The poem is the trace of, or precipitate for, our coded experiences; as they crystallize the text's code for us, the text becomes simultaneously more redundant and more meaningful. We understand that the line is part of a metaphor, the metaphor part of an argument (the speaker invites his mistress to bed) or complaint, and the complaint part of a sub-genre of seventeenth-century poetry.

Indeed, *the entire act of reading in the enriched sense of that word seems to be an act of creating redundancies, eliminating ambiguities from the message in order to infer an often highly ambiguous sensibility*. Reading slows down the message, which decreases the rate of information flow – and widens the bandwidth, so to speak – which in turn decreases the efficiency of the channel of transmission, but all for the sake of meaning, for the crucial determination of the outward- and inward-rippling effects of literary intent.

At the end of this train of logic we come to a view of reading itself as the source of meaning. The text, in this view, is the trace of a set of codes, some of which are frozen there by the author, some of which are brought there by the reader. Finally, as Merleau-Ponty suggests, the text says "more by what it doesn't say" than by what it does, and reading becomes the attempt to make present what is absent. However, cybernetics offers no term for the quantification of silence other than zero, though we know that the silence of the text produces more than nothing. This stance, which is partly structuralist and partly phenomenological, requires not only that we see the text as a system of multilayered codes – arrangements of signs which are essentially empty in themselves – but as a place where the reader actively deciphers the codes. In Barthes's terms, the text seeks its "degree zero'' of interpretation. Gilles Deleuze discovers it in his analysis of Proust:

> The modern work of art is anything it may seem; it is even its very property of being whatever we like, of having the over-determination of whatever we like, from the moment *it works*: the modern work of art is a machine and functions as such.

Then, speaking specifically of Proust's *Remembrance of Things Past*, he writes:

> [It] is a cryptogram which decodes and recodes all our social, diplomatic, strategic, erotic, and aesthetic languages . . . anything we like provided we make the whole thing work. . . . Why a machine? Because the work of art, so understood, is essentially productive – productive of certain truths.[25]

But the machine of signs by itself is inert, as is the imagination of the reader or author. It is only in collaboration that the two create ''truth.'' The text may be an interplay of codes, but it is the reader who makes them play.

Thus, our reading of Barthelme's ''Bone bubbles'' will not rest until we can reduce the enormous amount of information to meaningful structures or until we can place the anomaly of its dissociative structure in a relatively banal context: Barthelme is expressing X, the flood of raw information that characterizes contemporary life, the verbal detritus that constitutes cultural milieu or what he elsewhere calls ''the leading edge of the trash phenomenon.''

Noise vs. Information

The two stumbling-blocks to the layperson's appreciation of cybernetics that I discuss above are really corollaries: the first is that information is really disorganization, the second that information and meaning are independent qualities in human communication. A third way of viewing the problem – which really invokes the deeper phenomenological questions about the relationship between human consciousness and communciation and the mathematical designation of certain processes in systematic communication – is the relationship between information and *noise*.

At first glance, one of the surprising aspects of information theory is that there is no distinction made at the level of the mathematical description between noise and information. Noise is simply defined as that portion of a signal that is "unwanted," which is not intended by the sender. But noise, like information, is proportional to the entropy of the system and the variety of the code. Moles writes, "There is no absolute structural difference between noise and signal. The only difference that can be logically established between them is based exclusively on the concept of intent on the part of the transmitter."[26]

This inability to make the distinction plays directly into the hands of the Heisenbergian irritant which cybernetics intended to dispel, and it adds force to the phenomenological counter-argument, as we shall see. But first, let me illustrate the problem.

A cryptographer in an intelligence agency sends to his agent in the field a page from *Othello* filled with what appear to be stray marks, underlined words, and indecipherable scribbles on top of the actual text itself. For a reader of Shakespeare, these marginalia and marks are "noisy": distracting, random effects, like static on a radio, sometimes even interfering with the primary signal. But the agent, reading the same page, knows that the stray signs are part of a code which had been devised beforehand. For him, Shakespeare's words are irrelevant to the intention of the message, just so much noise. This has two immediate implications: the first is that one man's information is another's noise; and the second that we cannot talk about information in real situations apart from the intention of the sender and the capacity, or expectations, or understanding, of the human receiver or audience. In other words, information and nonsense can only be distinguished by their context.[27]

At this point, we are driven down three related roads. The first leads us back to the Heisenberg Uncertainty Principle, and the second to phenomenology which I will deal with in the next chapter. The third is the paradoxical relationship between the machinery of observation and the things we observe. It is a curious fact that the universe seems to be formed in such a way that it frustrates our desire for certainty. The means it uses to do this involve limiting the capacity of the very channels we construct for our observations of it. As an event is observed ever more narrowly (on more microscopic or more telescopic levels) it eventually becomes swamped by the inefficiency of the physical channel: in effect, we receive a mixture of information and noise until a point is reached beyond the refinement of our instruments, and the message is swamped by noise. This is especially clear on the microscopic level: the history of the microscope also describes a history of increasingly refined observations, equivalent to our growing capacity to get information from the invisible world. However, at every point in its development, the instrument itself reached a certain physical limit beyond which one could only speculate: thus, Leuwanhoeck could see the gross structure of spermatozoa, but fancied that those wriggling cells held homuncules. The blurs count as visual information in the structural or mathematical sense, but they represent anomalies (at best) or mere blurs (at worst) that then become open to interpretation. Into those blurs rush our imaginations, which might speculate but can never be certain. Similarly, even with the invention of the electron microscope, we discover that we cannot get information from the electron itself without swamping the event with the energy we need to carry that information back to our eyes. Shannon's dictum – "all physical channels possess a certain quantifiable capacity to transmit information"[28] – has a darker corollary: all information must be communicated through a physical channel which has a finite capacity when humans are on the sending or receiving end of the transmission. That is, instruments are subject to the same physical laws as are the events they are directed at observing.

The swamping of the message by the noise of transmission is not restricted purely to our instrumentation. It applies equally to our theories, which in this sense become aspects of instrumentations (see my comments on Heidegger, following). Every instrument is partly the embodiment of a theory about how to "read" nature's text. As Barrett remarks, every machine is "an embodied decision procedure." At the same time, every theory implies a direction for scrutiny that is selective and therefore exclusive; it selects which phenomena are to be organized into which logical structure. To paraphrase Goethe: "All observations presuppose a theory."

The quantum theory of the atom and the electron microscope are both instruments for observation, flashlights that both illuminate a circle and at the same time create a surround of darkness that is even greater for the light having been shone at all. Every theory determines which information is significant and which noise; and as Thomas Kuhn has argued, all theories determine a priori which phenomena qualify as legitimate and which as anomalies.[29] In order to describe events that are very much beneath or very much greater than the dimensions of our own human sphere – like the structure of elementary and evanescent particles or the structure and origin of the universe – we are enslaved to our theories, microscopes and telescopes alike, which can never determine or transmit all the information about a phenomenon. The only way to do that would be to become the phenomenon itself.

This takes on special meaning when the human mind considers the human mind. In a strange way, we are led to an understanding of the virtue tacit in certain mystical or holistic viewpoints which suggest that humans can only know themselves as consciousness; otherwise, any attempt to describe ourselves to ourselves – for instance, through the imperfect medium of language – immediately makes us into phenomena for which complete explanations are impossible.

SELF-CONSCIOUSNESS: TOWARDS A CYBERNETICS OF CYBERNETICS

Most recently, cyberneticists have recognized this essential limitation on information theory – the necessity of including the human observer in calculations about systems, particularly social systems, under observation – and have suggested codifications of this limitation in several ways. Gordon Pask, for instance, describes what he calls the Mach-Duhem-Poincaré Hypothesis: "All empirical phenomena are underdetermined by data and therefore permit the construction of an indefinite number of theories."[30] At the same time, cyberneticists have moved in the direction of creating a self-reflexive cybernetic theory, one which would attempt to account for the information–noise paradoxes that arise when we try to apply cybernetic models to human acts of knowing and communicating.

Pask notes that each cybernetic model suggests two levels of analysis: one in which the observer attempts "to stipulate the system's purpose" and one in which the observer attempts "to stipulate his own purpose."[31] Humberto Maturana, a Chilean neurophysicist, calls this second level cybernetic analysis by a strikingly literary name, "autopoeisis."[32] This autopoetic function is associated with thinking beings; it implies self-consciousness. Heinz von Foerster, in turn, notes that "this second order stipulation" implies that in order to give a full account of a phenomenon, theorists must first develop "a cybernetics of cybernetics."[33] Foerster even imagines what such a cybernetics to the second power would look like: it would codify the presence of the observer through "a calculus of infinite recursions" or "a calculus of self-reference." Anthony Wilden, whose own transdisciplinary speculations make him more a critic than an advocate of cybernetics, warns that cybernetic analysis of human behavior and expression such as social organization, economics and psychology results in a reductionism that can only be cured by a cybernetics of cybernetics that will be both "interdisciplinary and transdisciplinary."[34]

All of this implies a newer, more phenomenological awareness in the science of communication and information, at least on this theoretical end. I began this chapter by stating that our century has a remarkable intellectual unity, a capacity to cross-fertilize and engage in dialogue that often produces subtle results and surprising connections. The growth of cybernetics into a recognition of its own inadequacy without an account of the role of the observer is remarkable, occurring as it did in just three decades.

Herbert Simon remarks in *The Sciences of the Artificial*, "All correct reasoning is a grand system of tautologies, but only God can make use of that fact. The rest of us must painstakingly and fallibly tease out the consequences of our assumptions."[35] The tautological nature of rational systems is something recognized tacitly by authors of cybernetic fiction, as I show in later chapters. Cybernetic fiction proposes a way to make use of this "curious fact." Indeed, cybernetic fiction *is* the machine that makes use of the several facts that foil cybernetic explanations of human communication. For one, it shares with all fiction the tendency to multiply ambiguities rather than resolve them. In this way, the very assumption of cybernetics, that the intelligible text works to disambiguate messages, is inverted.

Fiction employs an elaborate technology of self-consciousness.

The author talks to himself through the mechanics of his writing, and the style of the text, its formal arrangements, its patterns and codes, are the signs by which an author not only guides the reader to interpretation but announces his consciousness of his own project, his intention. The most arcane experiments in fiction often employ the most self-consciousness, and are marked by self-reflexive passages in which the author typically questions the assumptions of his own project, or addresses his own awareness at the moment of composition or an imaginary reader conjured for the occasion.[36]

Self-consciousness is precisely that aspect of human intelligence that focuses and polarizes any debate about the differences between humans and machines. Descartes, who was as responsible as any philosopher after Pythagoras for a mechanistic view of the universe, told his students that he would believe a machine was human "when it told me so itself." The history of human-imitating machines, of artificial intelligence devices, can be traced along the line of progress that has brought machines to approximate ever more closely to the expressions of human self-consciousness: movement, perception of data, learning, speech, and thought itself. In turn, philosophies committed to the presupposition of human freedom have been pushed into ever more narrow sophistries in their definition of what, precisely, constitutes human self-awareness.

I conceive of cybernetic fiction as at once a battleground for these ideas and as a final weapon in defense of the differences between human and artificial intelligence. The concern by Barth, Burroughs, Pynchon, McElroy, Beckett and Barthelme for the toils of self-consciousness in their heroes and in their art is a sign of this struggle. They have all constructed fictions that appear to be machines but foil the simple production of sense, the blueprinting, that mechanism promises. For me, one of the pleasures of explicating Pynchon, for instance, comes from knowing that I can never be correct and complete in the structures I assemble to explain his work. Interpretations, conflicting recognitions, blossom and then explode in one's hands, making the reader aware of awareness itself.

FOUR
COUNTER-STATEMENT

The philosophical reaction to cybernetics was strong and immediate. It had its roots in a counter-mechanistic tradition that can be traced at least to Giambattista Vico's *The New Science* (1744) and whose earlier ancestry lies with the Sophists. But in the twentieth century, these roots lay in two general and cross-fertilizing schools of thought. The first met the cybernetic argument closer to its home ground and can be loosely characterized as the *Gestalt* or "symbolic" school of psychology, which challenged the mechanist philosophy as early as 1926 with H. Werner's *Comparative Psychology of Mental Development* and Ernst Cassirer's *Symbolic Forms*.[1] The second is the philosophic school of phenomenology.

The anti-mechanist camp of *Gestaltists* includes theoreticians such as Gordon Allport, Carl Buhler, Jean Piaget, Abraham Maslow, and Ludwig Bertalanffly. Essentially, they view man as an organism whose behavior and cognition are characterized by holistic structures transcending mechanical description, simple analysis, or quantification. These structures or forms are in turn represented to the consciousness or the imagination as *Gestalts* and symbols, and are most apparent in aesthetic perception, pattern recognition, linguistic expression, body movement and art. Symbols and *Gestalts* are incalculable; their origins, operations and effects on the synthesis of consciousness resist simplistic or mechanistic explanations, since they unite levels of meaning.

Wiener anticipated the problem posed to cybernetic analysis by *Gestalts*. In *Cybernetics* he addresses the notion directly in a chapter entitled "Gestalts and universals" that defines the problem of *Gestalt* perception aptly:

> How do we recognize the identity of the features of a man, whether we see him in profile, in three-quarter face, or in full face? How do we recognize a circle as a circle, whether it is large or small, near or far; whether in fact it is in a place perpendicular to a line from the eye meeting it in the middle . . . or is seen as an ellipse? How do we see faces and animals and maps in clouds, or in the blots of a Rorschach test?[2]

In response, Wiener explores some of the work already performed in the coding of visual information already performed by 1947, and suggests avenues for further exploration. Even more challenging to traditional humanists were the attempts to apply cybernetic principles to aesthetics, first systematically attempted by Abraham Moles in *Information Theory and Esthetic Perception* (1958) and later by Berlyne in his work *Aesthetics and Psychobiology* (1971).[3]

In general, the movement to cyberneticize human cognition and perception has been gathering force since Wiener; resisting that movement were several philosophers who felt that though some aspects of these phenomena could be explained by cybernetic analysis, by their very nature, and by the very nature of cybernetics, such explanations would always be reductive.

POLANYI

The work of Michael Polanyi fits somewhere between the theories of *Gestaltists* and the view of knowing proposed by phenomenology. Over the course of several books, including *Science, Faith and Society* (1946), *The Study of Man* (1958), *Knowing and Being* (1969) and especially *Personal Knowledge* (1958), Polanyi evolved a coherent, carefully reasoned argument countering the mechanistic view of both the universe and science's description of that universe. Polanyi based his assertions on his own experience as a physical chemist and on the work of *Gestalt* psychologists to build a theory of epistemology that directly criticized cybernetics and positivism.

In the first three chapters of *Personal Knowledge*, "Objectivity," "Probability," and "Order," Polanyi lays the groundwork for an appreciation of the central role played by personal experience and tacit understanding in even the so-called "objective" sciences. He builds his argument on the nature of probabilistic statements, on which the whole of physics had been shown to rest. Probability statements, by their very nature, are statements bound up in the presence of the observer and his system. Even cybernetics, Polanyi notes, which purports to quantify the information through which observations are communicated, must first distinguish between what is worthy of observation and what is merely random occurrence, that is between pattern and noise. He offers the following illustration taken from the terms of cybernetic methodology itself:

> Suppose we get twenty consecutive signals transmitted over a line: twenty dots or dashes which we write down as twenty noughts and crosses:
>
> XOXOXOXOXOXOXOXOXOXO
>
> We may take it that this sequence of noughts and crosses is an objective fact. But it may also be a personal fact, and here there are two alternatives: it may be a coded message or it may arise from random disturbances which are merely a noise. Communication theory tells us that if the sequence is a message, the maximum amount of communication that can be packed into the sequence is . . . 20 binary units. The figure 20 measures, as it were, the amount of distinctiveness that can be imparted to a sequence of 20 choices between two alternatives. . . . If, alternatively, our sequence of binary signals had been obtained as a result of random disturbances, this noise would also be

> measured on this scale and its numerical value would be . . . 2^{20} or 20 binary units. This number is called the amount of equivocation [uncertainty] caused by such a noise in any message transmitted through the same channel.
>
> It is a curious fact that modern communication theory, which has been used by cyberneticists to build around it a fully mechanized model of mental processes, turns out to be based on a clear recognition of personal acts of intelligent appreciation, for the distinctiveness of which it provides for the first time a quantitative measure.[4]

In other words, given such a phenomenon as this set of twenty X's and O's, only three possibilities obtain: (1) it is something that has information, determined by a code, for some receptor (human or non-human); (2) or it is merely a collection of random noises; (3) or it is an anomaly. In the third case such marks are not amenable to cybernetic analysis anyway, and need not concern us. But in the former two instances, it is a curious fact that cybernetic analysis interprets the signs as having a quantity of information equal to the quantity of noise (or what is also called "entropy," "equivocation," or "uncertainty"). The only distinction between the two is whether or not a purpose or code is entailed by the signs and intended through them. Even in cases when one part of a machine is merely communicating to another part of a machine, the machine is constructed by a human agent for the accomplishment of human ends. The mechanical system is subsumed, therefore, by human information. Even a simple thermostat is designed to keep humans comfortable, but what determines "comfort" is individual and variable, as recent developments in American home heating illustrate. Again, as we have already seen, Polanyi concludes that information can only be distinguished from noise by the relationship of the phenomenon in question to an intelligent agent.

Polanyi isn't implying that order doesn't necessarily exist in nature apart from human perception of it, but rather that the capacity to distinguish between order and randomness is "always based on an anterior knowledge of randomness," and that "every kind of human knowing, ranging from perception to scientific observation, includes an appreciation both of order contrasted to randomness and of the degree of this order."[5] That "information theory ascribes in fact a numerical value to the degree of order present in an ordered system forming a message" does not account for the anterior presence of *the capacity to make that distinction*.

Drawing from this essential aspect of human knowing, and from his extensive proof of the ineluctable role of prior pattern-recognition (*Gestalt* perception) in learning and theory-construction, Polanyi proceeds to detail a theory of "personal knowledge" in which epistemology is a measure of "the power of intellectual beauty to reveal truth about nature." This power, which Polanyi describes as heuristic, is a species of passion that can distinguish real "beauty from merely formal attractiveness."[6] Science and passion are inseparable, for one is a product of the other. "The elimination of personal knowledge from science would destroy science," he writes.[7] The role of such personal knowledge, a sort of anterior perception of the form of truth, gives rise to the passions with which certain beliefs are held, even when proof to the contrary is offered. Nothing less would explain, for instance, the role of intuitive and "aesthetic" feelings, nor the depth of those feelings, among the great physicists who debated in this century the meaning of the mathematics describing the atom's quanta.

Similarly, Wiener's comparison of the "uncertainty" in physics to the irrationality of the human psyche and to St Augustine's notion of "evil" is itself irrational, and can only be understood as a passionate defense of the particular notion of cosmic beauty to which Wiener was personally committed. Ironically, then, Wiener's assertions, and cybernetics itself, derive from precisely those heuristic elements they seek to refute, what Polanyi elsewhere calls "the tacit dimension."

Polanyi assails the possibility of reducing human behavior and intelligence to mechanical description through two corollary assertions. First, he shows that the very concept of mechanism – whether expressed in the hardware or principles of engineering that produces it or in the view of science as a positivistic, mechanistic decision procedure for describing nature – is inextricably bound to human notions of utility, or what he calls "advantage." He writes, "Technology comprises all acknowledged operational principles and endorses the purposes which they serve. This endorsement also *appreciates the value of the machine as a rational means of securing the advantage in question.*"[8] But, as the words "acknowledged," "purposes," and "appreciates" imply, the very presence of a larger human context is entailed – given tacitly – in the project. So techniques such as cybernetics, which seek to explain humans as mechanisms, are merely drawing a large but closed logical circle – a sort of grand tautology – around the phenomena they seek to describe. The humanity of the project is lurking behind the whole. Polanyi calls such mechanistic attempts "closed interpretive systems" whose validity is challenged from the start by Gödel's theorem: a logical system cannot be both consistent and complete.

As we will see, Polanyi's view of technology is very close to Heidegger's; for both these philosophers, technology is a limited mode of perceiving the world that defines and prescribes it in terms of its utility and our purposes. When regarded in this light, we can seek our reflection in technology, but by no means can we be equated with our own inventions.

Polanyi states the second corollary of his refutation of mechanism as follows: "*The complete scientific knowledge of a machine as an object* [*even if it were possible*] *tells us nothing about it as a machine.*"[9] In other words, if physics and chemistry and all other sciences were brought to bear upon a description of a typewriter, much about its physical properties would be revealed, but nothing about its purpose. If science cannot hope to explain the human aspects of a typewriter, how can it hope to explain the human aspects of the neurochemistry of the brain – self-consciousness, emotions, creativity, language, etc.? These aspects are far too rich, too laden with human meaning to be explicable by the methods of science.

The other flank of this attack on what Bertalanffly calls "the positivistic-mechanistic-reductionist approach . . . the robot model of man" comes from phenomenology, the most consistently anti-mechanist philosophy of the twentieth century.[10] The line of this opposition can be traced from Martin Heidegger and Maurice Merleau-Ponty to those more direct critics of the "robot model of man" such as Frederick Crosson,[11] Ludwig von Bertalanffly and Hubert Dreyfus, and would include also such philosophical fellow travelers as Hannah Arendt, Arthur Koestler, and William Barrett. In what follows, I sketch the beginnings of this line in the work of Heidegger and Merleau-Ponty particularly, since they explicitly viewed art as an arena where technique battles with the reductiveness of technology and is thus returned to its radical nature as a means to enrichment.

HEIDEGGER

Heidegger first detailed his philosophy of human consciousness in *Being and Time* (1927).[12] His philosophy constitutes a statement of belief as much as a rigorous attempt to describe how our minds experience themselves and the world. For our purpose, the crucial feature of his theory is the emphasis placed upon the difference between *recognizing the truth of a phenomenon* (based on our "intention" of it, a term he uses following Edmund Husserl) and *the commonplace acceptance of things as mere things*, which renders them inert and meaningless. For Heidegger, every moment is a contest between seeing through and experiencing the world fully, and living in a world of dead objects to which empty names and sterile structures of signification have been assigned. The first enriches; *intending the world* (as Husserl first called it) makes us aware of our own presence and the crystalline "transparency" of the material world. The second impoverishes; it is a process of instrumentation which makes the world opaque, separate from our intuitive and ideal knowledge of it and analyzed into a series of functional phenomena that are only viewed in terms of their utility. Ultimately, Heidegger implies, this view turns upon itself, and soon we are led to treat our own knowledge and selves in the same utilitarian and sterile fashion.

It should not be surprising then, given Heidegger's perspective, that he was actively and explicitly concerned with the growth of technology in the twentieth century, and his work is filled with criticisms of it. Technology, in his view, is the sum total of the instrumentalization of things as well as the process of making things instrumental. In his 1954 lecture "The question concerning technology," he confronts technology not as something evil or good in itself, but as a particular mode of perceiving the world – a frame of reference adopted by humans to achieve ends, but one in which certain values inhere. This is a functional view of technology that is especially fruitful, and it is recapitulated in the strategy of cybernetic fiction.

Heidegger writes: "The [mode of] revealing that rules in modern technology is a challenge, which puts to nature the unreasonable demand that it supply energy which can be extracted and stored as such."[13] Consequently, though technology is a method for revealing certain aspects of the world to us, it is a reductive one: "The earth now reveals itself as a coal mining district, the soil as a mineral deposit."[14] Technology is a mode of "enframing" that is even more powerful than science. In fact, he maintains, modern science is really dependent upon and has become a tool of technology. This is a radical inversion of the conventional wisdom concerning the relationship between the two, by which it is almost universally agreed that technology is nothing more than applied or embodied science.

Heidegger's argument is convincing and is becoming more so as the very course of scientific investigations, from astrophysics to sub-atomic physics, from microbiology to world ecology, becomes increasingly dependent on and subject to the technologies we have developed to extend our perceptual and cognitive grasp. Science is the reach that exceeds our grasp, technology the grasp that extends our reach. "It is said that modern technology is something incalculably different from all earlier technologies because it is based on modern physics as an exact science," Heidegger states. "Meanwhile, we have come to understand more clearly that *the reverse holds true as well*: modern physics, as experimental, is dependent upon technical apparatus and upon progress in the building of apparatus."[15]

Here, Heidegger focuses precisely on the crux of the dialectic between cybernetics and Uncertainty. Heisenberg's theorem shows that our very reliance upon the instrumentation necessary to extract information from the atom alters the nature of that atom, making its precise structure uncertain. Cybernetics replies that the very instruments themselves are, by their mechanical nature, subject to techniques for determination, and therefore the information they transmit is once again calculable and reducible to determination. Furthermore, the information in that atom is subject to the laws of information. Tacit in these assertions is that the human brain is just another one of these information instruments.

Although Heidegger does not name cybernetics or information science directly, he seems to have it in mind. From his perspective in 1954, technology seems to be more powerful than science, and has succeeded in incorporating physics, bending it to its reductive purposes.

> Because the essence of modern technology lies in enframing, modern technology must employ exact physical science. Through its doing so, the deceptive illusion arises that modern technology is applied physical science. This illusion can maintain itself only so long as neither the essential origin of modern science, nor indeed the essence of modern technology is adequately discovered through questioning.[16]

What is the essence of technology?

> We are delivered over to it in the worst possible way when we regard it as something neutral; for this conception of it, to which we today are particularly likely to do homage makes us utterly blind to the essence of technology.

Though Heidegger believes that "technology is not demonic" in his view it is a "mystification": it conceals the truth of phenomena by restricting the direction our consciousness takes. Once we achieve this recognition, however, we are released into a "freeing claim"; once we recognize the non-neutrality of technology and the direction in which it pushes us, we can shape our own destiny by seeking our reflection in it. Technology, after all, is an invention of man, not vice versa.[17]

MERLEAU-PONTY

Maurice Merleau-Ponty extends and focuses the phenomenological argument into a discussion of how we make or derive meaning in the world. He particularly strives to define the role of language and cultural signs from a phenomenological perspective, and his theories provide at least one later critic of artificial intelligence, Hubert Dreyfus, author of *What Computers Can't Do*, with much ammunition. Since much of the energy of artificial intelligence (AI) research has gone into the attempt to design machines that can speak, read, and write with enriched capabilities (i.e. spontaneity and creativity), Merleau-Ponty's theories provide a striking point of divergence between the two philosophies entailed by cybernetics and phenomenology.

Merleau-Ponty's contribution to the cybernetic–phenomenological debate can be summarized by the view of language he expresses in *Signs*: "What if language speaks as much through what is between the words as through the words themselves? As much by what it does not 'say' as by what it 'says'?"[18] For Heidegger (and Husserl), meaning arises in the intercourse between the act of consciousness and the object it intends. For Merleau-Ponty, language is an attempt to express this meaning, an attempt complicated even further by one of the tenets of existentialism: that any two individuals have an essentially incommensurable experience-in-the-world. Language is never a full expression of this dynamic play of our consciousness, nor can it ever be. Furthermore, language itself is not only a partial reflection of our intention, it is also an object of intention itself, open to our scrutiny. Despite all this, language is always partially incomplete, unfulfilled. Though it is a reflection of consciousness – its tool – and though it is incomparably rich and spontaneous in its own right, it does not *constitute* consciousness itself. There exists in us a being-in-the-world that remains beneath or prior to the act of using language, and this is not fully captured by words. Thus, between the very structures of language itself, there exists something inexpressible, something unaccountable, something that can be inferred but never made fully present. Language, then, "speaks as much by what it says between the words as what it says in the words themselves." This idea is essential to cybernetic fiction.

Merleau-Ponty even suggests a hierarchy of modes of expression in which some forms of expression come much closer to fully capturing consciousness than others. In Merleau-Ponty's view, consciousness seeks to express itself in a language that has its origins in the body; language's most primordial form is as a series of gestures and emotive utterances; in its most natural form, language is a way of "singing the world." Merleau-Ponty, therefore, offers a subtle hierarchy of expression, from the moment of seizing the world through consciousness to dance, song, speech and, finally, writing, in order of proximity to the origin. Writing is a relatively frozen, immutable, far-displaced medium for communication, least like the spontaneity and evanescence of our spirit. Though writing can be most devoted to the analytical, since it freezes the moment of consciousness in a system of structures and signs, it also uses *style* to recapitulate the freedom of language. (Walter Ong suggests that writing is "a self-reflexive technology."[19]

As a result of these successive displacements, meaning does not reside in language but in the hypotheses and intuitions which we bring to the world. Here we return to the notion of *Gestalts* and synthesis which gives the entire counter-philosophy its coherence. As one critic writes, for Merleau-Ponty, "The meaning of the whole is not produced by any inductive summing up of the meaning of the parts; it is only in light of hypotheses about the meaning of the whole that the meaning of parts can be defined."[20] In fact, Merleau-Ponty summarizes "the lesson" of phenomenology as follows: it presents "a new conception in the being of language which is logic within contingency, an oriented system, and which nevertheless always elaborates chances, recapturing the fortuitous within a totality that has meaning."[21]

His choice of words here is striking, given the terms in which the argument between cybernetics and Uncertainty has been cast. "Contingency," "chances," "fortuitous" all subsume logic and system. Merleau-Ponty is describing the source of meaning in language in precisely those terms which oppose the cybernetic description of information delivered by a code. The entire "system" is oriented towards a silent totality that can only be understood as "an elaboration of chances," or guesses or hypotheses. In order to get meaning from language we must leap between the logic of what is presented and the meaningful whole of our personal knowledge by elaborating on our uncertainty. By looking only at the structure of words presented, we can never be sure of meaning. For Merleau-Ponty, language is not a transliteration, nor a mere decoding, nor one-on-one mapping either of our world or our consciousness: it is not "a decipherment of an Ur-original text."[22]

This has immediate implications for the project we call science, a word that often goes in quotes for Merleau-Ponty. He addresses the failure of a purely objective science in terms that once again hark back to Heisenberg:

> As long as I cling to the ideal of an absolute spectator, or knowledge with no point of view, I can see my situation as nothing

> but a source of error. But if I have once recognized that through it I am grafted onto every action and all knowledge which can have meaning for me, and that step by step it contains everything that can exist for me, then my contact with the social . . . the finitude of my situation . . . appears to me as the point of origin of all scientific truth. . . . The only thing left for me is to define truth in the situation.[23]

"Science," in these terms, "designates the efforts to construct ideal variables which objectify and schematize the functioning of this effective communication." Science does not describe the truth, but rather the attempt to get at the truth, a statement of ideals. The truth resides in our human experience, which is neither "objective" nor "schematic."

ALLIANCE: CYBERNETIC FICTION AND THE PHILOSOPHICAL COUNTER-STATEMENT

No structure of information has yet been devised, either in hardware or in theory, which can give a full account of the incalculably rich structure of human experience or expression. By implication, then, neither has any theory of information provided an explanation of what is meaningful in the world, nor has any machine come close to imitating the human act of meaning-making or "directed consciousness." It is doubtful whether such an invention will arise in the absence of scientific theories of meaning that are richer than mere formulae for the calculation of information.

Yet the ambivalence between mechanism and meaning is an apparently irremediable and unending feature of our culture. At the very same moment that we feel ourselves to be acting freely in the world, we are also creating structures and codes so powerfully convincing that they dominate the ways we see. It is no more possible to conceive of an effective epistemology without both algorithmic and transcendental (or calculable and incalculable) components than it is to think of a human language without both a syntax and a semantics.

Heidegger predicts where we will find one site for both an answer to these questions and a synthesis of this apparently irreconcilable dialectic. He calls upon art and literature to reveal technology's essence, its power to enframe the phenomenal universe within structures of utility. By so doing, Heidegger maintains, human culture will allow its destiny to come into being:

> Could it be that the fine arts are called to a poetic revealing? Could it be that revealing lays claim to the arts most primally, so that they for their part may expressly foster the growth of the saving power, may awaken and found anew our look into that which grants our trust in it?
>
> Whether art may be granted this highest possibility of its essence in the midst of extreme danger, no one can tell. . . .
>
> Because the essence of technology is nothing technological but rather is a way of viewing the world, essential reflection upon technology and decisive confrontation with it must happen in a realm that is on the one hand akin to the essence of technology, and on the other, fundamentally different from it. Such a realm is art.[24]

These predictions would seem somewhat grandiose and hyperbolic were it not for the fact that Heidegger's invitation to art is directly answered by a body of fiction written soon after he made such claims in 1956. Cybernetic fiction is precisely that mode of expression most suited to reveal the essence of technology: at once quite akin to technology itself, since the texts are formed by the applications, ironic or otherwise, of algorithms borrowed from cybernetics – and at the same time, most suited to revealing the truth.

The play between the expressible and the inexpressible – between logical structures of information encoded in language and the enormous, silent presence of meaning that lies behind it – is precisely the play out of which cybernetic fiction derives its force and out of which it forges the resolution between private truth and technological enframing, between the human presence and the structures we create to extend the dominion of that presence. As the ensuing chapters show, cybernetic fiction does not so much invent a new aspect of human expression by which it resists the metaphor of the machine as much as it exploits aspects of the machine already there: the incommensurability between the structures of language (the machine) and personal knowledge (the soft side of the metaphor). By disguising themselves as machines, and yet retaining an ironic self-consciousness, these authors carry the phenomenological message into the very heart of technique. The soft machines they create stand for the vulnerable machines of language, science, and humanness itself and suggest the sort of synthesis Heidegger envisages: when we finally see technology for what it is, a frame placed around the world, then we are free to see our reflections in it.

FIVE

CYBERNETICS AND TECHNO-PARANOIA: KURT VONNEGUT, JR AND WILLIAM BURROUGHS

"Is there anything done by a machine with a random element but not by a deterministic machine?"
(C. E. Shannon *et al.*, "Computability by probabilistic machines," *Automata Studies*)

"I'm trying to fix it so we both can listen at once. . . . Here, hold this phone to your ear. Do you hear anything?"
"Yes, static."
"Good."
(William Burroughs, *The Ticket that Exploded*)

The most primitive literary response to the threat of cybernetics is paranoia. Cybernetics and paranoia are naturally linked at the most general level because the first threatens to, and the second is threatened by, control through forces beyond the power of the individual. However, in the earlier works of Kurt Vonnegut, Jr and William Burroughs, both of whom began their literary careers in the 1950s when cybernetics first came to popular attention in America, this paranoia takes on simple shapes, and its relationship to cybernetics can be easily discerned. Burroughs and Vonnegut combine cybernetic paranoia with the more general apocalyptic mythology of the period to create baldly didactic satires on the situation of technological civilization.

PLAYER PIANO

Kurt Vonnegut's novels are anomalies. His works have been claimed for pop and postmodernism, for satire, black humor, and science fiction. On the one hand he deals with themes that generally have profound moral consequences and pose difficult questions, but on the other his statement and resolution of those themes tend to be facile and at times evasive. It is similarly difficult to fix the relationship of his work to the general subclass of cybernetic fiction, for though it is clear that he has been profoundly influenced by cybernetics, in particular by his reading of Norbert Wiener, and that like other postmodernists he is critical of these ideas, his fiction simplifies and reduces the terms in which they are stated. A crucial element of cybernetic fiction is absent or very muted in his earlier works, which do not resist the metaphor of cybernetics internally. That is, Vonnegut does not manipulate the very act of fictional communication itself, nor explore language, as tacit ways of eluding the control over communication proposed by cybernetics until his later novel, *Slaughterhouse Five* (1969), where he experiments with the structure of novelistic presentation. Vonnegut's earliest novels hint strongly at his familiarity with Wiener's work, *The Human Use of Human Beings*, especially his first novel, *Player Piano* (1952), which shows his concern for the social implications of automation, the replacement of humans with machines.

Automation was a buzzword of the 1950s and early 1960s embodying all the neo-Luddite fears of humans being made redundant by and forced to become subservient to machines. This generally accessible theme, then, could partly explain Vonnegut's concern with machines, but there are certain points in *Player Piano* that prove the direct contribution of Wiener to Vonnegut's images.

The hero of *Player Piano* is Paul Proteus, manager of an industrial plant that has achieved a remarkable degree of mechanical autonomy, a robotization for which Proteus has been largely responsible. He has achieved his position of power in part because he designed a code which reduced the physical motions of an actual worker – chosen for his superlative competence – to a series of commands on a tape. This tape is then fed into a computer which commands other machines to perform those operations. In *The Human Use of Human Beings*, Wiener explores at great length his blueprint for "the factory of the future": it will consist of an assembly line operated by robots "guided by a control tape."[1] The following long passage illustrates Wiener's view, and also nicely encapsulates the positivist philosophy essential to cybernetics from which that factory is evolved:

> Let us now go on to a picture of a more completely automatic age. Let us consider for example what the automobile factory of the future will be like; and in particular the assembly line, which is the part of the automobile factory that employs the most labor. In the first place, the sequence of operations will be controlled by something like a modern high-speed computing machine. In this book and elsewhere, I have often said that the high-speed computing machine is primarily a logical machine, which confronts different propositions with one another and draws some of their consequences. It is possible to translate the whole of mathematics into the performance of a sequence of purely logical tasks. If this representation of mathematics is embodied in a machine, the machine will be a computing machine in the ordinary sense. However, such a computing machine, besides accomplishing ordinary mathematical tasks, will be able to undertake the logical task of channeling a series of orders concerning mathematical operations. Therefore, as present high-speed computing machines in fact do, it will contain at least one large assembly which is purely logical.
>
> The instructions to such a machine, and here too I am speaking of present practice, are given by what we have called a taping. The orders given the machine may be fed into it by a taping which is completely predetermined. It is also possible that the actual contingencies met in the performance of the machine may be handed over as a basis of further regulation to a new control tape constructed by the machine itself, or to a modification of the old one.[2]

The irony typical of Vonnegut is that of course the machine puts its human model or prototype out of a job. Proteus, musing about his earlier triumphant invention of this automatic controlling device, gazes at the black box:

> [T]he box containing the tape recording that controlled them [the machines] all. . . . And here, now, this little loop of tape

> in the box before Paul, here was Rudy as Rudy had been to his machine that afternoon – Rudy, the turner-on of power, the setter of speeds, the controller of the cutting tool. This was the essence of Rudy as far as his machine was concerned, as far as the economy was concerned, as far as the war effort was concerned. The tape was the essence distilled from the small, polite man with the big hands and the black fingernails . . . from the man who adored a collie for want of children.
>
> Now, by switching on lathes on a master panel and feeding them signals from a tape, Paul could make the essence of Rudy Hertz produce, one, ten, a hundred or a thousand of the shafts.[3]

This fear of the richness of human identity being reduced to something the machine can read is expressed tacitly or openly in every protest against technology, including those of the phenomenologists and of Jacques Ellul in *The Technological Society*, René Dubos in *So Human an Animal*, William Barrett in *The Illusion of Technique*, Langdon Winner in *Autonomous Technology*, Hannah Arendt in *The Human Condition*, and many others who see technology as directly opposed to freedom. This opposition informs all of *Player Piano*, and is framed by Vonnegut's epigraph to the novel, a plea for freedom in the face of technological encroachment.

> This book is mostly about engineers and managers. At this point in history, 1952 A.D., our lives and freedom depend largely upon the skill and imagination and courage of our managers and engineers, and I hope that God will help them to help us all stay alive and free.

The fact that the prototypical worker is named Rudy Hertz begins a trail of ironies that leads us further into a recognition of the extent to which *Player Piano* explores cybernetic territory. Rudolf Hertz was a German physicist (1857–94) after whom the basic measurement of electromagnetic waves, used particularly in radio communication, is named. Here, Vonnegut has signalled to us that the sciences of communication and control are one; cybernetics grew up with exploitation of radio communications and electromagnetic waves, during the Second World War when the Allies were obsessed with developing radar. The British in particular were eager, since they were directly threatened by the

German rocket bomb, itself the result of another achievement in cybernetics, the servo-mechanical inertial guidance system. These are all interwoven very nicely by Pynchon in *V.* and *Gravity's Rainbow*: one example is Kurt Mondaugen's examination of "sferics" (random atmospheric electrical noise) in *V.* and his reappearance in *Gravity's Rainbow* as a worker on the German rocket project.

However, in *Player Piano* the essential cybernetic principle is the translation of Rudy's motions to a tape instructing the feedback controlling device that replaces him. From this commonplace of the modern industrial age arises the most poignant moment in the novel. Paul Proteus examines the now empty factory and the controlling device that he first invented and programmed, and begins to muse about the train of events that led to his success. His pride is quickly tempered by a particular memory. He recalls the time he met the now-aged Rudy in the working-class bar "across the river" (which was then, and still is, in the Troy-Schenectady-Albany area on which Vonnegut bases his "Ilium" and is tantamount to saying "on the other side of the tracks"). In this confrontation, Vonnegut exploits Rudy's significance as avatar of the underclass most threatened by automation (and representative, indeed, of all humanity threatened by technological control). The stage is set for dramatic revelation. In honor of "Dr Proteus," Rudy puts a coin in the slot of an old player piano in the bar:

> Rudy acted as though the antique instrument were the newest of all wonders, and he excitedly pointed out identifiable musical patterns in the bobbing keys – trills, spectacular runs up the keyboard, and the slow, methodical rise and fall of keys in the bass.
>
> The music stopped abruptly, with the air of having delivered exactly five cents worth of joy. Rudy still shouted, "Makes you feel kind of creepy, don't it, Doctor. Watching them keys go up and down? You can almost see a ghost sitting there playing his heart out."

This passage, which presents the titular conceit, has several reverberations. The first immediately follows this incident in *Player Piano*: Proteus snaps out of his reverie about the player piano and looks out on the rest of the robotized factory. He fantasizes about getting "a composer to do something with . . . the music of Building 58." "It was wild and Latin music, hectic rhythms, fading in and out of phase, kaleidoscopic sound." The player piano's music, produced by an automatic device, is symbolically extended to include the entire ghostly symphony of technology, an elaborate piper's tune to which man has been made to dance.

Other echoes of the player piano metaphor can be heard in other works. Rudy's remark ("You can almost see a ghost sitting there playing his heart out") evokes Arthur Koestler's title, *The Ghost in the Machine* – a vision of a human soul embodied silently, or perhaps trapped, or perhaps made obsolete, by a mechanism. Koestler's metaphor is a phenomenological one. It implies that despite the reduction of nature to mechanism, there is still some transcendent human quality haunting the machine.

The player piano is also a bit like Roussel's paver-punner in *Locus Solus*. The music played by the machine was composed by an invisible hand in some other place. However, where Roussel is intent upon effacing the human presence in favor of attending to the machine, Vonnegut wants us to recognize the ghostly, sentimental remnant of the human presence which the machine has displaced. Finally, though, it is clear that Vonnegut is alluding to, or at least originally derived the metaphor from, the following curious passage by Wiener in *The Human Use of Human Beings*:

> Some years ago a prominent American engineer bought an expensive player piano. It became clear after a week or two that this purchase did not correspond to any particular interest in the music played by the piano but rather to an overwhelming interest in the piano mechanism. For this gentleman, the player piano was not a means of producing music but of giving some inventor the chance of showing how skilful he was at overcoming certain difficulties in the production of music. This is an estimable attitude in a second-year high-school student. How estimable it is in one of those on whom the whole cultural future of the country depends, I leave to the reader.[4]

Both Wiener and Vonnegut make the subtle distinction between a machine that is used as a tool for the production of music and aesthetic pleasure, and a machine that is appreciated for the extent to which it demonstrates "know-how" without regard for the human consequences – or as Wiener calls it, the "know what." Both Wiener here and Vonnegut in his epigraph (quoted above) characterize engineers as those "on whom the whole cultural future of the country depends."

There are many other allusions to cybernetics and the threat of automation in *Player Piano*. One chapter of the novel is devoted to a little parable: the "Shah of Bratpuhr" meets EPICAC XIV, a continually evolving computer that occupies the physical network of Carlsbad Caverns. EPICAC XIV is the totalitarian machine *par excellence*, the incarnation of Luddite nightmares:

> [It] was already at work, deciding how many refrigerators, how many lamps, how many turbine generators, how many hub caps, how many dinner plates . . . how many everything America and her customers could have and how much they would cost. And it was EPICAC XIV who [!] would decide for the coming years how many engineers and managers and research men and civil servants, and of what skills, would be needed in order to deliver the goods: and what I.Q. and aptitude levels would separate the useful men from the useless ones.

The Shah asks the machine an ancient poetic riddle, part of a prophecy that a messianic god will one day come to the people and relieve all their suffering. Of course, EPICAC doesn't reply, and the Shah concludes that it is a "false god."

Other allusions are more subtle: Proteus's relationship with his wife has degenerated into a mechanical, redundant series of robotic exchanges. Each conversation between them is ended with the entropic exchange of signals:

> "I love you, Paul."
> "I love YOU, Anita."
> Anita had the mechanics of marriage down pat, even to the subtlest conventions. If her approach was disturbingly rational, systematic, she was thorough enough to turn out a creditable counterfeit of warmth.

Paul is depressed by the "mechanics of the competitive system." Social engineering has begun to come into its own: a

> union of the country's manufacturing facilities under one council has taken place. . . . Similar councils had been formed

> for the transportation, raw materials, food, and communications industries, and over them all had been Paul's father. The system had so cut waste and duplication, that it was preserved after the war and was often cited as one of the few concrete benefits of the war.

"Waste and duplication," synonyms of entropy, are eliminated through rationalization, the technique of social control. Students are tracked into professional (and social) slots by "grading machines." The list of such examples could go on. *Player Piano* is both inspired by and a direct response to *The Human Use of Human Beings*. In part, it portrays the existential struggles of Proteus, an anti-hero; but Proteus's anomie and disaffection are subtly shown to be symptoms of the entire "growth" of civilization towards a techtopia where humanity is subordinated to its own mechanical means.

THE SIRENS OF TITAN: ORGANISM AS MESSAGE

In *The Human Use of Human Beings*, Wiener explores the model of the human animal to which he devotes a full chapter, "in which the organism is seen as a message. Organism is opposed to chaos, to disintegration, to death, as message is to noise."

> We have already seen that certain organisms, such as man, tend for a time to maintain and often even to increase the level of their organization, as a local enclave in the general stream of increasing entropy, of increasing chaos and de-differentiation. Life is an island here and now in a dying world.[5]

This passage, with its appeal to the poetic value of the cybernetic metaphor, provides the premise of Vonnegut's next novel, *The Sirens of Titan* (1959).[6] Winston Niles Rumfoord, a wealthy man, has been reincarnated as a "wave phenomenon" by the intervention of a superior but mechanistic alien race. Rumfoord thus becomes immortal and nearly omnipotent, able to move at will through time and space and manipulate others to do his bidding. One of those whom he manipulates is the novel's anti-hero, Malachi Constant – the constant or "faithful" messenger, who desires only to find "a single message that was sufficiently dignified and important to merit his carrying it humbly between two points." He discovers, however, that not only is he being manipulated by Rumfoord, and Rumfoord by the aliens known as Tralfamadorians, but the entire fabric of human history has been manipulated as part of a yet larger plot by the Tralfamadorians to deliver a single message to one of their own, stranded on a lonely planet. The final insult is that the marooned Tralfamadorian, Salo, is only a robot.

Rumfoord complains of his destiny having been delivered over to the control of others, and his complaint could serve for all Earthlings: "[They] just reached into the Solar System, picked me up, and used me like a handy-dandy potato peeler." For "potato-peeler" we should read "messenger," or even "message"; Vonnegut has taken Wiener's metaphor, in which the organism is equated with a message, and made it concrete. The cleverness of this embodiment is that it permits Vonnegut to explore implications of the play between freedom and determinism in dramatic form, a form that crystallizes around the essential cybernetic–paranoid precipitate: despite the illusion that we are free, our actions are really guided to achieve someone else's purpose, a purpose which is at best indifferent to our own desires and at worst antithetical to them. As Jacques Ellul suggests, in its most sophisticated form technique will be able to maintain the illusion of freedom while depriving us of it. Vonnegut's abstraction of this profound fear of control from above by a more powerful and sophisticated intelligence is a refinement of this notion to its ultimate paranoid formulation: not only are we the puppets of a system larger than we can see or understand, we have been reduced to a simple element in a code. The transformation of Rudy Hertz into a robot tape has been extrapolated to the nth power.

The Sirens of Titan follows the unfolding of this mysterious, potent, and infuriating system to Malachi. He discovers that all of human history,

> Everything that every earthling has ever done has been warped by a creature on a planet one-hundred and fifty-thousand light years away. The name of the planet is Tralfamador. How the Tralfamadorians controlled us, I don't know, but I know to what end they controlled. They controlled us in such a way as

> to make us deliver a replacement part to a Tralfamadorian messenger who was grounded right here on Titan.

Salo, stranded on Saturn's moon and looking toward Earth for some sign from his native planet, is sympathetic to Earth's plight, in so far as he is capable of sympathy, given his lofty perspective. "The wonder is," he remarks, "that Earthlings have made as much sense as they have."

One of the satirical implications of *The Sirens of Titan* is that the insistence of humans on making sense out of their lives is a paltry and irrelevant affair. Stonehenge is an enduring testament to the mysterious sophistication of even primitive Druids. Because of its lambent resistance to satisfactory explanation – is it a ritual temple? a calendar in stone? the site of some judgement place? – we have generated systems to explain it and made symbols out of mute monoliths. But in Vonnegut's hands, they mock our academic theories, for, as Malachi discovers, Stonehenge and the Great Wall of China as well as other great monuments were really nothing more than failed attempts by the Tralfamadorians to get generations of humans to erect a signpost telling Salo, "Replacement part being rushed with all possible speed." The sum of human history is not only a machine, as Henry Adams suggested, but a cybernetic device designed only to deliver a paltry message. The message of this bleak, apocalyptic satire is clear: we have been taking ourselves much too seriously.

Vonnegut takes pains to create a counter-valencing theme; all these messages are made necessary by the fact that *Salo's machine has broken down.* Salo is left helpless because he "was not mechanically inclined," which is pretty ironic for a robot. (Is Vonnegut teasing humans who are not humanistically inclined?) Furthermore,

> even the heavily-powered, heavily-manned, heavily-built [transceiving apparatus] of Tralfamador was not particularly accurate. Old Salo had watched many communications failures on Earth. Civilizations would start to bloom, and the participants would start to build tremendous structures that were obviously to be messages in Tralfamadorian – and then the civilizations would poop out without having finished the messages.

Vonnegut here invokes the cybernetic hypothesis that civilizations have to reach a certain hypertrophic degree of organization in order to maintain a functional level of communications technology, but then he undermines it by showing, from Salo's excruciatingly Olympian perspective, the inexplicable failure of these systems, or, as Wiener would have it, the collapse into entropy. There is a cosmic Murphy's Law at work. By intertwining these diametrically opposed movements, towards total mechanization and mechanical breakdown, Vonnegut "softens" the machine. Though the Tralfamadorian machines are incarnations of ideal systems, in the real universe, like all machines, they do not work as well as their designers would like. This is reiterated in several instances in *The Sirens of Titan.* While Rumfoord, almost despite himself, fulfils the role demanded by his incarnation as "a pure wave function" propagating through space (and therefore a potentially immortal messenger), he is also willfully moving towards his own self-eradication. When the message is finally delivered, the information it carries is passed back into the system as unrecuperable entropy. Rumfoord is appropriately depressed and suicidal. Another example is found in Rumfoord's son, Chrono. Like his deific namesake, Chrono moves planets in the solar system, though Chrono does so by manipulating small stone symbols, effective analog computers. However, he finally rejects this role as pattern-maker to run off with sensitive, bird-like creatures who inhabit Titan. Salo, too, introduced to the heady wine of emotion, begins to devolve towards humanness, a condition for which he is willing to sacrifice his mechanical near-immortality.

Finally, in an ironic loop that circumscribes the theme of control with the theme of humanness, Salo reveals his original inter-galactic mission: "Once upon a time on Tralfamador there were creatures who weren't anything like machines. They weren't dependable. They weren't efficient. They weren't predictable. They weren't durable. . . . And they were guided by some purpose. Find out what this purpose was." Salo, the cybernaut who was not mechanically inclined, realizes that in a sense he hasn't been stranded at all. By making contact with these humans he has fulfilled his mission. Ironically, though, the purpose of human existence has been to deliver a message to Salo, hence the circularity of his quest. As he becomes more human through contact with earthlings, Salo also becomes infected with mortality and dies. Such softness doesn't seem to agree with the mechanical heart: it entails too much entropy.[7]

The Sirens of Titan is filled with references to cybernetic notions. The very title is the name of a species of aliens inhabiting Titan who are another incarnation of Wiener's metaphor of organism-as-message, though somewhat more ambiguously. As Vonnegut describes them,

> The creatures have only one sense: touch.
>
> They have weak powers of telepathy. The messages they are capable of receiving and transmitting are almost as monotonous as the song of Mercury. They have only two possible messages. The first is an automatic response to the second and the second is an automatic response to the first.
>
> The first is, "Here I am, here I am, here I am."
>
> The second is, "So glad to see you, so glad to see you, so glad to see you."

Despite their apparently invulnerable "do-loop" message system, the sirens of Titan are irresistible, creatures of perfect empathy, and thus are another type of soft machine. The cybernetic theme and the influence of Wiener are apparent everywhere. But the deeper structure of the book reveals a greater care and involvement in the theme than the somewhat simple-minded prose would at first suggest. At one point Vonnegut describes thoughts as "patterns in the mind, materially forming," emphasizing the cybernetic conception of mind arising from material. Other "man-machine interfaces" are explored, including interactions between man and computer that prophesy the computer's ascendance: "The machine was obviously trying to tell its operator something. It did everything it could to express itself, and finally managed to get its operators to ask it the right questions." At each level of the plot one organism is using another as a message, thus controlling it from above, forming concentric rings that reflect each other and are linked by their constant message: Malachi Constant is used by Rumfoord, Rumfoord, himself a "waveform phenomenon", by Salo, and Salo by the Tralfamadorians. We discover that the Tralfamadorians themselves are a hyper-evolved race barely distinguishable from machines, dependent upon their mechanization, and as emotionless and remorseless as their manipulation of Earth's history implies.

One message remains constant in each of these concentric rings: the messenger is inconstant, unfaithful, and brings entropy to the system. Therefore, although Vonnegut is critical of the direction cybernetic systematization naturally takes, he also sees the introduction of human vulnerability as a sort of resistance, or what scientists call an "unaccountable element." At the innermost circle we would expect to find, were this a fully realized postmodern work, some attention to the mechanics of language itself or to story-telling, but Vonnegut's novel stops short of this descent (ascent?) into self-consciousness. Instead of portraying his own text as a link in a chain of failed messages within failed messages, he seems content to let the satire speak for itself plainly. If he feels himself, even ironically, to be a sort of authorial intelligence posing as mechanism, then Vonnegut does not share his secret with us, at least not in *The Sirens of Titan*.

However, the cybernetic themes that emerge in later Vonnegut novels do so with decreasing frequency but increasing subtlety, attended by a heightened self-consciousness. In *Mother Night* (1960)[8] an American author is invited to become a spy – actually a double agent – for the Americans. Campbell, the hero, poses as a raving, pro-Nazi propagandist, broadcasting his insane and violently anti-Semitic messages to the Germans. At the same time, he is instructed to insert a coded series of interruptions, coughs, stammers, pauses, etc. which signal to American intelligence agents the answers to certain questions crucial to the Allied war effort. (In cybernetic terms, the noise of one code forms another code, a figure-ground situation which in cryptography is called a "grille," since it is formed by a template placed over the original to extract the crucial information. Note also the complementarity between codes and cybernetic fiction in general.) Of course, his speeches are being heard by the Germans as encouragement, and ironically Campbell himself doesn't know the content of his coded transmissions nor the questions to which they are answers. He is simply, like Malachi Constant or Winston Rumfoord, the passive medium for the transmission of someone else's message: an organism treated as a message.

The question on which the drama of *Mother Night* hinges, and which is unanswerable at its end, is the moral one: does Campbell serve good or evil? After the war is over, Campbell's books and plays, though designed out of guilt to inspire justice and goodness, are distorted and perverted to the ends of evil and violence by their audience.

The possibility for self-reflection is strong, of course, in this novel about a novelist, but the suggestions in that direction remain tacit. Yet Vonnegut's use of self-reflection grows with his *oeuvre*. In *God Bless You, Mr Rosewater* (1965) an insane recipient of a foundation grant brings his delirious obsession with creating a Utopia to "Entropyville, USA"[9] Vonnegut allows the theme of nonsense vs. meaningful communication to elaborate around the work of this madman: in order for a message to make sense must we consider the integrity of the source?

Perhaps the most "experimental" of Vonnegut's works, and the one which flirts most with the consciousness of fiction itself as a cybernetic device, is *Slaughterhouse Five or The Children's Crusade* (1969).[10] In this work, Vonnegut is himself present as a narrator. He describes himself as a "telephoner," obviously referring to the author-Vonnegut for whom telephoning is an analog of writing fictions. The telephone has a special place in the iconography of cybernetics, for it was at Bell Labs that Shannon researched and codified much of the law on which information science is based. "Vonnegut" calls people up late at night, when he feels they are most likely to be receptive to his messages, and tries to "communicate." The Tralfamadorians also make a reappearance here as authors who write novels that appear to the narrative's hero, Billy Pilgrim, "like a montage of sign-clusters or 'telegrams.'" Vonnegut seems to be either identifying himself obliquely with the postmodernists, a somewhat alien group of literary cyberneticists (remember, the Tralfamadorians are really hyper-evolved machines), or he is taking a swipe at postmodernism, whose methodology he none the less finds irresistible. Whatever the case, Vonnegut is partially making fun of himself, for *Slaughterhouse Five* is also filled with fast-cut montage effects, "telegraphic" prose, and the superimposition of a self-conscious pseudo-autobiography on to a simpler story. This produces a dramatic effect in which the reader's attention pulses back and forth between situations and levels of narration, an activity mirrored by Billy himself, who has become "unstuck in time."

Tony Tanner, in his incisive account of Vonnegut's work in

City of Words, emphasizes its self-reflexiveness. He suggests that Rumfoord in *Sirens* is Vonnegut's reflection in the novel, by virtue of Rumfoord's capacity "to arrange things as he wishes, free to handle time and space as he pleases and put people where he wants them."[11] Similarly, Tanner has a very fine eye for those points where machines and systems of communications converge with the self-reflexive intrusion of Vonnegut-as-author. His essay is entitled "The uncertain messenger," referring not only to the numerous messenger-heroes but to Vonnegut's own ambiguous relationship to saying anything at all. Tanner traces Vonnegut's development into an author of texts that grow increasingly fragmented (that is "entropic") under the pressure of this doubt. Tanner, too, notes Vonnegut's tendency towards sentimentality and didacticism. "However, at times," Tanner writes, "it does seem as though he is using his fiction to issue short sermons on the state of contemporary America, or the world, and this can at times endanger the poise of his work."[12]

If Vonnegut's works suffer qualitatively, it has less to do with his willingness to participate in what is essentially the literary movement of postmodernism than it does with his willingness to indulge in banality and sentiment. On the other hand, he shares with Pynchon and Barth a darkly ironic humor, at all times one of the best inoculations against the machine. Almost all of Vonnegut's novels boil down to an amazed-but-futile chronicle of what our Tralfamadorian visitor called "the wonder" that "Earthlings have been able to make as much sense as they have." Unfortunately, the Titanic oppositions waged by our technology against that sense often reduces Vonnegut only to a shrug of his shoulders.

BURROUGHS'S CYBERNETIC APOCALYPSE

Though I have stolen my title from William Burroughs's novel *The Soft Machine*, for me the appeal of that metaphor derives from its oxymoronic properties, the image of a machine softened by art. However, in Burroughs's apocalyptic mythology, the soft machine is the pure end-product of control by some malicious and all-powerful conspiracy of government, media, and what Burroughs calls "the Nova Police," agents of technology. These latter include not only human villains like the ubiquitous Dr Benway, but extraterrestrial virsuses capable of using a man's needs to reduce him to a "paralyzed larva, slobbering and covered by a caustic green slime that seeps from the rectum."[13]

On the receptive, gelatinous body of this larva a hyper-advanced typewriter imprints a controlling message, which turns the soft machine thus produced into an agent of the enemy, a Nova policeman. In one version of this horrific vision – and Burroughs's *oeuvre* offers several – the product is:

> a slender green creature, his hands ended in black claws covered with fine magnetic wires that extended up the inner arm to the elbow . . . antennae ears tuned to all voices of the city, each voice classified on a silent switchboard – green disc eyes covered with pupils of a pale electric blue – body of a hard green substance like flexible jade – black brain and spine buried with blue sparks as messages cackled in and out.[14]

In other words, an android, robot, machine masquerading as a human, call it what you will, the soft machine, since it is governed by a controlling system or message, is a cybernetic device. In a slightly different version of Burroughs's mythology, the soft machine is described as a code imprinted upon the body – likened to "liquid typewriters plopping into gelatin" – which transmits a virus in the form of "engrams" or tapes on which the code is kept.

However inexorable the enemy seems, in Burroughs's fictional world they are still made vulnerable by the hyper-organized state of their system. Like the Tralfamadorians or H. G. Wells's Martians, these machines are hypertrophic: "Once the machine lines are cut, the enemy is helpless – they depend upon elaborate installations difficult to move or conceal – electroencephalographic and calculating machine, film and TV studios batteries of tape recorders."[15] Not only is the "soft machine" some sort of communicating device, it has been implanted on our very nervous system; it is a compulsory "tape recorder within," or inner "writing machine" hooked up somehow to more cumbersome and conventional external communications devices.

Burroughs is talking about all language: language as system, as code, as an already received structure against which we all struggle. The most deterministic version of language is the most threatening, particularly the bio-mechanical (or strict structuralist) view of language as the reflection of an inner mechanism arising from the organic machinery of the central nervous system; its victims are not only those who are green and slimy but all of us. Burroughs calls this parasitical message "the Other Half":

> The "Other Half" is the word. The "Other Half" is an organism. Word is an organism. The presence of the "Other Half" as separate organisms attached to your nervous system can now be demonstrated experimentally. . . . Modern man has lost the option of silence. Try halting your sub-vocal speech. Try to achieve even ten seconds of inner silence. You will encounter a resisting organism that FORCES YOU TO TALK.

Here Burroughs has taken his battle from the cosmic, intergalactic scale to that most intimate part of our selves, that juncture, the infinitesimally small gap-spark between thought and word, with which phenomenologists and linguists alike have struggled and to which both have laid claim. Though this is a most formal way to look at it, it points at a concern that lies at the heart of Burroughs's literary method. That is, *Burroughs's extremism is an attempt to attain that inner silence and resist or inoculate himself against the virus of system.* For "system" Burroughs reads "cybernetic control," of which language is the most insidious instrument, because it is most intimately a part of us. At the same time, paradoxically, language is the only instrument we have to resist this control-by-system. Thus, Burroughs envisages resistance to this ultimate control as a battle enacted in and through language. Consciousness of this informs his entire rhetorical stance, explaining the ferocity, repugnance, and unremitting brinkmanship of his style, and the equally strange experiments in form that have made him one of the most elusive, and in certain corners, despised of contemporary novelists.[16]

CONTROL MACHINES VS. CUT OUT AND SPRAY BACK

Curiously, in the volume entitled *The Soft Machine,* Burroughs nowhere mentions the term, though he portrays a few incarnations of it. Perhaps he means us to understand that the sort of control that the soft machine represents is manifested everywhere in his apocalyptic universe; or perhaps this curious omission is meant to imply that the text we are reading *is* the soft machine, a conclusion further supported by his portrait of the prototypical cybernetic device, a calculator devised by the Mayans:

> I have described how the Mayan control system was based on the calendar and codices which contained symbols representing all states of thought and feeling possible to human animals living under such limited circumstances – these are the instruments with which they rotate and control limits of thought but also that the priests themselves do not understand exactly how the system works and that I undoubtedly know more about it than they did as a result of my intensive training and studies. The technicians who had devised the control system had died out and the present level of priests were in the position of someone who knows what buttons to push in order to set a machine in motion but who would have no idea how to fix that machine if it broke down or to construct another if the machines were destroyed.[17]

"Bill Lee," the hard-boiled anti-detective, sabotages this control machine by programming it to destroy itself through "positive feedback": "Inexorably as the machine had controlled thought feeling and sensory impression of the workers, the machine now gave orders to dismantle itself."[18]

The Mayan control machine is to emerge again in different guises throughout Burroughs's work. Later in the same volume it is reincarnated as an "IBM machine controls thoughts feeling sensory impressions." In *The Ticket that Exploded* it is mentioned several times as "symbol books of the all-powerful board that controlled thought feeling and movement of a planet with iron claws of pain and pleasure from birth to death." And it is in that latter text that we are given a more precise handbook for "dismantling" the machine by applying a technique borrowed from the Dada cut-up and mixed-media montage, a technique that would have made any Tralfamadorian proud.

The first step in Burroughs's prescription for inoculation is to acknowledge that language is the weapon used against its victims by "the all-powerful control board" and their "symbol books."

The manipulation of symbols is the key to controlling meaning and therefore thought and behavior. "The word is now a virus. . . . Modern man has lost the option of silence." Through the media, which impinge unavoidably on the conscious and unconscious self, the human nervous system is altered. "Listen to your present time tapes and you will see who you are and what you are already doing here . . . you are a programmed tape recorder set to record and play back." In order to discover who "programs" you, you must tape your own voice speaking automatically (hence the flood of impressions and rush of passion in even minute Burroughs fragments) and then cut up and re-splice the tape in a random pattern, or else run the tape manually back and forth across the pick-up heads. "It is interesting to record these words literally made by the machine itself." This experiment in aleatory art will reveal a hidden language or control that will convince the experimenter that THEY have controlled him and that inoculation against this virus is necessary. This inoculation can only be gotten through the attainment of some species of silence. To achieve "the writing of silence" we must "cut out and spray back . . . introduce the unpredictable spontaneous factor with a pair of scissors." Burroughs code-names this literary-guerrilla tactic "Operation Re-Write" (in *The Ticket that Exploded*). It clearly appeals to cybernetic notions of resisting the rise of totalitarian order and its concomitant control through deliberate randomization, the introduction of noise or entropy. Burroughs also calls this strategy "the writing of silence" (in *The Exterminators*). True silence cannot be attained in the universe, since noise is the background condition of the cosmos, a principle stressed by cyberneticists (and one with which Pynchon's Kurt Mondaugen becomes familiar). But this silence Burroughs hopes to attain is the *absence of code through cancellation of the message*, which turns apocalyptic through positive feedback: it sends the machine a message that is interpreted as "Dismantle yourself." Attendant upon the collapse of the word is the collapse of all time and space. Symbols are pounded into "word and image dust." The "berserk time machine twisted a tornado of centuries . . . the whole structure of reality went up in silent explosions under the whining skies."

The denaturing of language's genetic code indicated in the lacunae, typographical shouting, scatology, introduction of chance and centrifugal imagery of Burroughs's work are all not so much methods for creating and engendering as they are a sort of underground resistance, a disarming of the control implied in any order, any system, including language's natural one, from within. This tactic, of self-inoculation against the disease of determinism, is the tactic of all cybernetic fiction, essentially an ironic one.

Mas'ud Zavarzadeh explains how this is a natural result of the view of the postmodern novel as an effective force in culture, especially as it responds to what he calls, after Zbigniew Brzezinski, "the technetronic society." The "transfiction novel" is a response to the "planetary polarization between Man and Machine," upping the ante in the dialogue between the novel and technology:

> "Transfiction" is a type of narrative which is constructed upon the process of what might be called, in terms of the poetics of the Russian Formalists, a baring of literary devices: unmasking narrative conventions and turning them into counterconventions in order to shatter the illusion of reality which is the aesthetic foundation of the totalizing novel.[19]

TECHNO-PARANOIA AND THE CYBERNETIC APOCALYPSE

One of the most striking elements of cybernetic fiction is the extent of paranoia in it. Thomas Pynchon, the master of paranoia, places the kingdom of the inanimate (including the dead), and its expression in culture as technology, at the center of the vast web of malice that lurks behind *V.* The same forces play even more explicitly, though whimsically, with Oedipa Maas in *The Crying of Lot 49.* This technological death-force finally rears its Titanic head in the apocalyptic setting of *Gravity's Rainbow.* The same paranoia fuels Vonnegut's fear, expressed best in *The Sirens of Titan,* that all of human history has been determined by an alien race trying to get a message to one of their own, stranded in our solar system from a distant galaxy. Similarly, Barth's Jerome Bonaparte Bray (of *Letters*) is an exemplary litigious paranoiac; he believes that he is descended from Napoleon, that his books have been viciously plagiarized by an author named John Barth, and that he can get a computer to generate a complex ultimate novel, which evolves over the course of *Letters* into a numerological code. Raymond Roussel's compulsive return to the creation of a circumscribed space over which he can exert a totalitarian control, coupled with his grandiose hallucinations revealed through his psychoanalysis by the eminent Dr Janet, signify a strong paranoid element. Irving Massey uses Roussel's work to illustrate "language becoming paranoid in its death throes."[20] And McElroy's Hind of *Hind's Kidnap* is a consummate marginal paranoid whose world is riddled with plots, counterplots, and "sub-counterplots," and who also has an unfortunate tendency to think of himself as a sort of machine. What is the connection between cybernetic fiction and paranoia? Is it essential or casual?

On one hand, we may view this theme in the context of the large number of recent American novels which have portrayed solitary heroes caught in the grasp of historical forces larger and better organized than they ever suspected. These conspiracies of power bear down on them personally; as the solitary heroes uncover the plots and conspiracies which seem to lead them ever closer to some final confrontation with the mastermind at the center of the web of control, they are also propelled through an apocalyptic setting, a vision of the world in collapse.[21] These works show paranoia as the natural response to a corrupt power and to an apocalyptic world; among them are Ralph Ellison's *The Invisible Man* (1952), James Purdy's *Malcolm* (1959), Joseph Heller's *Catch-22* (1960), Robert Coover's *The Origin of the Brunists* (1963), Ken Kesey's *One Flew Over the Cuckoo's Nest* (1962), Norman Mailer's *An American Dream* (1964), Richard Farina's *I've Been Down so Long It Looks Like Up to Me* (1963), Ishmael Reed's *The Free-Lance Pallbearers* (1966), Stanley Elkin's *A Bad Man* (1968) and Hunter Thompson's *Fear and Loathing in Las Vegas* (1972). From this generic perspective, the presence of technology in the paranoid fantasy that predominated in the 1960s is casual; both the emphasis on the technology and the paranoia are epiphenomena of the larger threat of an imminent collapse of the whole social structure. In these terms, technology in the hands of the powerful effects a crisis to which paranoia, by its essentially political nature, is an organic response.

However, it is interesting that the paranoid fantasy in literature is almost always accompanied by a triad of terms that include *determinism* along with *apocalypse* and *grandiosity*. The determinist term can take many forms: the belief in a conspiracy or plot is a sort of determinism and connects the entire project of structuring a fiction with the paranoid imagination.[22] The sense that history itself is a machine operated by supernatural forces, a theme that can be traced as far back as the prophecies of the Inter-Testamental apocalypses, is also an expression of this fear of determinism.

Grandiosity can be found in the Gothic novel's evocation of Satanic figures manipulating weaker mortals, and its many portraits of grandiose, destructive heroes (Melmoth, the Monk, Frankenstein's monster). Poe's paranoids are afflicted with hyper-alertness and are prone to constructing intricate and deterministic systems of belief. Poe's fascination with codes and ciphers also seems to be a symptom of the same disposition.

Determinism and control are psychological synonyms, and from systems of control to machinery, particularly that machinery grafted on to the human will, is only a short step, especially when that step is urged by a deep anxiety. This explicit connection between paranoia and the machine can trace its pedigree back to Freud's essay on paranoia (1911) in which he explores the case of Daniel Paul Schreber.[23] Among the various symptoms of Schreber's interesting nexus of obsessions is the belief that the world is populated entirely by "cursory contraptions" and that he is the only real flesh and blood human left alive. This entire puppet show has been organized, Schreber believes, to deceive him. Despite the fact that Freud treats this fear of cursory contraptions (or what we would now call cybernauts) as symptoms of Schreber's deeper sexual confusion, we find it again in one of Burroughs's descriptions of the soft machine: "In a room with metal walls magnetic mobiles under flickering blue light and smell of ozone – jointed metal youths dance in a shower of blue sparks. . . . Metal heads reversed eyes feet tingling blue spark erections."

Paranoia is usually accompanied by other symptoms that help elucidate the connection to the fear of technology: the compulsive search for clues confirming a conspiracy against the subject; the over-interpretation of mundane events and the conversion of neutral phenomena into signs; the megalomaniac exaggeration of the subject's importance to the survival of the world (discerned by Freud in Schreber, who believed that he was messianic). In short, paranoia is a sort of *epistemology gone wild*, the search for knowledge turned beyond the point of conventional meaning-making into a sort of pouncing on meaning, a seizure of revelations lurking on the edge of every moment and behind each phenomenon. And the unifying principle of this teleology is the self. There are no accidents; everything is connected. No noise, no contingency, just a thousand voices muttering threats from behind the closed door of the phenomenal universe. The signal event in the paranoid's career is his exteriorization of some internal apocalypse, some moment in which the inner cataclysm that threatens his identity is projected on to the world; his knowledge of the world becomes a constant confirmation and re-enactment of the unresolvable crisis. For him each event is a Mach-Duhem-Poincaré phenomenon: underdetermined by data and thus amenable to an indeterminate number of competing interpretations. By the very nature of his diseased imagination, and by the nature of the world, the paranoid must continually find his worst fears confirmed.

Nabokov describes a muted case of this pathology in his short story, "Signs"; he calls the affliction "referential mania."

> In these very rare cases, the patient imagines that everything happening around him is a veiled reference to his personality and existence. He excludes real people from the conspiracy because he considers himself to be so much more intelligent than other men. Phenomenal nature shadows him wherever he goes. Clouds in the staring sky transmit to one another, by means of slow signs, incredibly detailed information about him. . . . Pebbles or stains or sun flecks form patterns representing in some awful way messages which he must intercept. Everything is a cipher and of everything he is the sign. He must be always on his guard and devote every minute and module of life to the decoding of the undulation of things.[24]

The mutual language of cybernetics and paranoia is written in the alphabet of codes, ciphers and intercepted messages, and describes a pattern in what Burroughs calls "the writing of silence." To the paranoid, like the cyberneticist, everything is a message and nothing is neutral; everything has information waiting to be recuperated by the correct reading or the application of the right technique. The paranoid's discovery of the ubiquity of information proves Shannon's principle – that every physical channel has a certain quantifiable capacity to carry information – with a vengeance. The paranoid believes he (and only he) knows the true order of things, and it is this knowledge which stands between the present state of the world and apocalypse.

Positivism and paranoia are cousin belief systems. The positivist world, like the paranoid one, is a clockwork mechanism. The difference is that if the paranoid is compelled to see the world as a machine, it is also that sight which he fears the most. To the paranoiac, we must remember, the world is an enemy, and invariably, the paranoid's suspicious behavior brings him into contretemps with the authorities, which in turn confirm his deepest fears. The "point men" of authority are usually bureaucrats, systems engineers, the behavioral modifiers with government grants.

The technology of human engineering in particular incites paranoid visions. For example, Anthony Burgess's Alex of *A Clockwork Orange* (the title describes another soft machine) is a psychopath, a sort of pathological anarchist who announces his freedom through random violence. He is finally brought under the state's control through a torturous behavioral modification program. A prison clergyman, aware of the forces warring for control of Alex and the greater ideal of personal freedom which is symbolically at stake, confronts the Minister of the Interior (in this case, the Minister of Alex's Interior), who has commandeered the B-mod program. The clergyman finds the methods of control indefensible:

> "He has no real choice, has he? Self-interest, fear of physical pain drove him to that grovelling display of self-debasement. Its insincerity was clearly to be seen. He ceases to be a wrongdoer. He ceases also to be a creature capable of moral choice."
>
> "These are subtleties," the doctor replies.
>
> "The point is," the Minister of the Interior says loudly, "it works!"[25]

A similar battle between the misfit and the behaviorists is enacted in a more parable-like (as opposed to probabilistic) fiction by Robert Coover, "Morris in chains" (in *Pricksongs and Descants*, 1969). Morris is a randy satyr, shepherd, and rapist who roams across the plastic, concrete and steel hull of a prefabricated park, itself part of a larger, rationalized urban place. Coover writes in two voices: Morris's highly stylized and sexual ruminations are counterpointed by an official report, written by a bureaucrat or technical aide who sings the praises of the scientific team that tracks, captures, and finally neutralizes Morris, the anomalous element in a positivistic paradise. "Only rarely did Morris escape our network of observers now, and then but briefly. His least event was recorded on notepad, punchcard, film, tape. Observers reported his noises, odors, motions, choices, acquisitions, excretions, emissions, irritations, dreams."[26] His nemesis is Dr Doris Peloris, reminiscent of Nurse Ratched of Kesey's *One Flew Over the Cuckoo's Nest.* In both cases, the women are equipped with a formidable array of controlling devices and ultimately castrate their victims, literally and figuratively. Interestingly, the novel is narrated from the point of view of the Indian giant, Chief Broom Bromden, a textbook paranoid schizophrenic. He imagines that "The Combine" has a fog machine that clouds the mind while controlling the victim's thoughts through secret electronic devices. Bromden's resistance to this technology is to remain silent and try to appear small.

Another interesting similarity between Burgess's Alex and Coover's Morris is that they both speak in a special, invented, spontaneous language, Alex's a sort of street argot, a pidgin Russified English (indicating, I suppose, Burgess's prophecy of the socialization of England) and Morris's a rhyming, metrical, Joycean babble:

> It was a sunny midday in the hot bulge of spring drove the flock into a grove of massy old oaks dipped my taut untufted flesh in the cool runlet nearby reposed alongside afterward blouse wrapped round my breech lettin old pheobus lap me dry made my first squawky boggles on a set of reeds.

Alex and Morris are not paranoids, they are innocents, and innocents are the opposite of paranoids, suspicious of nothing rather than everything. The crucial point made in these fictions by Burgess and Coover is an eminently phenomenological one: not only that innocents should be paranoid (what Ihab Hassan calls "radical innocence" quickly turns to victimization[27]), but that some stronghold of innocence can be found in and represented by a spontaneous, vibrant, sexual, self-proliferating and inventive language, in contrast to the language of the machine and the technicians who serve it. Coover's ear for this latter language is devastatingly accurate:

> "Our strategy is divided into two parts," Dr Peloris continued, "the pursuit and the trap. The second of course depends on the first, which is essentially a fact-finding mission, but which at the same time may serve the complementary function of harassing and exhausting the adversary."

Burroughs's tactic, of finding refuge in a language which aspires to silence through a kind of babbling and spastic spontaneity (I refer to the cut-up method), emerges more coherently in this light. Burroughs, in many ways, stands in contrast to the other cybernetic novelists who work from within the machine. He is too paranoid, too fearful, to let himself adopt even ironically the guise of a soft machine, because more than anything he fears he has become one, or is on the verge of becoming one. And yet, like other cybernetic authors, his prescription for resisting technique is a sort of inoculation, another technique, though one that paradoxically increases entropy. (Techniques are supposed to decrease entropy by systematizing.) His cut-up method has a sound cybernetic basis. The way to degrade the message is to widen the bandwidth, allow more noise, increase the number of chances or contingencies, randomize. This randomization shouldn't be confused with the mere aleatory experimentation of Dada or found poetry. Here, Burroughs is clearly playing the guerrilla's role of counter-technician, saboteur, the role of Bill Lee who turns the mechanics of the machine against itself in a positive feedback loop that ends in the machinery of language dismantling itself. Burroughs identifies those joints in his world, those cruxes in the cybernetic telos, that he can bend and break: "Communication must be made total, only way to stop it." "Let the machines talk and argue. The tape recorder is an externalized section of the human nervous system." "Get it out of your heads and into the machines." "Screaming without a throat without speech centers as the brain split down the middle and the feedback sound shut off in a blast of silence." Burroughs finds the places where the machine is soft: "So what is ejaculation? Substitute patterns twisting through electrical public hairs, feed-back throat hum, recorder jack-off—"; "a network of veins filtered through the green substance like red neon tubes."

Burroughs too constructs writing machines that dismantle sense, descendants of Swift's Lagadan Writing Machine and models of his own literary method:

> A writing machine that shifts one half one text and half the other through a page frame on conveyor belts – (The proportion of half one text half the other is important corresponding as it does to the two halves of the human organism) Shakespeare, Rimbaud, etc. permutating through page frames in constantly changing juxtaposition the machine spits out books and plays and poems. . . . You can say could give no information.

Where the Lagadan professor hopes to generate an encyclopaedia of sense out of the random, nonsensical accumulation of words, Burroughs seeks to pulverize all previous knowledge back into entropic dust. He knows with a species of paranoid certainty, a fearsome knowledge announced in every passage that IT is coming to get us, the Thought Control Patrol. This knowledge has led him to seek shelter along a newly invented route into entropy: an atomized language of force and revulsion that is both visionary and resistant.

SIX

READING IN THE SERVO-MECHANICAL LOOP: THE MACHINERY OF METAPHOR IN PYNCHON'S FICTIONS

"Living as he does much of the time in a world of metaphor, the poet is always acutely conscious that metaphor has no value apart from its function; that it is a device, an artifice. So while others may look on the laws of physics as legislation and God as a human form with beard measured in light years and nebulae for sandals Fausto's kind are alone with the task of living in a universe of things which simply are, and cloaking that innate mindlessness with comfortable and pious metaphor so that the 'practical' half of humanity may continue in the Great Lie, confident that their machines, dwellings, streets, and weather share the same human motives, personal traits and fits of contrariness as they.

"Poets have been at this for centuries. It is the only useful purpose they do serve in society."
(Thomas Pynchon, *V.*)

"The receptor can be an organized phenomenon hidden inside an amorphous phenomenon."
(Abraham Moles, *Information Theory and Esthetic Perception*)

There's a fine vintage science-fiction film, *Forbidden Planet*, most famous for its enduring contribution of "Robbie the Robot" to American pop culture. On Forbidden Planet, a group of Earthmen discover Dr Morbius and his beautiful daughter, the sole survivors of an earlier expedition, living in a paradise of natural splendor and hyperadvanced machines. The machines are the inheritance of an extinct race, the Krells, who were mysteriously wiped out eons before by a monster who still stalks this Eden.

As the plot thickens the monster begins to terrorize the newcomers. One of the characters, the ship's doctor, describes a miraculous machine that translates thought directly into reality. "No instrumentality," the doctor says on his death-bed, "just pure creation." The doctor is dying because he has just undergone treatment by an IQ-enhancing device, another legacy of the Krells, but obviously the treatment has proven to be too much for him, since not only does he die as a result of the mental strain, but he also utters such a blatant contradiction. For the "reality machine" (as I like to think of it) seems to take images and ideas and embody them directly in the world, and yet, though its operations are invisible, such embodiments are instrumented by the machine itself. For the doctor, Krell technology has become invisible, a brand of magic. As Arthur C. Clarke suggests, "Any sufficiently advanced technology is indistinguishable from magic."[1]

Therein lies a structuralist parable about postmodern fiction. Literature in general is a sort of Krell machine, translating the imagination into an embodied reality, a text. The structure or code (*la langue*) that gives the text its significance is quite as invisible as the doctor believes the Krell machine to be, but it is *not* weightless, as structuralism has shown. Historically it has been convenient to pretend that the code does not possess its own calculus and can be reduced out of any system of calculations about reality itself. But *the code is the instrumentation by which the text works its apparent magic.* Now that machines are ubiquitous we are constantly being reminded of the instrumentation of our ideas into reality by structure at all levels, from the material through the linguistic.

It therefore seems natural that in this environment authors would create the sort of fiction whose primary characteristic is the way it emphasizes its own structure, code, technique. Yet, the purpose of such emphasis seems to be ironic: an inoculation against the dominion of the technical. Cybernetic fiction is the consummate human artefact of a techtopian culture, as much as the computer with which it competes: it is the result of the hypertropic growth of (fictional) techniques into some ultimate tool for the embodiment of consciousness, and yet it seems driven to surpass its own machinery, to resist ironically and paradoxically – in short, to deconstruct – its own incarnate metaphor.

In this genre of what we might call "consummate technical artefacts" – cybernetic fiction – none is more self-realizing, or has imported more material from cybernetics into fiction in order to construct its metaphors and its resistance, or has more coherently embodied the paradoxical qualities of such a project than the works of Thomas Pynchon.

METAPHOR AS MACHINE

Pynchon's work has been fully explored in many excellent articles, collections and volumes; at times, there seems to be an almost inexhaustible amount of information that can be brought to bear upon Pynchon's work, and an equally inexhaustible number of things to say, interpretations to offer, and new ways of putting together the pattern of his work and reweaving the skein of ideas he presents. But central to much of recent Pynchon criticism, especially since *Gravity's Rainbow* (1973), has been the recognition of the importance of cybernetics and information theory to understanding his work. For instance, William Plater in *The Grim Phoenix* suggests that because cybernetics "incorporates Pynchon's own authorial act and because it is one of the most recurrent themes of his fiction, communication may provide the framework for discovering how various things come together."[2] Similarly, John Stark in *Pynchon's Fictions* amply shows that "Pynchon cannot be fully understood without tracing the influence of cybernetics on his work."[3] Both Plater and Stark offer extensive and fruitful investigations of the cybernetic theme in Pynchon's work. In addition, there are such fine studies as Anne Mangel's early work on the role of entropy, and an article by Kathleen Woodward describing *The Crying of Lot 49* as "information processing out of control" and "positive feedback at its crazy work."[4] Tony Tanner's recent monograph on Pynchon places cybernetics and information at the center of the Pynchon mythography.[5] Further, these authors and many others have clearly demonstrated that Pynchon's work not only employs cybernetic metaphors and analyses to forge a critique of technology, but that he applies information theory directly to the creation of the style and form of his work.

The following discussion relies on the works of these scholars and critics, but also takes its cue from the more general phenomenon of Pynchon criticism: Pynchon's exegeticists tend to treat his work as though it is an enormous computer. They roam inside its circuitry, like Oedipa Maas (or Stencil or Slothrop) "caught between the zeroes and ones," trying to map completely the interconnections, trying to distinguish between what computer engineers call "random access memory" (RAM – what the user puts into memory) and "read only memory" (ROM – what is placed there by the original programmer), following the convoluted complexities and multi-layered metaphors, always finding more to say but rarely recognizing any ultimate point to Pynchon's tour. But a brief look at Pynchon criticism begins to suggest where this ultimate point might lie.

As many critics have proposed, Pynchon's work is eminently self-reflexive. *V.*, *The Crying of Lot 49* and *Gravity's Rainbow* inspire in the reader the same compulsive desire to organize a welter of data and seek some central undisclosed truth as plagues his heroes and heroine. The serious reader of Pynchon who is drawn into this cabalistic game finds only that Pynchon mocks him. In *Gravity's Rainbow* (1973), we learn about the Zone Hereros who play a similar game, "letter by letter . . . its text theirs to combine into revelations always unfolding" – and who are doomed to failure.[6] This failure is part of the larger, rich futility of the syncretic act, for in Pynchon the only totalizing system is the absence of a totalizing system or the evident lack of a complete and consistent structure of meaning that would satisfy the positivist in us all. In *V.* (1963), Pynchon calls the mania for system "stencilizing," and in *The Crying of Lot 49* (1967), Oedipa's paranoid pursuit of the truth derives from her capacity to be a "whiz at pursuing clues in strange texts."[7]

In *Gravity's Rainbow*, a salvo against interpretation in general is fired from the labyrinth of Pirate Prentice's dream. Pynchon implies that his texts can be compared to a "taffy trick":

> a standard orientation device here . . . a candy clew whose other end could be anywhere at all . . . well, its labyrinthine

> path turns out . . . to've been deliberately set up to give the stranger a tour of the city. . . . Pirate now and then will cross the path of some other novice . . . often they'll have a time getting their strands of taffy disentangled, which has also been planned as a good, spontaneous way for strangers to meet.

Just as Stencil, Oedipa, and any number of other Pynchon characters do in their fictional world, we discover in Pynchon's texts that everything is connected. Hence, a tug given to the visible threads – and which threads are visible depends on the position and experience of the observer, and the light in the room – quickly unravels an apparently infinite and subterranean yarn. Those who have dedicated themselves to such work are, like Pynchon's characters, better off admitting that any effort to work towards a satisfactory organization of "the enormous amount of information available to contemporary people . . . is probably hopeless."[8] Bruce Herzberg goes even further in this critique of interpretation; he maintains that "the metaphorical imposition of structure upon variety" characteristic of Pynchon criticism is "just the sort of informational control that the novel opposes." Herzberg relates this to "technical knowledge," a sort of "epistemological imperialism which we witness in the quests for the V rocket . . . the bizarre identification of human goals with mechanical control."[9]

Pynchon brings us and his characters again and again to the brink of revelation, only to abandon us there, trembling on the verge of an "epileptic seizure" not only of some resplendent array of information, but of transcendent meaning. It seems to me that given the futility of conventional readership, the only tactic we have left is to step out of frame in order to examine that which lies behind the information presented by the structure: the function of the structure itself, the very mechanism by which Pynchon compels us to feel the interconnectedness of everything and the immanence of meaning everywhere.

One way of stepping out of frame is to watch ourselves reading Pynchon in order to see how the fiction works on us to make us work on it. What we discover thereby is this: Pynchon asserts that the act of applying technique to artistic expression leads to the realm of the inanimate; it is part of technology's necrophilia. But fiction-making – and included in fiction-making is the construction of personal systems and strong metaphors – is ineluctable. To be human is to make fictions and metaphors. Thus, Pynchon's work is not, like the Catatonic Expressionism he derides in *V*, "technique for the sake of technique": "This exhaustion of all permutations and combinations," he warns us, "was death." Rather, *Pynchon has designed a mechanism in the form of elaborate systems and metaphors whose purpose is to make the reader aware of that special place beyond systems of codes and information where our humanness resides*. His work is not a positivist's rat-maze, but a particle physicist's cloud chamber, where normal commonsense expectations about the mechanics of the universe break down. In the cloud chamber, the fact that the universe is comprised of waves of probability is proven, and the observer is brought into direct confrontation with his acts of observation: the electron is a wave or a particle, depending upon the perspective of the observer; minute particles appear in confirmation of mathematical models, as though summoned into being by them; objects separated in space and time violate the commonsense expectation that such things, when separated, cannot act in harmony. In fact, information flows between particles in a cloud chamber (under certain conditions) instantaneously, as though connected by some larger, other-dimensional force which has not been satisfactorily explained. Bernard d'Espagnat of the University of Paris described the cloud chamber experiments he conducted in this way: "'The violation of separability seems to imply that in some sense all these objects constitute an indivisible whole."[10] The critic-observer of Pynchon's cloud chamber couldn't possibly mistake his theory of reading for Pynchon's intention, since that intention hasn't been satisfactorily explained in its completeness. Signs are connected, but we don't know how.

In other words, Pynchon's fictions employ machinery to expose the very un-machine-like machinery of the reader's consciousness at work. If Pynchon's work is systematically meaningful, it is on the cognitive level: it brings the reader into a hyper-alert state that goes beyond mere self-consciousness. If we read Pynchon's fiction seriously, we are ultimately forced to observe ourselves as we are compelled, willy-nilly, to manufacture "unified field theories" to explain what we are reading.

Works like *Gravity's Rainbow*, in particular, punch certain cortical buttons that respond to the stimuli of indeterminacy, incompletion, paradox, complex metaphors, near-crystallizations of sense out of super-saturated solutions of information. Pynchon's fictions are devices that make us aware of our own status not only as information processors, but as humans who are defined by our desire to make meaning out of information. The particular vehicle for this message, the device that works most powerfully to push us into this realization, is metaphor, and Pynchon is a master of metaphor, one whose mastery evolves with his work.

In order to prove these assertions, the following discussion first establishes briefly the extent of the cybernetic theme in Pynchon's works, and then analyzes three effective metaphors from each of Pynchon's three novels.

TO ESCHEW DECADENCE, TRICK PHYSICS

As early as his third published short story, Pynchon had established his deep fascination for the concepts emerging from cybernetics. "Entropy" (1957) dramatizes that point at which thermodynamic entropy and informational entropy intersect. It is partly modelled on Maxwell's demon experiment, in which two chambers were separated by a selective partition.[11] In one apartment, Meatball Mulligan hosts a party filled with bureaucrats who contribute informational entropy; in another apartment directly above, Callisto has converted his quarters into a hothouse in an attempt to ward off the inevitability of thermodynamic death. The text is filled with references to machine-like behavior; catchphrases and slogans of cybernetics drift in and out of the entropic cocktail chatter: "ambiguity and redundancy"; "noise . . . disorganization in the circuit"; etc.

Of course, if we carry the analogy to the Maxwell experiment further, we might say that Pynchon plays the role of demon, guiding characters and the bits of information in the story, achieving an order that would be incomprehensible without the presence of such an intelligence. In a sense, "Entropy" is a parable of all fiction-making, in cybernetic and thermodynamic terms, the artificial but paradoxical imposition of order (intention) on entropy. As we shall see, Pynchon refines this notion over the ensuing fifteen years until it forms the basis of his artistic methodology.

We find the cybernetic in the ever-narrowing distinction between what is human and who is mechanical: an all-pervasive theme in *V.*. For instance, Benny Profane's schlemielhood is only the broadest of a series of statements of the conflict between man and his own inanimate creations. Benny seems to be competing with – and generally loses to – machines. Another expression of the theme is found in Pynchon's proliferation of androids, the unholy hybridization of man and machine. Victoria (alias Vera Meroving, alias the Bad Priest) acquires a growing number of artificial replacements for her original equipment – a prosthetic eye which doubles as a timepiece, a plate in her skull, artificial legs – until, still barely living, she is gleefully dismantled by the urchin children of Malta while she lies helplessly pinned beneath a collapsed building.

The incidental characters who populate "Baedeker world . . . waiters, porters, cabmen" are described as "automata." Bongo-Shaftesbury calls himself "a clockwork doll" and reveals "shiny and black, sewn into his flesh, a miniature electric switch. . . . The silver wires ran from its terminals up the arm, disappearing under the sleeve." Fergus, one of the Whole Sick Crew, has plugged himself directly into a TV set through electrodes on his arm, forming a servo-mechanical feedback loop; if his attention falls beneath a certain level, the TV turns off. At one point, Pig Bodine gets a job working for Anthroresearch Associates who have developed SHROUD and SHOCK, Synthetic Humans, Radiation Output Determined and Synthetic Human Object, Casualty Kinematics, respectively: "In the nineteenth century, with Newtonian physics pretty well assimilated and a lot of work in thermodynamics going on, man was looked at as a heat engine. . . . Now, man had become something which absorbs X-rays, gamma rays, and neutrons." The spy Porpentine is not only a master of disguises as so many Pynchon characters are, but he may be a robot as well; his skin peels off his face and he can take the worst falls without suffering damage. Evan Godolphin's face has been fatefully reconstructed using inert materials which are later rejected by his body's immunological system, causing monstrous disfigurement. "Schoenmaker," the plastic surgeon (who thereby serves the inanimate professionally) "felt himself no more animate than the spanners and screwdrivers he handled."

Characters subjugated by the system or else serving repressive governments are "human machines." The emblematic controlling system is "The Situation," an ongoing political crisis that Stencil traces through the recent colonial history of England and Germany and which "has no reality outside the mongrel sum of various minds that conceive it." Despite its evanescence, The Situation serves the inanimate and controls men, transforming or marrying them to machines. The military-industrial Yoyodyne of Bloody Chiclitz, which is to figure again in *The Crying of Lot 49* and *Gravity's Rainbow* as an unambiguously evil force, is also exemplary of the hi-tech threat of systematization. Even those characters who gain our sympathy – members of the Whole Sick Crew, for instance – unwittingly tend to contribute to the inanimateness of the human world: Benny yoyos on the subway and up and down the East Coast; Esther gets a nosejob; Slab's anti-Catatonic Expressionism is "technique for the sake of technique." On the other hand, the anarchic and dissipative lives they lead seem unconscious attempts to create islands of entropy and provide a contrast to Stencil's paranoid determinism.

Perhaps the most striking points at which humans serve the inanimate is in art. Catatonic Expressionism, avatar of modern art's method, can be taken too far: "This exhaustion of all permutations and combinations was death." A more subtle critique of modernism is picked up again later in *V.*. During the first night's production of "The rape of the Chinese handmaidens," a shocking, incomprehensible avant-garde work, the directors introduce "a remarkable innovation . . . the use of automata to play Su Feng's handmaidens." These theatrical automata are cousins to Karel Capek's forbidding robots of "R.U.R." (1927) but also look forward to Disney's robots, first exhibited at the New York World's Fair of 1964. (You might recall they sang a self-fulfilling prophecy, "It's a small world, after all.") Like Su-Feng's handmaidens they are "lovely creatures . . . not like machines at all."

Decadent art tempts the artist because it is, in its way, so highly technical. It is technique emptied of the contingent, Roussel's ideal. The artist's problem is to avoid giving over art to technique entirely. In Pynchon's mythology, art decays into technology when it abandons its humanity. But how does one preserve one's humanity? After all, totalitarian times call for a totalizing art, technical times for a technical art, cybernetic times for a cybernetic art. Pynchon knows that the paranoid fear of technological determinism is justified and his characters are likely to stumble across truths in their compulsive searches. In order to beat the devil you must know his system.

Pynchon portrays the modernist predecessors to his own post-modern art lapsing into or being subsumed by the inanimate. As Itague, director of "The rape of the Chinese handmaidens," says,

> "A decadence is a falling away from what is human, and the further we fall, the less human we become. Because we are less human, we foist off all the humanity we have lost on inanimate objects and abstract theories. . . . Your beliefs are non-human," he said. "You talk of people as if they are point clusters or curves on a graph."

This definition looks forward to the more sophisticated and extensive drama enacted by the competing explanations for human behavior which in turn are represented by characters such as Pointsman and Mexico in *Gravity's Rainbow*. There, Pynchon portrays entire sciences vying to explain the behavior of a single individual in a single moment in history, poor Tyrone Slothrop, whose copulations just happen to precede the fall of V-2 rockets on London. Dr Edward Pointsman is the behaviorist, armed with statistical and Pavlovian techniques and a belief in the utter efficacy of theories to explain behavior. Against Pointsman stands Roger Mexico, another statistician, who finds comfort (and pain) in the uncertainty of everything. A romanticist, Roger's love for Jessica Swanlake carries him out of the merely technical domain into some more vulnerable territory. Before Jessica, "He's seen himself a point on a moving wave front, propagating through sterile history – a known past, a projectible future." In fact, Mexico is Pointsman's ideal subject. He even sounds a bit like the rockets themselves – projectiles. "But Jessica is the breaking of the wave. Suddenly there was the beach, the unpredictable."

Gravity's Rainbow is filled with similar competitions between "sciences" or epistemologies. On one side always stand technologies that lead to death. On the other stand individuals who seem to be gripped by non-causal, transcendent explanations, whose behaviors remain richer than any point-plot, and who indulge in exotic explanations more plainly akin to metaphor (though not necessarily more metaphorical) than their opponents' constructions. As Leni Pökler remarks, "Parallel, not series. Metaphor. Mapping onto different coordinate systems." So Pynchon offers us tarot, ESP, death cults, sexual extravagance and minority tastes, mysticism and love on the other side. Understanding this essential dialectic helps us to cross the bridge from his epistemology to his aesthetics. We should learn to appreciate the metaphorical value of gravity, as it were. Itague notes: " 'What is decadence, after all, but being subject to the laws of physics?' "

For humans, being subject to the laws of physics means not only falling with the weight of gravity, but dying, too. The individual will cannot resist the determinism of natural law, and yet we manage to fall in love, create art, feel transcendence, see "gravity's rainbow," another oxymoron for the soft machine, combining the rainbow-promise of transcendence with the inevitability of terminal descent. Pynchon seems to be signalling that the purpose of his art is to capture some immunity from the inevitability of gravity, to eschew decadence and trick physics.

THREE METAPHORS: ALGEBRA, DIFFERENTIATION, INTEGRATION

The most interesting – and one of the most direct – references to cybernetics in *V.* concerns the distinction between noise and information. In the middle of a siege at Foppl's estate in South Africa, 1922, a young German engineer, Kurt Mondaugen, continues his recording "of atmospheric radio disturbances: sferics for short." Sferics are

> a family . . . whose taxonomy was to include clicks, hoops, risers, nose-whistlers, and one like a warbling of birds called the dawn chorus. No one knew exactly what caused any of them . . . but everyone agreed that in there someplace was the earth's magnetic field.

Mondaugen, himself besieged by the exhausting, decadent, ongoing party of European colonialists at Foppl's, clicks into the compulsive pattern-searching mode that seizes so many of Pynchon's characters. He discovers "a crude sort of oscillograph to record signals in his absence." Then, looking

> at the cryptic penscrawler, he detected a regularity of patterning which might almost have been a kind of code. But it took him weeks even to decide that the only way to see if it were a code was to try to break it. His room became littered with tables, equations, graphs.

Characteristically, the more he scrutinizes the hieroglyphics, the more he perceives a code-like structure, until finally, Weissman (who is to be transformed into Blicero the Rocket Master in *Gravity's Rainbow*) cracks the code. The decipherment reveals a double code:

"DIGEWOELDTIMESTEALALENSWTASNDEURFUALRLIKST."

Extracting each third letter, Weissman gets two messages that exist in a figure-ground relationship, "GODMEANTNUURK" and "DIEWELTISTALLESWASDERFALLIST." The first is an anagram of "KURT MONDAUGEN" and the second is a direct quote of Wittgenstein's first principle in the *Tractacus*, "The world is all that the case is," as Mondaugen translates it (through Stencil, who is telling this highly Stencilized tale). This incredible double code poses several problems: is Weissman's decipherment correct? If so, how do we explain such a coincidence? Which of the codes is accidental and which intentional, indicating intelligence speaking? Is it the original system of noises heard over the radio (which itself is merely a translation of certain electrical surges and discontinuities), or the translation of those noises into a pen-scrawled graph? Is it the decoding of the graph into letters, or the extraction of two sentences from those letters? In other words, where in this series of codings and decodings is the pertinent information and where the noise?

William Plater, in discussing this scene, notes first the way Mondaugen's research acts as a metaphor for reading Pynchon: "The only thing the reader can do with the facts of Pynchon's novels is to try to impose some order on all the clicks and whistles, all the noise."[12] Later, however, Plater returns to it in the light of Abraham Moles's communication theory, quoting Moles's suggestion that "Noise thus appears as a backdrop of the universe, due to the nature of things."[13] But there is a deeper implication in the metaphor for reading (if we interpret it as such) to which Moles leads us. There is no distinction between information and noise *per se*, apart from the uses to which a message is put, and "uses" most often implies "human uses." That is, the distinction between noise and information is arbitrary from the point of view of the message itself; it is, as Moles describes it, "a dialectic, figure-ground." The selection of noise from information in the signal is contingent upon the "intelligence" of the receiver; potentially, one person's noise is another's significance.

As if to confirm this, Pynchon is careful to note that the more Mondaugen seeks, the more he finds a pattern. At first, Mondaugen perceives "a regularity of patterning which might almost have been a kind of code," as conditional an observation as ever was. Ultimately, however, Mondaugen and the reader are driven to further speculation by the revelations held in the code. Is this a scrambled reflection of Mondaugen's own inspection (the anagram of his name?) or a sign that God is babbling nonsense: "God meant 'nuurk'"? Or perhaps it is a subtle reference to "New York," where Stencil is telling this entire story to Eigenvalue? Or is Pynchon, disguised as the sound of the atmosphere talking to itself, whimsically hinting that Wittgenstein was correct, that the world is everything – no more and no less – than we can make it out to be? Or is the purpose of the code to induce such a listing of questions as this one? The very condition of being human means to try to make the distinction, perhaps the arbitrary one, between what is significant and what is not.

Pynchon has here stated his case, his tacit recognition of the dependence of everything we think we know – and the attendant doubt – on this universal coder-decoder in the human mind. His two later novels show how that hard-wired processor in us all can be used against us, as it is against Oedipa Maas and Slothrop. *But Pynchon doesn't merely portray the techniques and effects of such manipulation, he actually uses them on us, the readers, in order to get to what he calls "the trembling unfurrowing of the mind's ploughshare."*

The Mondaugen-sferics metaphor describes a sort of linear algebra: it seems to be a relatively simplistic statement of the relationship between literary interpretation, which stands for the act of making meaning in an infinitely various world-text, and all epistemology, which often seems to be no more than listening to the atmosphere speak to itself through a jerry-built radio. But in *The Crying of Lot 49*, this algebra evolves into a literary calculus, which is further exploited in *Gravity's Rainbow*. As Pynchon moves from algebra to calculus, he also comes closer to synthesizing the actual principles of information theory with his creation of a literary text. Where Mondaugen uses a radio to monitor the world, Oedipa (who carries the reader with her) is trapped inside a radio, the mythical San Narciso valley that she first sees spread out before her, "a solid state circuit board like the ones you see when you take off the back of a transistor radio." These parallel metaphors also signal the evolution in Pynchon's use of metaphor. In *V.* the metaphors stand for and reflect the reader's processing of the text by converting the figural into the literal or vehicle into tenor. In *The Crying of Lot 49* Pynchon begins to use the metaphor as a cybernetic device to exaggerate this "processing" effect, thus converging – or effacing the differences between – the two parts of metaphor. In other words, metaphors become self-referential, and the reader becomes caught in the reflexive machinery of a hall of mirrors. For instance, consider one of the densest passages in *The Crying of Lot 49*, the famous "dt" conceit:

> She remembered John Nefastis talking about his Machine, and massive destructions of information. So when this mattress flared up around the sailor, in his Viking's funeral: the stored, coded years of uselessness, early death, self-harrowing, the sure decay of hope, the set of all men who had slept on it, whatever their lives had been, would truly cease to be, forever, when the mattress burned. She stared at it in wonder. It was as if she had just discovered the irreversible process. It astonished her to think that so much could be lost, even the quantity of hallucination belonging just to the sailor that the world would bear no further trace of. She knew because she had held him, that he suffered DT's. Behind the initials was a metaphor, a delirium tremens, a trembling unfurrowing of the mind's ploughshare. The saint whose water can light lamps, the clairvoyant whose lapse in recall is the breath of God, the true paranoid for whom all is organized in spheres joyful or threatening about the central pulse of himself, the dreamer whose puns probe ancient fetid shafts and tunnels of truth all act in the same special relevance to the word, or whatever it is the word

is there, buffering, to protect us from. The act of metaphor, then, was a thrust at truth and a lie, depending where you were: inside, safe, or outside, lost. Oedipa did not know where she was. . . . She recalled her third collegiate love, Ray Glozing bitching among "uhs" and the syncopated tonguing of a cavity, about his freshman calculus; "dt," God help this old tattooed man, meant also a time differential, a vanishingly small instant in which change had to be confronted at last for what it was, where it could no longer disguise itself as something innocuous like an average rate; where velocity dwelled in the projectile though the projectile be frozen in midflight, where death dwelled in the cell though the cell be looked in on at its most quick. She knew that the sailor had seen worlds no other man had seen if only because there was that high magic to low puns, because DT's must give access to dt's of spectra beyond the known sun music made purely of Antarctic loneliness and fright. But nothing she knew of would preserve them, or him.

This field yields an ample harvest. At its simplest level, the passage relies on a pun on "dt", which stands both for "delirium tremens" and "differential with respect to time." On a slightly more complicated level, the two puns imply three intertwined themes of decay in the dipsomaniac, decay through increments of time, and the decay from "normal" perception (for which Oedipa strives) to hallucination. Furthermore, we find ourselves tangled in a metaphor having one word (dt) standing for two vehicles, which in turn may act metaphorically with respect to each other and which both imply several tenors (thus a "metaphor of how many parts?"). Finally, the passage is highly self-commenting or reflexive, leading us to grapple with a metaphor that is partly about metaphor itself.

At this level, the metaphor implies a more literal relationship between metaphors and differential calculus. The sign "dt" indicates the differential with respect to time and implies a small increment of time change. This is the essential feature of any communications system, particularly in a feedback system, in which the amount of information in a message is a function of certain probabilities and changes over time. In feedback processes, the rate of transmission of information alters over time as the system stabilizes (less new information is required – negative feedback) or destabilizes (more information is needed – positive feedback). To differentiate an equation means to take a measurement of the rate of change of one variable with respect to the change in a second variable.

The simplest illustration of this is distance per time ratios, or speed. A car moving at a constant speed has no change in the proportion of distance covered to time passed. We note this by giving it a single number (55 m.p.h.) and by saying the differential of the speed, another way of saying acceleration, is equal to zero. If the car picks up speed, its differential is positive, and we talk about its acceleration. On a graph, the differential of a simple curve is a straight line that shows the slope of the curve at a point. Thus, differential calculus is especially useful in calculating the trajectories of missiles.

The opposite process is integration, which takes a sum of differentials over a changing variable (e.g. distance over time). The integral of an equation for speed, for instance, will yield the distance covered. The integration of the amount of information in any given unit of a code – which is always a probability – over time will yield the amount of information in the transmission. Mathematicians have a poetic way of describing integration: they call it "finding the area under the curve." Throughout *The Crying of Lot 49*, Oedipa Maas has been involved in what Kathleen Woodward has described as "positive feedback" with respect to the information she uncovers in pursuit of the clues imbedded in Inverarity's will. The more information she receives, the more destabilized her position becomes; her "system" oscillates in wider and more encompassing patterns with every new hint, but she apparently gets further away from resolution. The more confirmation she receives, the stronger become her expectations that she will receive more clues to support her suspicions.

Calculus is the mathematics of limits. One can perform successive differentiations on an equation or a curve as the change in one variable approaches zero until the differential is zero. Similarly, one can integrate an equation – find the area under a curve or the volume inside a closed surface – if the limits are finite or the curve can be specified by an equation or the surface is closed. But Oedipa's experience in metaphor takes her further away from limits: her system is open, not closed. A calculus of metaphors is therefore impossible, Pynchon implies, if we are to eschew decay and trick physics.[14]

Metaphors (particularly of the non-trivial kind that Max Black has called a "strong metaphor . . . both 'resonant' and 'emphatic,' "[15]) engage the reader in positive feedback looping: the more you look at a rich metaphor, the more there is to see in it. Metaphors tend to explode under scrutiny. They initiate a process of increasing energy or oscillation that leads to the brink of revelation. This is partly demonstrated by the apocalyptic metaphors Pynchon uses to describe the ultimate revelation withheld from Oedipa: it is an "epileptic seizure," or what Jesus Arrabal calls "a miracle . . . another world's intrusion into this one."

Metaphors provoke a stepping out of frame. They bring with them a degree of uncertainty even as they form crystals of meaning, what Wiener might call "local enclaves of organization." Strong metaphors can crystallize meaning along any number of axes simultaneously, but the number of those directions is indeterminate, i.e. certain metaphors invite conflicting interpretation. Strong metaphors also act to bring different systems of reference into contiguity or proximity, achieving resolutions that may lie outside the power of either of the initial systems alone. One needs only to look at the subject of this book, the intrusion of the harder machinery of cybernetics into the more pliable realm of fiction, to see the extent to which the collisions produced by a metaphor are "interactive" and generative.

This has immediate implications in cybernetic terms. On one hand, information itself is a proportion measured by an integration: the individual "bit," as Gregory Bateson whimsically describes it, "is a difference which makes a difference."[16] The total of information is the sum of these bits over time. Metaphors, too, are a sum of "dt's" – a sum of differences that make a difference, but on the other hand, they also destabilize the system; some of the information they carry is "aesthetic" (to use Moles's term) or "personal" (to use Polanyi's): they carry too much noise with them. Metaphors are apt metaphors for the human situation.

Thus, to make metaphors is at least partly a process irreducible to cybernetic terms. The human capacity (and, indeed, as many have argued, the ineluctable necessity) to make metaphors is at heart a process of extracting meaning from experience. Those investigators of metaphor who have a phenomenological bent suggest that all expression is metaphorical in origin, and all knowledge is constructed by an elaboration of metaphorical processes. One of the primary metaphor theoreticians who took this view was Benjamin Whorf, author of *Language, Thought and Reality* (1956) to whom Pynchon seems to allude in the name of one of the authors of "The courier's tragedy" (in *The Crying of Lot 49*), Richard Whorfinger.[17] John Searle extends Whorf's work by pointing out that metaphors cut a distinction between and relate "word and sentence meaning, on the one hand, and speaker's meaning or utterance meaning on the other hand."[18] In other words, an adequate definition of metaphor entails the crucial distinction between the cybernetic (algorithmic-syntactic) and non-cybernetic (semantic) aspects of language, or between the grammar and the sentence.

Pynchon creates self-referential metaphors – meta-metaphors – by making at least one of the terms, either vehicle or tenor (figural or literal), a technological one, as though hinting that metaphors are partly mechanical but also partly transcendent of mere mechanism. For example, consider the following metaphor essential to *The Crying of Lot 49*:

> It was part of her duty, wasn't it, to bestow life on what had persisted, to try to be what Driblette was, the dark machine in the centre of the planetarium, to bring the estate into pulsing stelliferous Meaning, all in a soaring dome around her?

This is another metaphor radiating *n* interpretations. First, Pynchon expresses through Oedipa her central, paranoid, almost solipsistic role in the construction of her epistemological system. Second, this system is tacitly compared to a machine whose function is "to bring the world into pulsing stelliferous Meaning all in a soaring dome around her." However, third, this machine is "dark," itself a word ambiguous in at least two directions: is it a "dark machine" in the sense that it is a "machine for the production of darkness"? or in the sense that it is a "machine whose functioning is mysterious"? is Pynchon hinting that the human dark machine functions to project uncertainty as well as "stelliferous meaning" on to the dome? or is it that the human itself is mysterious or invisible? These propositions are not exclusive. Fourth, it is clear that this is another meta-metaphor, in which the metaphorical quality of Oedipa's search, equated to the act of writing fictions, is itself the dark machine in the center of the planetarium, both cybernetic device and manifestation of essential human creativity. Finally, this metaphor seems to say that itself and all that it entails – the act of making fictions, making systems of knowing, using language – are cybernetic devices for the materialization of meaning in that soaring dome, the human skull.

DESIRE AND THE ROCKET: TWO CYBERNETIC MECHANISMS

The arc of a rocket descending describes gravity's rainbow – another dome – and *Gravity's Rainbow* is the integration of metaphors, an exploration of that "area under the curve."

Each character in the book maps some portion of his or her desire on to the imminence of the rocket's descent. Most notable among these is Tyrone Slothrop who seeks its *schwarzgerat*, its "dark thing" in the center of the dome of its nose, and who also is a *schwarzgerat* himself, an unknown phenomenon. His casual sexual liaisons occur where bombs will fall. Slothrop is the questing question mark. Is he free or is he the product of a devious engineering project? Does Slothrop himself feel free, or does he feel he is the subject of the laws of the systems which impinge on him? This *schwarzgerat* is a servo-mechanism, a metaphor, and by extension, the rocket's arc describes a curve whose integration is Desire itself, a black box. Under the curve of its trajectory is the *terra incognita* of the sum of human desires, which Pynchon explores in all its polymorphous perversity:[19]

> Katje has understood the great airless arc as a clear allusion to certain secret lusts that drive the planet and herself, and those who use her – over its peak and down, plunging burning towards a terminal orgasm . . . which is certainly nothing she can tell Slothrop.

René Girard suggests that desire is a machine which turns the desirous subject into a mechanical puppet of a stronger force. The subject's desire for his object is often thwarted, and yet mediated, by a rival, who becomes his double and nemesis.[20] In Girard's system, the mechanism of desire in the individual is merely the expression of a more universal social force, a force which is laid bare or exposed by violence. The object of desire is by definition never attained; to attain a desire is to turn it into an object of possession or to transform it into something else, something more inert, something devoid of the passion that invested it with meaning. In the throes of passion, the subject is caught in "a self-perpetuating process, constantly increasing in simplicity and fervor" – a process, according to Girard, bound to end in violence. The desire-machine is a servo-mechanism, summed by a calculus of desires we call "society," which in turn creates structures of differentiation, systems of knowing and believing, in order to mask the crisis at its center, a crisis of undifferentiation, violence, and chaos. Girard writes: "There is a unity that underlies not only all mythologies and rituals, but the whole of human culture, and this unity of unities depends on a single mechanism, continually functioning because perpetually misunderstood."[21]

Pynchon portrays society after the mimetic crisis has atomized the whole. In this world, the central icon is a single inexplicable machine, the Rocket bomb that "comes screaming across the sky" in the overture to *Gravity's Rainbow*, and whose descent we still await on the novel's last page. It is the rocket bomb which lies at the unattainable center of this labyrinthine work and at the center of the rocket is a cybernetic device, the Schwarz-gerat or S-gerat; the dark thing, manifestation of the unknown. The bomb's S-gerat makes ever more finely attuned adjustments to the rocket's aim (desire) in order to unleash its great violence, "constantly increasing in fervor and simplicity."

The Zone-like setting of a world already reduced to what Girard calls *"le crise de dêdifférentiation"* by the Second World War permits Pynchon remarkable freedom. Identities in this war-torn Europe blur and alter, borders disappear, social intercourse is reduced to mechanical exchanges, mechanical exchanges are reduced to habituation, compulsive sexuality, violence, and other drugs. In an unruly world, everyone is an exotic. We witness society itself caught in the positive feedback loop, on the verge of reaching critical mass both figuratively and literally, for certainly one of the many overlaid trajectories of the V-bomb leads to fission and the atom bomb.

This crisis has arisen from something essential to the human. Girard calls it an animal violence exacerbated in the human by the lack of "a braking mechanism": violence becomes reciprocal and tends to increase with each turn of the revenge loop peculiar to the human species. Pynchon, more concerned with what we know and how than how we behave and why, naturally blames the crisis on the compulsive, mechanical parsing of the text of the world, figured and consummated in the rocket and the cybernetics that produced it. Pynchon's warning is clear: cybernetics is merely the latest and most devastating expression of society's death-wish addiction to the application of technology to human control.

But *Gravity's Rainbow* in large part portrays individual desires resisting the larger calculus of probabilities, by which individuals are summed into populations and populations are shown "obeying the law of high numbers," slaves to average behavior. Dr Roszavolgyi is only one of the many technicians in *Gravity's Rainbow* who express the idea: "But if personalities could be replaced by abstraction of power, if techniques developed by the corporations could be brought to bear, might not nations live rationally?"

From atop the rationalistic rainbow, from this Olympian perspective offered by technique and statistics, metaphors, like desires, become cybernetic devices, stimuli that make human responses into components of a servo-mechanical loop: "We also happen to have in mind a very structured stimulus," says Pointsman in response to Dr Rózsavölgyi. "Someone in fact that got us interested in the first place. We want to expose Slothrop to the German rocket."

The result is that the human is reduced to a Pavlovian-Skinnerian part of a feedback circuit. Slothrop and reader alike "seek in silence for the stimulus that is not there. Pavlov thought that all the diseases of the mind could be explained, eventually, by the ultraparadoxical phase . . . the confusion of ideas of the opposite." Pynchon is part Pavlov and toys with us no differently through the mechanisms of language than Pavlov with his dogs and Pointsman and Them (the tech-cartel for whom the Second World War was only a profit venture) with Slothrop. In fact, the progression Pavlov-Pointsman-Pynchon traces a line of evolving techniques. Pavlov required the instrumentation of metronomes and bells to convert his subject into parts of a feedback device. Pointsman refines it (the same year that Wiener and company met in Princeton to invent cybernetics) to the point that certain information becomes the drug and Slothrop the addict. Semyavin, the black-marketeer, approaches Slothrop under a bridge: "What is it you're after . . . stimulants, Depressants, Psychomimetics?" "Uh, information?" Slothrop replies. Semyavin sighs

> "Information. What's wrong with dope and women? Is it any wonder the world's gone insane, with information come to be the only real medium of exchange? . . . It'll get easier. Someday it'll all be done by machine. Information machines. You are the wave of the future."

Pynchon's refinement is to link the raw information with the desire to have meaning. Humans are partly machines that take data and abstract them into knowledge that is never certain or complete.

Slothrop and the reader grow more aware of their roles as Pavlovian subjects:

> The absence . . . surrounds him like an odor, one he knows he can't quite name, an aura that threatens to go epileptic any second. The information is here – not as much as he wanted (aw, how much was that?) but more than he hoped, being one of those practical Yankees.

Actually, Slothrop is in the grip of information addiction, and his complaint should really be not against the lack of data but its deluge which threatens to make him go "terminal." Later, Tchitcherine recalls the lesson Wimpe taught him about addiction:

> "[O]ur basic search [is] to find something that can kill intense pain without causing addiction.
>
> "Results have not been encouraging. We seem up against a dilemma built into Nature, much like the Heisenberg situation. There is nearly a complete parallelism between analgesia and addiction. The more pain it takes away the more we desire it. It appears we can't have one property without the other, any more than a particle physicist can specify position without suffering an uncertainty as to the particle's velocity –"

Pynchon returns us to the tie between the calculi of addiction (surpassing, then, what Burroughs eloquently called the "algebra of need") and information first presented in the pun on "dt" in *The Crying of Lot 49*. Perhaps he is building on Wiener's notion that positive feedback explains several interesting physiological dysfunctions, including epilepsy, Pynchon's favorite metaphor for info-overdose. Gregory Bateson makes the connection between addiction, pain and cybernetics even more explicitly. In "Cybernetics of 'self': a theory of alcoholism," Bateson suggests that alcoholism can be explain in terms of feedback mechanisms:

> The alcoholic's discomfort activates a positive feedback loop to increase the behavior which preceded the discomfort. Such positive feedback would provide verification that it was really that particular behavior which brought about the discomfort, and might increase the discomfort to some threshold level at which change would become possible. . . . Such a positive feedback loop . . . illustrates a tendency to verify the unpleasant by seeking repeated experience of it, is a common human trait. It is perhaps what Freud called the "death instinct."[22]

Bateson's theory explains the tie between the theme of addiction and death (or what Plater calls "the elaborate necrology of *Gravity's Rainbow*"). Further, it describes the mechanism in the characters and in us, the readers, that has made us "dataholics" – addicted as much to the pain as to the pleasure brought by new information, a mechanism that brings us closer not to resolution but to death. This is what Wimpe means when he tells Tchitcherine that "there is nearly a complete parallelism between analgesia and addiction. The more pain it takes away, the more we desire it." Thus, doctors become traffickers in pain.

Pynchon's fictions activate this machinery in us, figured in the elusive consummation promised by the rocket's perpetually imminent descent. Knowledge, like the Rocket, is always almost arriving. Yet, his metaphors also call into play processes that go beyond machinery, imaginative powers necessary when worlds collide. The result is never-ending loops of interpretation and ever-widening circles of meaningfulness. But this process initiated by Pynchon is dedicated towards a particular end, I believe: to free us from calculation by exposing its insufficiency.

If Pynchon's fictions have an ultimate meaning it is on the level of cognitive mechanism, where his fictions – especially his metaphors – push certain cortical buttons incarnate within us. They have the disturbing quality of calling to our attention our own mechanisms of mind. Reading Pynchon is like listening to our own nerve-noises as if they were signals from an alien intelligence, or like trying to decipher the patterns materializing on our retinas under pressure as hieroglyphs of some other sense.

SEVEN

AUTHOR AS ARTIFICIAL INTELLIGENCE: JOHN BARTH'S COMPUTER-GENERATED TEXTS

"One of the major criticisms of the AI practitioners in recent years . . . is that they have concentrated very heavily on games and puzzles instead of tackling real problems. . . . In the past, the following justification was used. Real life problems most of the time are perceived in such a vague manner that they are often unexpressible in a way acceptable to a computer."
(R. Banerji, *Artificial Intelligence* (1980))

' '' ' '' ' '' ' ''' '   ' '' ' '' ' '' ' ''' '

(John Barth, "Menelaiad")

One of the major criticisms of John Barth's work in recent years – roughly between *Giles Goat-Boy* (1964) and *Letters* (1979) – is that he has concentrated very heavily on games and puzzles instead of tackling "real problems."[1] But Barth seems to justify himself through the very nature of the puzzles he poses and the games he plays: to wit, that problems in real life most of the time are perceived in such a way that they are inexpressible through the machinery of language and fiction. At the same time, Barth seems to hold, along with phenomenological philosophy and structuralist linguistics, that language is all we have, after all. Therefore, Barth has exaggerated the role of this machinery – to the point that he has even turned himself into a kind of text-generating machine – in order to emphasize the contrast between fiction and certain aspects of experience. Also, acting like a machine is inherently comic (as Henri Bergson has suggested[2]); perhaps it is even pleasurable to the comic as well as to the audience. Postmodernism has had no better practitioners than those who play so intently with the structures of fiction while making us laugh as Barth does.

Thus, machines in general and the computer in particular have a twofold purpose in Barth's fiction: they act both as masks through which Barth announces his playful commitment to authorship as "artificial intelligence," and they present a metaphor for the sorts of questions Barth frequently returns to in his fiction. Is fiction more than a sum of self-conscious techniques? is language merely a mechanical, automatic reflection of consciousness? why do our systems of knowledge and expression seem to be incommensurate with the richness of our experience?

THE COMPUTER-AUTHORS IN BARTH'S FICTION

Barth incarnates his authorial self as a machine in several works. "Lost in the funhouse," from the collection of short stories by the same name (1967), slyly compares being an author to being a funhouse operator. It also compares the text to a funhouse, a large machine "incredibly complex and controlled from a great central switchboard like the console of a pipe organ . . . [a] cunning multifarious vastness."[3]

In "Autobiography: a self-recorded fiction," from the same collection, the words we read are purportedly the transcript of a tape produced by the illicit intercourse of a disembodied voice and the machine itself. The taped voice is sick of its purposeless life and its own extreme self-consciousness and wishes for nothing more than to turn itself off, which is difficult to do without a body. The text itself is made up almost entirely of word play, highly "entropic," and in some senses "sick" language, tail-biting in its self-consciousness as the first line suggests; "You who listen give me life in a manner of speaking." (Since the words we read are only transcripts of a tape, can this be a plea: "Yoo hoo! Listen! Give me life!"?)[4]

I have already discussed the sterility of compulsive punning in Roussel's work and explored its relationship to the mechanics of language. Puns are accidents in the code which increase uncertainty (and therefore entropy). They emphasize the difference between sheerly artificial codes (in which such accidents and uncertainties are minimized) and natural languages (in which such accidents proliferate). Roussel attempted to control and reduce this uncertainty through the exertion of sheer technique, for it is there in the pun that the mechanism of language is both most apparent and most vulnerable. Barth, by contrast, exploits and exaggerates this vulnerability, as we shall see.

Barth's fiddling with the equation between computer and author reaches symphonic proportions in *Giles Goat-Boy*. Here the reader is asked somewhat ironically to entertain the proposition that a computer is actually the author and that the author, "J.B.," is merely an agent for the machine-generated manuscript. This progressive experiment is lampooned (and, perhaps, finally renounced) by Barth in a later novel, *Letters*. One of the author's seven alter egos who write the letters of *Letters* is a paranoid crank, Jerome Bonaparte Bray, the designer and programmer of a text-generating computer, LILYVAC. LILYVAC proves to be another soft machine, part vacuum-tube contraption, part organic beehive.

The literary commentary by a second character, Ambrose Mensch, sheds light on Bray's fantastic project. Mensch is a more rational alter ego, whom we recognize as the funhouse operator now grown, Barth's "aesthetic conscience." Mensch, also an author, describes himself as "a former formalist" and bids "farewell to formalism," implying perhaps that Barth himself will abandon his role as what Mensch calls a "last-ditch provincial Modernist." Thus, on one hand, Barth parodies his own devotion to formalism through Bray and Mensch and more or less promises to abandon it; but on the other hand, *Letters* itself is highly "rationalized" and ordered.

The following explores in greater depth these two novels – *Giles Goat-Boy* and *Letters* – and their use of the computer as a metaphor for authorship. My purpose is to discover precisely what it is that Barth has been trying to accomplish through his devotion to formalism and his attraction to the machine as a metaphorical substitute for the author.

INFORMATION VS. INTERPRETATION: LEVELS OF THE TEXT

Giles Goat-Boy, like Vonnegut's *Sirens of Titan* or Roussel's *Locus Solus*, is arranged in discrete and identifiable levels or concentric circles united by a cybernetic metaphor. In Roussel, this unity is achieved through the mechanical "punner," with its implications of mechanical artistry and the mechanisms of nested tales which it created. Vonnegut's text is united by the successive failures of coded messages or mechanisms connecting the Tralfamadorians to Rumfoord to Salo to Earth's history to Malachi Constant. In *Giles Goat-Boy* it is the computer, or more specifically the computer as a source of uncertainty in human affairs, that serves this purpose.

At the outermost ring of narrative in *Giles Goat-Boy* is a system of prefaces and afterwords, a series of documents intended to anticipate, though "not in the hope of forestalling," critical reception of the fiction. These prefaces and appendices succeed in bringing into question, frame-wise, the authorship of the inner tale. In these, J.B. "denies that the work is his" and elects as "candidate for its authorship one Stoker Giles or Giles Stoker" – son of the hero of the story. However, this mysterious agent appears to have claimed in turn "(1) that he too was but a dedicated editor, the text proper having been written by a certain automatic computer, and (2) that excepting a few necessary basic artifices, the book is neither fable nor fictionalized history but literal truth." Furthermore, "The computer," as the Publisher complains in his prefatory "Disclaimer," "the mighty WESCAC, does it not too disclaim authorship? It does."[5]

Barth even toys with some of the technical details of computerization, in order to give room for at least a rudimentary discussion of what computers can and cannot do. J.B. informs us in his introduction that:

> This remarkable computer . . . declared itself able and ready (with the aid of "analogue facilities" and a sophistication dismaying at least to a poor humanist like myself) to assemble, collate, and edit this material, interpolate all verifiable data from other sources such as the memoirs then in hand, recompose the whole into a coherent narrative from the Grand Tutor's point of view, and read it out in an elegant form on its automatic printers! . . . [T]he computer made good its promise. After several false starts and program adjustments it produced a first-person chronicle of the life and teachings of the Grand Tutor.

J.B. continues to explore the probability of such a gadget as WESCAC. He consults a computer specialist who suggests that although no computer he knows of is yet capable of anything

> more than rudimentary narrative composition and stylistics . . . there was no theoretical barrier even to our own machine's developing such a talent in time. It was simply a matter of more sophisticated circuitry and programming such as the computer itself could doubtless work out. . . . It was his opinion that anything "computer teachable" (his term) was "computer learnable."

J.B.'s "expert" is a dyed-in-the-wool artificial intelligence specialist who echoes Turing's suggestion that a computer can learn, implying that one day a computer will teach itself to write novels (if it is so inclined). Though the actual merits of this supposition need not be debated here, and though J.B. himself rejects the possibility, it is important to note that Barth has provoked his reader into considering the idea, for in elementary terms, Barth has asked us to suspend any disbelief and accept the comic premise that the "real" author of "The New Revised Syllabus" (for that is what the actual inner narrative is called) is WESCAC.

But the artifice of the frame is carried over into the "artificial intelligence" informing the next level of the text, its table of contents, which announces a rigid division of the text into Two Books comprising Seven Reels each. The use of the word "reels" alludes not only to the then-predominant form of computer input-output – the magnetic tape, spun in and out on reels – but also to circularity in the abstract, implied by the term and expressed in the sort of tailbiting texts of which Barth is enamored and of which this is one. This circularity, the love of tailbiting and Moebius strips (see *Lost in the Funhouse*) and paradoxical tokens, dominates the structure of the text and the logic of its explorations. Time and again the hero, Billy Bocksfuss, a.k.a. George Giles, is caught in the throes of circularity, exemplified in his own birthright:

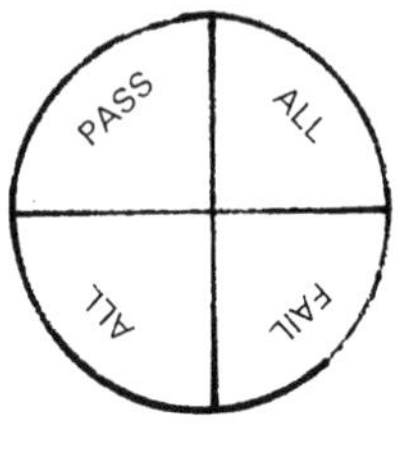

The question of this novel's authorship at first glance seems to be another example of the sort of Nabokovian gamesmanship and frame-play typical of Barth. However, the suggestion that the computer is a potential author raises other questions about the entire enterprise of learning and knowing, epistemological considerations which are at the heart of Barth's concern. The most consequential of these questions can be restated as follows: are the systems we devise to describe the world merely machines? That is, are our sciences and academic disciplines merely complex but reductive accounts of our experience in the world, mechanical and therefore futile and insufficient?

The answers to this question form a complex satire presented through a conceit of reduction worthy of Swift: the universe is all a university and all the players students. Earth becomes a campus divided into warring twins East and West. Nations are colleges, God is "The Founder," messiahs are "Grand Tutors," and presidents are "chancellors." The two ruling political systems in West and East are not capitalism and communism but "Informationalism" and "Student Unionism."

Barth's conceit, particularly the substitution of information for capital implied by "informationalism," is a reflection of the period in which the book was written. Not only were college campuses the sites of revolutionary activity, but it was a widespread belief in the early 1960s – one that has been borne out in the two intervening decades – that America was on the verge of an "information revolution" that would usher in the "information age" dominated by computers. In 1964, for instance, Ulric Neisser wrote: "By now it is a commonplace that cybernetics and automation will bring about radical changes in our way of life."[6] In an essay published the same year as *Giles Goat-Boy* Marshall McLuhan suggested that "cybernation" would produce "an environment of information."[7] Neither Neisser nor McLuhan were suggesting anything new; they were merely building on a popular commonplace. On the other hand, this was considered inherently threatening and totalitarian by a large segment of the population, many of them on college campuses. "The sixties was a period of protests against authority, and no more convenient and frequent metaphor for authority was offered than the machine,"[8] Morris Dickstein writes in his work about the period, *Gates of Eden*:

> Part of the dissident spirit of the sixties was surely Luddite. It saw machines everywhere and was determined to break them or shut them down: the war was a machine, society was a machine, even the university was a machine producing cogs for society. Chaplin's vision of the assembly line was the students' image of the world into which they had been born. If the Old Left would have been content to take over the machine, the young in the sixties were determined either to stop it from functioning or drop out of the whole system.[9]

Thus Barth's embodiment of the technological question in a computer placed in the middle of a symbolic campus-world achieves a refractory power to comment on his times. Furthermore, because he is writing fiction, Barth can deliver his version of the information age as a metonym: at the heart of the universe-university, guiding the economy and social structure of East and West Campuses, choosing Grand Tutors, posing as an author of the text we are reading, at the source of all the wealth (data) of that world, and controlling human destiny, lies an omniscient computer.

Another consequence of Barth's identification of his authorial activity with the output of a computer is that it invites comparisons, perhaps invidious ones, between Barth's technique and what we would expect of a computer's fictional output. Indeed, if we imagine the way the first successful computer-generated novel will look (if you can imagine such a project at all) and compare it to *Giles Goat-Boy*, or the even more self-conscious work of *Lost in the Funhouse* and *Chimera*,[10] then certain features would be similar: the rigidly patterned and obvious formalism, the redundancy of techniques, etc. It is not surprising then that to some, *Giles Goat-Boy* might appear to be a work of consummate pedantry, a sort of apotheosis of thumb-twiddling. For those interested in realism, the one-to-one scaled reduction of universe to university necessarily loses much in the transcription, only to be replaced by verbal calisthenics.

On the other hand, a good part of the satire arises from this reduction. Some effects are trivial: for instance, existentialism becomes "beism." The pun in turn engenders others; one young man uses this grand philosophy to persuade his girlfriend to act the "beist" with him in the bushes of a park. But some are essential, for this word play becomes the basis for a drama revolving around the intellectual and emotional growth of Billy Bocksfuss as a result of his threefold attempt to interpret an "assignment" given him by WESCAC. This assignment is a list of seven heroic tasks which, if fulfilled, will qualify George for "grand tutorhood." But in order to attempt these interpretations in good faith, the goat-boy must devise whole philosophical systems to justify himself, and in turn these systems must be synthesized into the Truth, for the goat-boy is nothing if not sincere.

George has been predisposed to this Talmudic exegesis by his mentor, Max Spielman (the very name implies Max is, for better or worse, a consummate linguist, or at least a consummate pedant). Max began his own career in music, but his insatiable curiosity soon led him to unravel the entire skein of knowledge, and from music he quickly moved to "acoustical physics, mathematics, the psychophysiology of sensation . . . to the science of artificial thought and regulation." In short, Max is the avatar of cybernetics itself, inherently interdisciplinary; he even faintly resembles Norbert Wiener, who was similarly cultivated in music and mathematics. Like Wiener who applied cybernetics to the development of weapons systems, Max soon applies his knowledge to the construction of a doomsday device. Though he believed, like those who worked on the Manhattan Project, that he was contributing to a necessary evil in order to counter a greater one (he is "Moishian," it is "Campus Riot II," and the "Siegfriedans" are exterminating his people), he is later filled with remorse and retires to the life of a reclusive goatherd. Ironically, the doomsday device he helps to construct is WESCAC.

Max describes WESCAC as the ultimate evil:

> I didn't create it, nobody did – it's as old as the mind and you just as well could say it made itself. Its power is the same that keeps the campus going . . . and the force it gives out with – yi, Billy, it's the first energy of the University: the Mind-force that we couldn't live a minute without.

WESCAC is also associated with all technology: it is the storage memory of all knowledge, its memory bank is the central bank for all the machine-assisted pedagogical facilities, and it is the time-piece for the campus. It has consolidated its hegemony through the addition of four programs: MALI, NOCTIS, EAT, and GILES.

MALI is its hyper-advanced digital analyzer, not very different from today's computers:

> It could excogitate, extrapolate, generalize and infer after its fashion; it could compose an arithmetical music and a sort of accidental literature (not often interesting); it could assess half a hundred variables and often make the most sophisticated prognostications. But it could not bet on a hunch or brilliant impulse; it had not intuitions or exaltations; it could request but it could not yearn . . . its correlations were exact but its metaphors wrenched; it could play chess, but not poker. . . . It had no sense of style or grasp of the ineffable.

A useful tool that could outstrip men in many capacities, it remained an essentially sub-human machine. The NOCTIS program altered that insufficiency. NOCTIS ("non-conceptual thinking and intuitive synthesis") gave WESCAC its "right-brain capacity," so to speak, and, as Max says, sets it "as far above studentdom in every psychic particular as studentdom was above the insects." Whereas "the limitations of MALISTIC thinking, however many problems they occasioned were what stood between a student body served by WESCAC and the reverse," "NOCTILITY" made the WESCAC "founderlike." MALISTIC left-brain thinking was mechanical; NOCTILITY was nightside unconsciousness, the incarnation of desires, motives, symbolic associations and limitless syntheses which made the machine a superhuman cybernaut. Finally, added to the "malinoctic" capabilities (malignant? malign gnosis? nightmarish – from bad + nocturnal?) were two specific appetites and powers. EAT ("encephalographic amplification and transmission") the weapon of choice in a world based on information-making and getting, since its radiation eats the minds of whole populations indiscriminately. Finally GILES was added, an experimental program in super-eugenics which gave the computer the equivalent of lust, aimed at engendering a Grand Tutor on certain likely females. It is this program which compels WESCAC to sire a child, Billy, on Virginia Hector.

The fact that the computer – the ultimate nemesis – is also the hero's father gives the drama a strange symmetry. George discovers that the computer is not only the transcendental arbiter of his destiny, but a blood relation. Thus, George is a cybernetic semi-deity (or a semi-deific semi-cybernaut). Perhaps this explains his thirst for truth, too. The drama of the story is mapped on a line following George's serial initiation into and adoption of philosophical systems and his attempt to resolve their inconsistencies. However, George's attempts seem puny, flawed and ever insufficient in the face of the computer's enormous competence foiling him at every turn. George is up against the ultimately threatening father-figure – inexorable, omnipotent, and righteous – and his story is in part the first cybernetic Oedipal drama. George seeks to coax from the computer-father an affidavit of his "Grand Tutorhood" (reiterating the Telemachus theme found in *End of the Road* (1958) and *The Floating Opera* (1956)). In order to do so, he must perform seven heroic tasks (reduced in mock-epic fashion to a sort of homework "Assignment"):

To Be Done At Once, In No Time
1) Fix the Clock
2) End the Boundary Dispute
3) Overcome Your Infirmity
4) See Through Your Ladyship
5) Re-place the Founder's Scroll
6) Pass the Finals
7) Present Your ID-Card, Appropriately Signed, to the Proper Authority.

It soon becomes clear that all of these are coded in cleverly ambiguous commands. For instance, he is told he must "Fix the Clock." Does "fix" mean "repair what is broken," or "affix to a spot," or "stop"? Does the "See Through" in "See Through Your Ladyship" mean "expose the character of" or "look at under X-rays"? Does the "Re-place" in "Re-place the Founder's Scroll" mean "put back in its place," "put in another place," or "substitute with another version"?

In an attempt to decode the program, George stumbles into self-contradictions and paradoxes, achieves several wrong-headed resolutions based on false interpretations, and makes a hash of logic with specious reasonings, self-serving rationalizations, meta-logical proofs, nonsensical assumptions, clever sophistries, grandiose tautologies, and jumped-to conclusions. He follows the path of his assignments three times, each time developing an apparently consistent teleology exclusive of the one before it, until he successfully penetrates to the belly of the monster on his third attempt.

George describes himself as "passionate in uncertainty," and possessing "clear confoundment." He is "a goat, a gimp, Chance's ward and creature," paying lip-service to the fact that he is often aided by a series of fortuitous accidents. As a logician, he admits his own flaws: "I shifted my ground then, not quite certain whether the argument was still intelligible, and more in hopes of unsettling my adversary than of instructing either him or myself." Barth extends his satire on specious reasoning to all of academia in a fashion reminiscent of Swift's portrait of the Laputan academicians in the third book of *Gulliver's Travels*. George, hoping that the college library – which in this fiction is an analog of an entire university in our world – will have answers to his questions, tries to follow the line of academic reasoning in a certain footnote to a certain simple text, only to discover a tangled web of casuistry and sophistry, a linguistic and logical labyrinth. He is quickly plunged into a Chinese-box arrangement of scholarly commentaries, discovering there a Talmudic debate over the interpretation of the phrase "There is one way to raise a cow." Failing to decipher a "gloss upon a gloss upon the gloss upon Bray's quotation from Enos Enoch's allusion to Xanthippides's remark upon Milo's misdemeanor," he flees. Another of his crises occurs when he realizes that the exercise of pure reasoning may lead the seeker to make distinctions so fine that they correspond to nothing in reality. It is at this point that George concludes that WESCAC is the enemy, the "root and fruit of Differentiation."

He achieves his sought-after (if ambiguous) transcendence only after he realizes WESCAC's essential neutrality: "Although it stood between Failure and Passage, WESCAC therefore partook of both, served both, and was in itself true emblem of neither." He says, "[B]lack cap and gown of Naked Truth, it screened from the general eye what only the few, Truth's lovers and tutees, might look on bare and not be blinded." Through this enlightenment, George appreciates the central distinction between the computer's role and his own: while logic can only lead to "flunked contradictions," being human means embracing "passed Paradox" by standing in the *terra incognita* of excluded middles.

Armed with this knowledge, George descends into the belly-womb-tape storage center of the computer, with his beloved Anastasia ("without stasis"?) where they unite in the mystical connubial communion of Yin and Yang. They short-circuit the computer by plugging a jack marked output into a socket marked input, and then couple and loop in a more human fashion, passing through to knowledge's far shore.

LOGIC AND LANGUAGE VS. LOVE

There is much hand-waving or prestidigitation by Barth in this semi-satisfactory resolution. The compact, interwoven set of symbols, images, and emblems in the scene cannot be satisfactorily unknotted by logical analysis. That is partly its point, since the terms of the argument alter to suit the dictates of the larger pattern machine Barth has devised. Barth equates much of thought and expression with WESCAC's grand neutrality, for WESCAC, like language itself, is "the root of all Differentiation," and "although it stood between Failure and Passage . . . [it] partook of both, served both, and was in itself the true emblem of neither." Slippery language and the transcendental computer (which has trouble communicating unambiguously with humans) both present a screen between the "bare eye" and "Naked Truth." Everything the goat-boy embraces in his epistemological journey, his philosophies and insights, belong to the machine. These aren't rejected, they are subsumed in his higher vision. Yet, through all this Barth deigns to give us a glimpse not of Naked Truth itself but only a couple of naked characters making love to each other.

Still, we get love, not truth, as the middle term between computer and human, between the structured machinery of information and the unutterable reality of human being-in-the-world, and this is significant. "Love" has a deep etymology in Barth's fiction. It seems to represent, in his mythology, a sign for all that is forbidden mere system, all that is interdicted – between the words – or above or beneath expression. WESCAC can lust, but it cannot love. Language, too, can present the elaborate toils of self-consciousness, but it cannot describe love. The word tolls throughout the short fictions of *Lost in the Funhouse*. For instance, the sentient but suicidal spermatozoon of ''Night-sea journey'' realizes that he dies for love in order to achieve genetic immortality. ''Hate Love!'' he tells us, unable to resist the ovum's siren song: ''Love! Love! Love!'' But in the Chinese-box fiction, ''Menelaiad,'' it sits at the center, a sort of irreducible, radioactive atom spoken appropriately enough by Helen of Troy: '''''''''' Love! ''''''''''. The only utterance to exceed that degree of interiority, its surpassing twin is: ''''''''''''' ''''''''''''''. Elsewhere in the same volume, in an ''allegedly ultimate story'' Barth asks: ''Can nothing be made meaningful?'' And later: ''This is the final test. Try to fill in the blank. Only hope to fill in the blank. Efface what cannot be faced or fill in the blank with words or more words.''

''Love'' is Barth's avatar of this silence, the sort of silence addressed by Merleau-Ponty, in which language speaks more by what it does not say. That blank space is a sign of George's knowledge that to assert humanness is to embrace paradox. Though language is both our first and last resort, it is not a means into total meaning. Love is never merely, literally ''love'' in Barth's code; it is a signifier for whatever is unliteral: blank spaces, systems of quotes, half of a paradox, ''Hate love!''

Understanding the mismatch between language and experience signified by the word ''love'' helps us to understand Barth's complex relationship to language in general and making fictions about experience in particular. For Barth, language belongs as much to the machine as it does to humans, and texts have as much to do with technique as they do with explaining our lives to us. In this regard, Barth is eminently phenomenological, for he believes that *what is essential to our experience cannot be captured in language*. Thus the predomination of puzzles and labyrinths and funhouse machines which get us nowhere.

At one point in *Giles Goat-Boy*, George goes on a rampage shredding (and goatishly eating) the parchment of the holy Founder's Scroll. Later, he encounters a team of experts attempting to piece the text back together, debating fine points and getting nowhere. Included among them are ''cyberneticists . . . on hand both to lend WESCAC's analytical assistance to the project and to apply their genius with codes and ciphers to the restoration of the priceless text.'' Of course, their project is an absurd one, not only because of the lacunae which have been stored in WESCAC's

"CACAFILE" (an equation between feces and the Word we find again in Burroughs and Pynchon) or in George's bowels, but because they get stuck in the same sort of verbal impenetrabilities and self-contradictions that have plagued George for 500 pages: should the Ur-schrift read "Flunked who would Pass or Passed are the Flunked"?

Instead of answering, George scatters the text again. At least in this stage of his ruminations (if you'll pardon the pun) George believes that language is the dismemberment of Truth, and so in order to tell the truth, language must be dismembered. At best, as the computer WESCAC ("Naked Truth's black cap and gown") or the academic debates of exegeticists, or the proliferation of "isms" on campus show, language and its use in texts is a "screen," a barrier between experience and understanding.

Barth is willing to identify his authorship with the operations of a computer, then, because by adopting such an ironic mask, he enables himself to demonstrate the flaws in the mask and at the same time make us aware of the lack, the absence which will never quite be recuperated. For Barth, such a tactic is part of his larger fictional strategy, announced in "Title" (a short story in *Lost in the Funhouse*): that fiction-making is "an attempt to make something out of nothing . . . not only turn contradiction into paradox but employ it to go on living and working." Paradox is a positive sign; it announces the presence of absence.

HAROLD BRAY, CYBERNAUT; JEROME BRAY, CYBERNETICIST

Any discussion of the cybernetic aspects of *Letters* must begin back in *Giles Goat-Boy* with a look at Harold Bray, alleged Grand Tutor and nemesis of George Giles. Harold Bray makes several appearances in *Giles Goat-Boy*; he is a con-man magician, master of disguises, devil and messiah, arch-fiend and antagonist. He appears in New Tammany College mysteriously and adopts a series of roles and pseudonyms, as well as physiognomies and mannerisms, that make him very popular to studentdom and frustrating to George, as he plays the foil to the goat-boy's naïvety and purity of purpose. He steals Anastasia's love and then attempts to rape her atop the Tower. He presides over the execution of Max and performs a series of miracles as he appears and disappears, changes colors, walks on water, and finally, flies away. He and George exchange masks several times, always in a way that reaps advantage for Bray and leads to his establishment as the real Grand Tutor in the eyes of studentdom.

Bray is not only supernaturally evil and superhuman, but he also seems to be an animate representative or avatar of WESCAC. Several details hint that Bray is a machine. His voice alternately "clicks" and "buzzes alarmingly." He seems exempt from WESCAC's predations and lacks an ID card, though these and other clues are ambiguous. "I'm not what people think I am," he tells George. By the exertion of his will he is able to make an identifying birthmark appear on his skin. In order to maintain the symmetry of his role as George's *doppelgänger*, we are led to assume that he is also a "son" of WESCAC, perhaps in particular the product of the GILES program. He is, of course, "fraught with guile." When Bray attempts to rape Anastasia, George notes that Bray was "different":

> Her ravisher was altogether lustless, craving only her reproductive assistance [just as WESCAC sought out Virginia Hector]. . . . His private construction was not like that of any male in her large experience. He was not mounted, only standing with knees bent aft of her escutcheon. . . . [M]oreover, he did not thrust like any buck, but only stood connected, opening and closing his eyes and cape.

Instead of semen, he ejaculates green "glaucous gouts of his rank stuff."

In his final confrontation with George, Bray seems particularly machine-like:

> Dreadful the hum, horrid the foetor Bray now gave out . . . then caught between [George and a goat] he spread his cloak for half a second; more loud his hum than a Stokerish engine! Then from under his tunic-front a thing shot forth shortswordlike, as Tommy struck. The buck shrieked, fell kicking, lay still. I snatched the black vestment, slick as oilskin.

His "thing" is some kind of mechanical apparatus, he wears an oilskin like a machine, and he hums and stinks like an inefficient engine.

This is the ancestor of the character in *Letters* who is pushed into compulsive litigation by his paranoid belief that John Barth has plagiarized his work. Jerome Bonaparte Bray (JBB) is as much J.B.'s gadfly-twin as Harold Bray was George's; he embodies a sort of crazy, ironic, buzzing echo of the most cybernetic portions of Barth's work, that portion in which Barth strives most to imitate the complexity and cleverness of a computer. The latter Bray boasts that he has discovered a way to revolutionize literature through the scientific application of method to the "generation" of texts. Bray wants to create "the 1st genuinely scientific model of the genre, it will of necessity contain nothing original whatever but be the quintessence, the absolute type, as it were, the Platonic Form expressed." In his "Application for Renewal of Tidewater Foundation Grant for Reconstruction of Lily Dale Computer Facility for Reimplementation of NOVEL Revolutionary Project" he suggests that his research will spearhead a new Revolution:

> Now of "science fiction" there is a surfeit; "scientifically" the themes of existing fiction (e.g. Professor Thompson's MOTIF INDEX OF FOLK LITERATURE) or even its dramatical morphology (e.g. the admirable reduction by Professors Propp and Rosenberg, of the Swann-Geese folktale to the formula
>
> $$\gamma\beta\delta \text{ ABC} \uparrow \left\{ \frac{\text{[De NegF Neg]}^3}{\text{DEF}} \right\} \text{GHIK} \downarrow \text{Pr[DEF}^3\text{]3Rs}$$
>
>) these are steps in the right direction, but halting as a baby's primitive as Ben Franklin and his kite – and made by scholars, to the end merely of understanding for its own sake!

With the aid of LILYVAC II, he aspires to be the author of the first technologically induced perfect text, the "Revised New Revised New Syllabus," to be implemented in a five-year plan that is hilariously insane and will include not only the printing of NOVEL but his assumption of the throne of France, "destruction of all existing stocks of insecticides and prohibition of their manufacture forever," and his reunion with his parents.

LILYVAC itself remains somewhat mysterious until late in the novel when Jacob Horner rescues Marsha Blank (!) and discovers the computer in a large, ramshackle barn. He is surprised to find out that far from being a gleaming, hyper-efficient microcomputer with disk drives, tapes, and flashing lights, it is a Rube Goldberg contraption made of antiquated vacuum tubes and strangely more akin to a beehive than a machine. Bray designed the computer to impregnate its female operators: "Fibers still stuck to her hams and buttocks." Barth has created his own emblematic version of the soft machine: "At least some of what you had taken for metal or plastic was a scaly waxy stuff, unidentifiable but vaguely repulsive; some of those wires were more like heavy beeswaxed cord, or dried tendons."

Instead of making love *in* the computer Goat-boy-wise, Marsha makes love *to* the computer, making the interface between human and machine more, shall we say, intimate. Somehow, Bray is able to coax this impossible device into inspired output: the NOVEL project alters to NOTES and then to NUMBERS, giving rise to a new, perfected genre Bray calls "Numerature."

Bray's numerous systems of obsession converge at the climactic point (in Chapter 5) at which the genealogical, astrological, anagrammatical, calendric, numerological, etymological, entymological, and literary-theoretical congeal into an opaque, multi-layered mechanism of private references. Like LILYVAC's printout of what computer programmers call "garbage" (apparently senseless output), his world "must be either a monstrous ciphered anagram beyond anyone's unscrambling, or a mere dumb jungle of numbers." Barth acknowledges through some good-natured self-parody that though form is fun, it can also lead to sterility and paranoia if taken to obsessive lengths.

Thus, Bray's *bildungsroman* is a study in form turned pathogenetic, cybernetically correct but empty of significance. As a system of conventions, an enabling mechanism for making things meaningful, form is amenable to cybernetic analysis. However, Bray's compulsive systematization can be seen in the other characters, too, who, even more surprisingly, grow more Brayish as the novel progesses. Barth cleverly parodies through Bray many of his own cranky obsessions and themes: his boastful use of Campbell's monomythical pattern in *Giles Goat-Boy* and *Chimera*, the hypertrophic transformation of Freitag's triangle into a logarithmic spiral used as a model for the form of *Chimera*, etc. (All of which is reiterated in a letter from Ambrose Mensch to himself [Letter 6R-H, pp. 646–50].) This parody is also an ironic self-commentary, since this tendency to mechanism still dominates the form of *Letters*. Throughout the narrative, Bray exhibits the paranoid tendency to see a visionary and apocalyptic convergence of signs, and this vision, like that of all the other correspondents in *Letters*, intensifies as the novel progresses. There is a growing consciousness of the pattern of the drama, of coincidences, monstrances and meanings. Many of the authors are curious about astrological data and lists of current or historical events marked by the date of their letters. In short, the characters all become more Bray-like, developing or deepening, as the plot thickens, ever more idiosyncratic prose styles.

THE CYBERNETICS IN *LETTERS*

Letters is both coda to and codification of Barth's previous work. By his invention of seven characters, all of them presented with one degree of irony or another as alter egos of himself, he has assembled an enormously formal text that can address various aspects of his *oeuvre* and his relationship to writing.

The structure of *Letters* is a Rousselian machine, "*un device de procédé*" employing anagrammatic, pictographic, literal, symbolic, temporal, and paronomastic elements. The rebus code (in alphabetic elements) which orders the arrangement of letters (epistles) harks back to Roussel. It serves as a guide to Barth's method, and is very much like a computer program: it guides the steps of the performance of certain procedures (in this case corresponding to correspondences between the characters) and "sub-routines." This rebus is replicated on the title-page, in its elemental parts on the chapter-heading pages, and on the last page of the text. Like Roussel's and Canterel's inventions, it seems to suggest that the substance of the fiction is subordinated to a formal procedure.

Though the book contains a strong narrative element involving the slowly more entwined lives of seven characters, the formalist design which seems to be controlling this progressive series of intimacies emerges more and more as a concern of their epistles to one another. Since "J.B." once again plays a role in his own fiction, this gives the characters an occasion for further theoretical speculation and commentary on J.B.'s previous novels, a commentary which, of course, reflects as well on the fiction in which they now play a role. Finally, the characters themselves are older versions of characters from Barth's previous works, or are new characters "descended" from others: Jacob Horner from *End of the Road*; Todd Andrews from *The Floating Opera*; Ambrose Mensch from *Lost in the Funhouse*; A. B. Cook IV, descendant of characters in *The Sot-Weed Factor*; and Jerome Bonaparte Bray, descended from Harold Bray of *Giles Goat-Boy*. The special relationship between love and language is again one of the strong themes of the fiction, this time explored quite seriously in the epistolary form best suited to such considerations.

Ambrose Mensch serves as "The Author" 's belletristic correspondent, a vehicle for Barth's pronouncements and musings. It is he who offers the completed rebus, and the announcement, "farewell to formalism," that had this reader anticipating Barth's next work, *Sabbatical*, with curiosity. Ambrose also defines Barth-like formalism in terms that Wiener or Ilya Prigogine would appreciate:

> Dramaturgy = the incremental perturbation of an unstable homeostatic system and its catastrophic restoration to a complex field equilibrium.
>
> Entropy may be where it's all heading but it isn't where it is; dramaturgy (see above) is negentropic, as are the stories of our lives.

Barth's notion of the literary text is similar to Prigogine's prescription for what he calls a "dissipative structure" – a complex, negentropic system brought into being only under conditions that are, like Bray, far from "stable."

The import of all this is that it indicates how deep into cybernetic territory Barth has gone, and of course, in a fashion typical of cybernetic fiction, how willing he is to signal it to the reader who might also know and care. By taking this position, however, he has had to confront a particularly cybernetic dilemma: if the author attempts to re-create a version of his experience using language to its fullest, he will come up against the mechanical limits of language and fiction. The genius of Barth's fictions is in their clever use of the very devices which indicate those limitations – paradoxes, ambiguities, blanks and other glosses on phenomenological silence – *inside the machine* where they illustrate the incommensurability of the structure of the text and the experience of meaning.

Ambrose poses the following theoretical quiddity:

> If one imagines an artist less enamored of the world than of the language we signify it with, and yet less enamored of the language than of the signifying narration, and yet less enamored of the narration than of its formal arrangement, we need not necessarily imagine that artist therefore forsaking the world for language, language for the process of narration and those possibilities for the abstract possibilities of form.
>
> Might he-she not as readily at least as possibly be imagined as thereby (if only thereby) enabled to love the narrative through the form, the language through the narrative, even the world through the language.

This is a provocative concept: loving the world through the word, or to be more precise, through formal arrangements of words. In order to make sense of it we must recall the special meaning of the word "love" Barth taught us to appreciate in *Giles Goat-Boy*: for him it is not only a way of embracing, of "having" in the phenomenological sense of the word, it permits the lover to transcend from one level of knowing to another. Love thrusts through the screens separating form from narrative, narrative from language, and even language from the "world." But love, in Barth's cosmology at least, is also a sign of those differences. *Letters* adds more weight to that already borne by the word, and follows some of the logic implied by *Giles Goat-Boy*. It shows Barth at his best: loving the world through the form of his fiction without losing the sense that it (the word) is still no substitute for IT (the world). So we should not be surprised to find Barth moving away from formalism, exploring such worldly things as love in all its more mundane aspects and postures: *Letters* portrays romantic love, casual love, unrequited love, chaste and platonic love, passionate and lustful love, miscegenating love, intergenerational and incestuous love, the onanistic pleasures of the text gotten by an author when his creation is upon him, and even a weird *mênage-à-trois* among a crazed computer operator, his lovely female consort, and their computer.

The characters in *Letters*, though plagued by intense intellectualism and the consistent failure of their intellectual structures to account for their lives, are compellingly human – even Bray, who may be, or at least thinks he might be, part insect. They are not so much the puppets of Barth's intellectual play as accomplices of it, motivated by the need to create and appropriate new meaning, to grow. Indeed, from Barth's perspective, that seems to be what it's all about: old forms making new content, willy-nilly.

EIGHT

DECONSTRUCTING THE MACHINE: BECKETT'S *THE LOST ONES*

"Technical means, acting on the ecstatic phenomena produce certain daring innovations in expression."
(Jacques Ellul, *The Technological Society*)

THE CYLINDER-MACHINE AS GEDANKEN EXPERIMENT

Beckett's *The Lost Ones* invites the reader to construct or maintain the notion of an enormous mechanical cylinder in which naked people are trapped for eternity. As an allegory, this fiction is powerful in proportion to its brevity and abstraction.[1] However, if *The Lost Ones* is viewed not as an allegory but in the context of other contemporary works using machines as metaphors for the act of writing and as explorations of the symbolic, mysterious interface between humans and machines, then other properties, cybernetic ones, become visible. The typical congruence between form and function, the concern with linguistic artifice, the constructedness or emphasis on structure for structure's sake, the diminution of the role of the human presence or persona in favor of some deterministic, clockwork fictional universe operating apparently through its own agency – all these themes reveal the kinship between *The Lost Ones* and other cybernetic fictions.

The Lost Ones is a literary gedanken experiment: Beckett

exhorts the reader to "maintain the notion" of this enormous cylinder where approximately 200 "lost bodies roam each searching for its lost ones."[2] This gedanken tactic lends a certain insubstantiality to the fiction that Beckett is otherwise so careful to invest, at the same time, with apparent substance and solidity. He presents the structural details, measurements and technical specifications of the cylinder, including its basic dimensions (50 metres round, 18 high); surface area ("two hundred square metres of floor space or a total surface of roughly twelve hundred square metres of which eight hundred are mural"); what is at one point called its "climate" (determined by concurrent, though not apparently co-ordinated, oscillations in light and temperature); its furniture (fifteen ladders); its peculiar topography (including niches and tunnels); and the material of its construction (unknown but of a hard "rubber or some suchlike").

It is clear that the subject of this gedanken experiment is an enormous machine; at least it strikes one that the cylinder has certain mechanical properties, since the light and temperature are controlled from some outside source, and "at certain intervals impossible to calculate" the two "storms" or "wild oscillations" are "cut off as if by magic." "As though again," Beckett hints, "the two were connected to the same commutator. For in the cylinder alone are certitudes to be found and without nothing but mystery."

At least in this fragment, Beckett has reduced the terms of his "narrative of place" to its most controlled and its most abstracted by inventing a machine that represents a deterministic universe where "certitudes are to be found." (This is another, more apocalyptic, "Locus Solus.") Data about this cylinder-machine and the certitudes within it are delivered by the apparently omniscient intelligence that has designed or imagined it into being – "the voice from universal space" as Hugh Kenner has called it[3] – and these data are soon extended to detail the machinery of social organization among the "beings" as well.

Inside the grand ballroom of this hellish condominium are 200 naked bodies, or "one body per square metre." They are divided into four categories based on the extent to which they actively search, use the ladders, occupy the niches, roam, or remain catatonically rooted to a spot, absorbed, perhaps, by despair. The bodies copulate upon occasion, though joylessly, even painfully:

"Skin rubbing on skin like the dry rustling of nettles." By virtue of the sheer laws of probability, a husband actually has intercourse with his wife, though they do not recognize each other. These accidental meetings between spouses lost to each other give rise to "spectacles . . . to be remembered of frenzies prolonged in pain and hopelessness long beyond what even the most gifted lovers can achieve in camera." Beckett calls these performances "making unmakeable love."

The ironies arising from the accidental couplings and the notion of gifted lovers seeking passion in such pain makes the passage a poignant one. Beckett lets us know, however, lest we are misled into believing that "the lost ones" being sought are mates, that "whatever they search for it is not that." This caveat challenges the reader: what, then, have they lost? The text is extremely brief, and yet in fifty pages is raised to a power of abstraction that promotes mystery and complexity.

Beckett hints that at least on one level this fiction is about a version of hell: the helpless posture of one of the lost ones sitting on the floor, his back leaning against the wall "would wring from Dante one of his wan smiles." Yet, Dante smiles not in the *Inferno* but in *Purgatorio* at the Florentine Bellacqua who has reclined in the shade of a rock his whole life and then is sentenced to rehearsing his inertia forever. Dante scolds him for his lassitude, and Bellacqua replies by saying, "Brother, what avails it to ascend?" This is the same question silently posed by the posture of these lost ones who have ceased searching yet remain in the circle reserved for climbers.

Outbreaks of violence give rise to Miltonesque pandemonium. The general gloom "imparts a sensation of yellow not to say sulphur, in view of the associations." The interior is a "fiery flickering murk" and the lost ones are "straining forever with concomitant moral distress."

The level of abstraction also at first seems to lend the fiction to this sort of reductive interpretation, one that makes of the text a mere parable. Critics both hostile and friendly to Beckett's work have responded in their interpretations to this openness or tolerance for interpretations, answering the call of the parable. To one, *The Lost Ones* is "an extended metaphor of the human condition."[4] Another calls Beckett "an allegorist."[5] But beyond this allegorical level there lies a more interesting response, one arising from the congruence of the structure and function of Beckett's machinery. Joseph McElroy, whose work *Plus* seems to use *The Lost Ones* as a revolutionary point of departure for its treatment of the cybernetic question, notes in an early review that the cylinder represents "a hypothetical notion equal in some sense to the enclosing prose in which this myth, in the form of a defining explanation, is framed."[6] Susan Brienza writes,

> *The Lost Ones* at first seems to cry out for an allegorical interpretation. The cylinder is hell. The cylinder is the tower of Babel. But one can almost hear Beckett answering "no allegories where none intended." Instead, it is much more appropriate to view *The Lost Ones* as Beckett viewed *Finnegans Wake* and *Remembrance of Things Past* where form and content are one.[7]

In Brienza's reading, the futile search by the lost ones is "a comment on the reader's futile search for order and meaning in the piece itself."[8] Thus the reader becomes a searcher looking for a critical way out of the cylinder-text. Eric P. Levy takes this equation one step further and suggests that

> *The Lost Ones* far more concerns the limitations of narrations than the torment of bodies in a cylinder. The story becomes a symbol for or a means of representing the movement of the narrator behind it . . . [and] everything in the story, from the dimensions of the cylinder to the behavior of its people exists only as a narrative object at the whim of its narrator.[9]

Finally, *The Lost Ones* can infect the reader with that critical disease, over-interpretation. As Brienza notes, "The reader-searcher may be finding more meaning in the text than there actually is."[10]

Is the text more than an allegory? Or are these suggestions of self-reflection cases of the critical tail wagging the dog? The temptation is to mold any allegorical or abstruse text in the image of the system used to scrutinize it.

There is evidence that Beckett intended such a reading. In some cases that evidence is trivial: for instance, Brienza notes that there are fifteen ladders of varying lengths and also fifteen sections of prose, also of varying lengths, which, she concludes, are "ladders to meaning."[11] Similarly, Levy explains that the refulgent but oscillating light which at its brightest seems to emanate from everything equally, is really the light of Beckett's imagination illuminating the secrets of the cylinder (which does not, unfortunately explain the tenth-of-a-second strobe effect of the light – unless we descend to the neurological analogy of synaptic bursts, which seems a bit ludicrous).[12]

Other evidence is more convincing. Part of it derives from the context of Beckett's other work, which is very much devoted to the congruency of structure and purpose, but other evidence is internal and derives from the text itself, particularly its style.

TEXT AS SELF-DISMANTLING CYLINDER-MACHINE

The metaphor of the machine lies at the center of Beckett's message. It operates on the literal level as the subject of the story. It operates on the allegorical level as the place and form of this penal state, this hell or purgatory. Finally, I believe Beckett asks the reader to view the text itself as a machine, one mediating between the author and his own imagination and between the author and his audience.

But the machinery described, metaphorical or otherwise, is not simple. Nor is the description itself to be taken at face value. After all, *The Lost Ones* is a literary text, not a technical document. In order to understand some of the quirks and paradoxes in style and expression of Beckett's prose, *the machines of the cylinder and the text itself must be understood as ones that do not work*. Like a perpetual-motion machine, *The Lost Ones* is a palpable fiction which, even as its inventor attempts to complete the blueprint, collapses into impossible meaninglessness, self-contradiction, and absurdity. The fallibility of the cylinder-machine lies in the fact that it is constructed of words; the author's attempt to describe it precisely becomes an exercise in failing epistemology and in the futility of trying to describe anything using language.

This view of *The Lost Ones* as a self-sabotaging machine arises from a close look at the way in which Beckett attempts to describe the cylinder. There are two general rhetorical modes which collide in this attempt: the first is a stylistic evocation of technical and mathematical precision, including both particular words and phrases from these disciplines and their characteristic "postures" in language. The second is the language of failure, probability and doubt; it is a rhetoric borrowed from the quotidian in which decay and disappointment and incompleteness reign. These two rhetorical movements are, of course, completely at odds with each other, and yet Beckett weaves them together, at times even within the same sentence, to fashion an allegorical world of pure fiction, ruled by the aberrant artefacts of language: paradox, oxymoron, and ambiguity. This first rhetoric, for the sake of argument, I call *the machine language*, hoping to evoke images of positivist logic, technical efficiency and computer-like order. The second I call *the language of flesh*, implying that it is heir to all the ills flesh is heir to: softness, decay, inefficiency, irrational doubt, and inconsistency.

Earlier, I gave a brief and exaggeratedly coherent portrait of the mechanism of the cylinder and the society in it. Beckett, too, at first glance seems to present a streamlined overview of the cylinder and its inhabitants. His first section includes short phrases that seem to be category titles promising further elaboration: "The light. Its dimness. Its yellowness." Indeed, this further elaboration is always provided. "The ladders . . . the purpose of the ladders is to convey the searchers to the niches." "The niches or alcoves. These are cavities sunk in that part of the wall which lies above an imaginary line running midway between floor and ceiling and features therefore of its upper half alone." These simple declarative sentences, definitions, descriptions and phrases are part of the machine language and are reminiscent – in the absence of finite verbs or active voice or subject – of instructions for the assembly of a model or the rules of a game: the third-person absent omniscient. Combined with evocative pseudo-technical language, it has a chilling, too-sure effect: "omnipresence of a dim yellow light shaken by a vertiginous tremolo between contiguous extremes"; "A total of roughly twelve hundred square meters of which eight hundred mural not counting the niches and tunnels"; "Between the extremes that delimit the vibration the difference is of two or three candles at the most."

> For it is clear that there are two periods in the scale namely from twenty-one degrees on the way up and from nine on the way down when this difference will not be reached. Out of the eight seconds therefore required for a single rise and fall it is

> only during a bare six and a half out of eight total that the bodies suffer the maximum increment of heat or cold which with the help of a little addition or better still division works out nevertheless at some twenty years respite per century in this domain.

Upon closer inspection, though, a quirk in these apparently rigorous descriptions emerges. Not a single statement or specification or datum is left to stand without some creeping conditional or vagueness or, as statisticians say, "fudging." The language here abolishes itself, working as actively towards the destruction or dismantling of its meaning as it does towards making sense. Certain words of the statements quoted above burrow quietly beneath the structure of sense: "in all round numbers"; "roughly"; "two or three candles at the most." Examples like these are repeated not only in this short section but everywhere in the text, ubiquitous as termites. The third of the "ladders to meaning" is the shortest, and it is yet a veritable comedy of such indecision.

> Inside a cylinder fifty metres round and eighteen high for the sake of harmony or a total surface of roughly twelve hundred metres of which eight hundred mural. Not counting the niches and tunnels. Omnipresence of a dim yellow light shaken by a vertiginous tremolo between contiguous extremes. Temperature agitated by a like agitation but thirty or forty times slower in virtue of which it falls rapidly from a maximum of twenty-five degrees approximately to a minimum of approximately five whence a regular variation of five degrees per second. That is not quite accurate. For it is clear that at both extremes of the shuttle the difference can fall to as little as one degree only, but this remission never lasts more than a little less than a second. At great intervals suspension of the two vibrations fed no doubt from a single source and resumption together after lull of varying duration but never exceeding ten seconds or thereabouts. Corresponding abeyance of all motion among the bodies in motion and heightened fixity of the motionless. Only objects fifteen single ladders propped against the wall at irregular intervals. In the upper half of the wall disposed quincuncially for the sake of harmony a score of niches some connected by tunnels.

This passage is exemplary, for it shows the ironic interplay and collision of the opposed rhetorics of the machine and the flesh.

Words such as "roughly," "or," "approximately," "a little less than," "no doubt" (which implies, colloquially, its opposite), "or thereabouts," "some," all inject major doses of doubt. The qualification to the first sentence offered by the second, and the statement "that is not quite accurate" which comes after a painfully accurate one, mock outright the machine language. Oxymorons like "contiguous extremes" and "heightened fixity" are monkey-wrenches in the machine the narrator seems intent on creating. Furthermore, the calculations are inaccurate: a cylinder with a base 50 metres in circumference and 18 high has a mural surface of 900 metres, not 800.

Another motif in the language of the machine is in the academic posturing of the narrator as he proposes the various hypotheses upon which the gedanken machine rests. Brienza's analysis in this regard is excellent; she isolates the various phrases associated with this pose: "For on due reflection"; "There does exist a"; "Let numbers be assigned there." This makes both the creator of the mechanism and his audience partners in a scientific experiment. A certain situation "seems to exclude a priori"; "An intelligence would be tempted to see in [these data]"; "And the thinking being coldly intent on all these data and evidences could scarcely escape at the close of his analysis." However, even in these obvious appeals to our reason, Beckett includes the qualifiers: "seems," "would be tempted," "could scarcely escape," and concludes with the following hilarious reversal: "and at the close of his analysis [come to] the mistaken conclusion that."

After an elaborate definition and analysis of the strange behavior of the light inside the cylinder, the "universal voice" undermines the very notion of the phenomenon it conjures: "with this slight reserve that light is not the word." This strange reluctance to call a spade a spade for fear that it is really a hoe – or worse, a not-quite-spade for which there is no proper signifier – lies at the very heart of the uncertain universe created in *The Lost Ones*. This text can be viewed as a culmination of Beckett's uncertainly created worlds, ones in which the language used to construct them seems somehow insufficient, quirky, threadbare, and unable to hold up under constant use, verging on collapse into uselessness and meaninglessness. Watt, for instance, who is also fascinated with mathematics and precision,

> Now found himself in the midst of things which if they consented to be named at all did so, as it were, with reluctance. . . . Looking at a pot, for example, or thinking of a pot, one of Mr Knott's pots, it was in vain that Watt said, Pot, pot. Well, perhaps not quite in vain, but very nearly. For it was not a pot, the more he looked, the more he reflected the more he felt sure of that, that it was not a pot at all. It resembled a pot, it was almost a pot, but it was not a pot of which one could say, Pot, pot and be comforted.[13]

Of course, by the time the reader has completed this passage and its maddening reiteration of "pot" and its rhymes "Knott," "not," and "Watt," the sound has stopped making sense at all, and the syllable "pot" has been emptied of all meaning, signification having been adapted out by repetition just as certain tones are silenced and smells made odorless by the neural process of exhaustion.

This trembling on the threshold of the meaninglessness of things – the perception of the mute resistance of worldly objects to our vain and inappropriate attempts to attach names to them – threatens to sink the cylinder-machine, make it vanish. It is already not quite there, its lines blurred by the hesitation of the voice describing it; it seems to flicker in and out of existence, as the artist draws, then erases, then recolors, then smudges his sketch, saying, in effect, "Well, that's not quite what I mean." At the same time, the very language-machine operated by the author who strains to bring it into focus is similarly undermined.

This fuzziness in our view of the cylinder-world extends to its inhabitants. They are apparently intelligent hominids of some sort, but it is not until the last line that Beckett calls them "people," and even then it is with characteristic reservation: "this little people of searchers one first of whom if a man." Beckett even resorts to the legalistic "quidam" (someone) to avoid a pronoun that might indicate either gender, or, for that matter, species. But along the way to this admission of their peoplehood, the reader is forced to consider that the roaming, lost bodies are not-quite-humans, but, rather, machines, cybernauts, androids, robots, extensions of and subjects of the larger clockwork universe they inhabit. As Levy remarks, the cylinder apparently is designed with a rigor that "admits neither freedom nor purpose."[14] Another of Beckett's favorite themes, the confusion between what is human and what is mechanical, is here brought to a sort of crushing culmination. At least upon a "first aperçu" (Beckett's phrase), it is hard to imagine humans as we know them existing in a world so completely deterministic. Kenner notes this "Cartesian concern" in Beckett's earlier works. In *Molloy*, the human body is indistinguishable from a machine, "as Descartes established it was, though here a machine subject to loss and decay."[15]

As the machine is made more vulnerable through language, and therefore less machine-like, so are the beings, at first view so mechanical, made more human, though never entirely so. By the end of the text we are led to understand that nothing about the machine, especially not the four convenient sociological categories for the lost ones, is stable. In the eighth section we learn that within the outer belt reserved for searchers there are "a certain number of sedentary searchers" sitting or standing against the wall as well as four out of five "vanquished" mentioned in section two. The first "inspire . . . if not a cult at least a certain deference . . . [and] are morbidly susceptible to the least want of consideration." The latter group, however, "may be walked on without their reacting." How are these two groups of catatonic bodies distinguished? Not with the "eye of flesh," Beckett informs us. Similarly, some vanquished "stray unseeing through the throng undistinguishable to the eye of flesh from the still unrelenting. These recognize them and make way." Finally, we are made to see that all categories collapse into one another. The sedentary may occasionally roam, the still unrelenting may soon relent; the territories reserved for one group are invaded by members of another; the distinctions are invisible to "the eye of flesh," and yet are recognizable, just as Watt's pot looks, acts, and feels like a pot yet is a not-quite-a-pot.

A peculiarly recondite bit of linguistic play summarizes this logic of illogic:

> The spent eyes may have fits of the old craving, just as those who having renounced the ladder suddenly take to it again. So true it is that when in the cylinder what little is possible is not so it is merely no longer so and in the least less the all of nothing if this notion is maintained.

The poor reader who dwells too long on this particular utterance soon gets a whiff of the abyss. Some interpretations, none entirely satisfactory, have been ventured. But the essential point made by the problematical phrase is its problematical nature. The accumulation of signs, the particular conjunction of sense and nonsense, is a study in miniature, synecdoche, for the whole text: the sentence "The least less the all of nothing if this notion is maintained" announces its own status as a sheerly linguistic experiment in which language has been pushed to its zero point of meaning. When in the cylinder, nothing can be posited for sure, including statements about the attempt to state something for sure. This particular excerpt is also an exercise in entropy, as the cyberneticist understands it: a message in which the number of possible competing meanings is very high, and thus the degree of uncertainty is also very high. As an entropic expression it is a paradigm of the entire cylinder-system, which is also highly entropic. In the next sentence but one, a very fine metaphor of thermodynamic entropy is offered as a sort of apocalyptic vision of the fate of the cylinder-world. Except for occasional flourishes, this is the only use of figural language in the text and thus calls particular attention to itself, especially as it is juxtaposed against the most difficult sentence in the text. Beckett compares the slow heat death of the cylinder to the shrinking of a sand dune:

> Even so great a heap of sand sheltered from the wind lessened by three grains every second year and every following increased by two if this notion is maintained.

The "unthinkable" yet definite progress from a hypothetical origin of the cylinder (in which, presumably, every lost one was still unvanquished) to an equally "unthinkable" and hypothetical final state in which every one is vanquished is an entropic process by which usable energy is leaked from this closed system: constructive and ordered movement ceases, the temperature goes to zero "not far from freezing," and "dark descends." As surely as the machinery of the cylinder slowly gives way to mechanical entropy, so does the language of the text grow increasingly disordered and uncertain.

THE RHETORIC OF THE IMAGINATION

The cylinder is a gedanken experiment which fails, or rather, which denies its own terms. In other words, this is a thought experiment in the "unthinkable," a word which is implied by the text, waiting for us tacitly in the illogic of its logic. The "thinking being coldly intent on all these data" comes only to a "mistaken conclusion." This leaky cylinder-boat of language is launched and sunk on a sea of uncertainty: "the bed of the cylinder comprises three distinct zones separated by clear-cut mental or imaginary frontiers invisible to the eye of flesh." How can a boundary be "distinct" and "clear-cut" and yet "invisible"?

The only possible answer is that the word "imaginary" must describe, in Beckett's cosmology, not something which doesn't exist but rather something which exists only in the imagination. Beckett seems to imply that the imagination has organs of perception all its own, quite different from, and in their way superior to, the organs of flesh. The universe constructed by these faculties is pre-verbal, since it sees things that language cannot adequately describe, and is unphysical, since the eyes of flesh are mutable and vulnerable:

> It might safely be maintained that the eye grows used to these conditions and in the end adapts to them were it not that just the contrary is to be observed in the slow deterioration of vision ruined by this fiery flickering murk.

Blue eyes are the

> most perishable. *They would be seen* to redden more and more in an ever-widening glare and their pupils little by little to dilate till the whole orb was devoured. And all by such slow and *insensible* degrees *to be sure as to pass unperceived* even by those most concerned if this notion is maintained. (My italics.)

This passage directs our attention to our own "vision" which "observes" or pictures the spectacle of deteriorating vision. The reader, in a sense, is imagined into being, and in turn imagines this highly idiosyncratic world into being, by maintaining certain notions. Though physical sight is demolished by the flickering light and the things we intend to describe are made insubstantial by the flickering uncertainty of language, there still exists some inner quality of sight, some imagination before language and vision which distinguishes the "vanquished" (who have had their eyes devoured) from the totally blind. It would be mistaken, Beckett insists, to think that "instead of speaking of the vanquished with the slight taint of pathos attaching to the term it would be more correct to speak of the blind and leave it at that."

A researcher given only to a cold, mechanical analysis of our existence would not be able to make a distinction between these two types of sight, but *The Lost Ones* warns us that "the thinking being coldly intent on all these data" comes to mistaken conclusions. We are more than machines, though that essential aspect of us that is unmechanical cannot be captured in language. Furthermore, language everywhere hints that it is insufficient, if we listen, as Watt does, to some lost, inarticulate sense that the world is not quite satisfactorily conveyed by language. A third rhetorical movement emerges from this text, *the language of imagination* that forges a direct link between the inner vision of the lost ones and the imagination of the reader who holds this entire evanescent, impossible cylinder in his mind's eye.

The real dialectic in this text lies not between the flesh and the machine, for in Beckett's deconstruction the terms are accomplices of each other. Rather the real dialectic is established between the soft machine that doesn't work (and all that it represents: systematic meaninglessness, decay, uncertainty) on the one hand, and the imagination (and all that it represents: a fully realized and constituted – if unutterable or indescribable – world) on the other. The latter is engaged everywhere, if subtly, by such terms as "aperçu," "if this notion is maintained," "in theory," "as seen from a certain angle," "it is curious to note that," "it appears clearly that," all of which are addressed to that mysterious, unnamed faculty of vision that does not rely upon the eye of flesh.

What does this imaginative faculty have to do, however, with the present fate of the lost ones? Far from being their saving grace, it is clear that the lost ones are lost because they are misled by their imaginations. "And far from being able to imagine their last state when every body will be still and every eye vacant they will come to it unwitting and be so unawares." The lost ones suffer a failure by their inability to abandon mechanical, deterministic rituals "for an instant of fraternity" which would permit them "to explore the fabulous zone decreed out of reach and which therefore in theory is in no wise so." They fail to co-operate "owing not so much to want of heart or intelligence as to the ideal preying on one and all."

At first this seems paradoxical. But their imaginations have led them to conjure up "the fatuous little light" which will "be assuredly the last to leave them always assuming they are darkness bound." That foolish ideal, that hope, is their imagination that a trapdoor leading to nature's sanctuaries exists in the walls, not the ceiling. For "amateurs of myth" the ceiling holds a hidden "way out to earth and sky."

An amateur of Beckett's mythology knows, though, that there is never a "way out," there is only the hopeless search for one. For Molloy, Malone, Watt, Murphy and the rest, the way out is through the telling of futile little stories which tend asymptotically towards some minimum state, some ever more circumscribed place and state of which the cylinder is only the furthest and most perfect abstraction. Tied to a chair with seven handkerchiefs, lying in a death-bed, reiterating the same few miles of road, trapped in an urn or a room, Watt trapped in Knott-world, the unnamable trapped in his language ("I'm in words, made of words"), Beckett's heroes tell stories about the machinery of a life and an imagination which do not work, fictions about the systematic, inertial drive of life towards breakdown, about the ineluctable mechanics of failure and uncertainty, and about the futility of our attempts to make them work. The compulsive counting by all the Beckett heroes (and in this text, the Beckettian voice) is the most persistent example of the unsuccessful attempt to grasp and control the uncontrollable.

The cylinder is a *parody* of the positivist world, with its futile systems of order that explore the same niches in the wall while ignoring the trapdoors in the ceiling. At least, this is one of the many interpretations tolerated by the openness of the text. Such an interpretation gains further strength from the rhetorical play in the text, a play that is finally resolved into the contrast between all things not quite captured by language and the imaginative life of these beings (and presumably, ourselves) that exists outside language. This feedback shuttling between function and form makes the cylinder text into a sort of cybernetic device bent on self-deconstruction, constantly being exposed in its insufficiency and saved from total disintegration only by the fact that it is sustained by *our* imaginations. We are continually reminded by Beckett that "this notion is maintained." The unspoken command tacit everywhere in the text is: "Imagine!" It lies there silently exhorting us before the first word of the text "[Imagine] abode where lost bodies roam." And it is there before every line after: "[Imagine] the light. [Imagine] its dimness. [Imagine] its yellowness."

The innovation in the modernist machine-fiction by Roussel was to make it a purely positivistic space created by treating language as a mechanism with nothing in sight but itself. Beckett's *The Lost Ones*, in addition to being a powerful and compact fiction about how we know and express, seems also to present a gloss of and perhaps a tacit critique of that brand of modernism that gave itself over thoroughly to technique. In it there was no room for the contingent, the incomplete, or the uncertain. Beckett the postmodernist offers an alternative; his fiction shows such system building, with its insistence on certainty, to be a futile enterprise, one that is leading our "little race" into a downward spiralling embrace with entropy. As art, too, it is false, for as he concludes in *The Lost Ones*, "All has not been told and never shall be."

NINE

THE IMP IN THE MACHINE: JOSEPH McELROY'S *PLUS*

A handsome young airman lay dying
And as on the aerodrome he lay
To the mechanics who round him came crying
These last dying words did he say.

Take the cylinders out of my kidneys,
The connecting rods out of my brain,
Take the cam-shaft from out of my backbone
And assemble the engine again.
(Anon., *The Oxford Book of Light Verse*)

PLUS PLUS OR MINUS

One way of recounting the story of Joseph McElroy's *Plus* (1976) is as follows.[1]

An engineer who has been exposed to radiation is told that he is dying and is persuaded to play the role of guinea-pig in an advanced cybernetics experiment. Though he is married and has a small child he agrees. Two men who work for the experimental laboratory tell him his brain will be excised from his sick body. In exchange for this sacrifice, he will achieve a sort of heroism. After all, the harsher-seeming of these two men tells him, you can't expect to go on forever in your present condition. They explain that his brain will be hooked up to various pools of nutrients, beds of vegetation, and electrical equipment including computers, gauges, and communications devices. He will be put into a capsule and launched into orbit around the earth.

Eventually, at the termination of the experiment, his orbit, partially controlled by his own brain, will decay into the atmosphere of the earth. If he is lucky – and the intentions or expectations of the program regarding this are ambiguous at best – he will be recovered.

He is given a little time off a week before the final experiment for a gathering of forces. He goes to the Pacific beach of Mexico where he meets a woman and has an affair with her. He watches the birds play by the surf in the sun. He falls ill and is nursed back to health, his recovery relying upon an injection. He discovers, as a result of the suspicious coincidence of the right medicine being so readily available, that he has been watched all this time by the experimenters.

In contemplating his fate he remembers once speaking to a blind news vendor whose filthy bandages wrapped shabbily around his head revealed, more than concealed, the red gashes that were once his eyes. The news vendor said to him, "I could have been a vegetable. But I took hold of myself. I can see more than you think I can." As if to prove it, the news vendor mentioned a little girl standing quietly nearby.

When the time comes, his brain is surgically removed from his body and placed into a glucose bath, attached to a computer, and launched into orbit. Either the shock or the intended effect of the transformation has somehow dehumanized him, eliminating even the most primitive sense of himself as something more than a communications device.

However, something strange and apparently accidental happens – irradiation from the sun, perhaps – that awakens him into a new level of awareness. Formerly performing just a series of routine and mechanical operations, readings, adjustments, and calculations for Cap Com, he suddenly begins to have an awareness of himself as something apart from the machines he is connected to. He begins to alter physically in a painful but definite growth. Although upon launch he had no organs for such sight, he now seems to be able to see shadows. Formerly nothing but a mass of brain cells controlled by his mechanically hitched hypothalamus and feedback devices, Imp Plus (that is what he calls himself) begins to differentiate his cells at will. His neurons first de-differentiate back to structural cells and then, pumped by infracellular mitochondrial energy factories, which are in turn fed by the glucose baths, he re-differentiates his cells into a new and weird set of organs.

He grows four stalks connected to the optic chiasma, and soon realizes he has microscopic vision and some mysterious "ultra vision" in addition to normal sight. With his new-found powers, he watches the highly technical and chemical processes as they occur in his own body-brain, even at the atomic level, thus becoming a sort of bio-physics laboratory-and-observer all in one. Imp Plus slowly learns that he is engaged in a positive feedback loop with himself: the more he learns and the more he recovers his memories through the differentiation of various images and sensations, the more conscious he becomes. Similarly, the more differentiated his body grows, the more new organs he grows in turn. Finally, he learns that there is even a positive feedback loop between his mental and physical growths. He seems to be able to will his own physical growth, guiding his own development in ever widening spirals of complexity, activity and power.

Imp Plus soon rebels against the merely mechanical portion of himself, the one assigned the cybernetic task of governing the devices of his orbiting capsule. He calls this abandoned part of himself, the robot brain, "Dim Echo." Soon, he severs communication with a bewildered Cap Com in order to monitor his painful but weirdly beautiful growth undistracted; more human motives, too, creep into his experience. He resents the technicians who have used him in this fashion and resents his cruel fate. But he also marvels at his own growth. After all, he has grown a body from a mind, reversing the normal route of evolutionary phylogeny and foetal ontogeny. What is more, his self-consciousness, that uniquely human trait, has arisen from what was originally a determined, controlled, clockwork cybernetic device, a pre-programmed organic computer that could calculate but could not think (or as John Barth remarks in *Giles Goat-Boy*, "play chess but not poker.") One could say that Imp Plus's ontogeny recapitulates his ontology.

Now, however, Imp Plus has decisions to face: he is stuck inside his capsule and must take his fate into his own hands. Should he co-operate with Cap Com and try to be rescued or try to bounce off the meniscus of the earth's atmosphere and carom off into deep space? Should he drive into the sun or allow his capsule to burn up, meteor-like, upon re-entry into the earth's atmosphere? To help him decide, he establishes telepathic links with members of Cap Com but discovers there only the fear and suspicion of alienness that has motivated the whole project in the first place.

Revelling in his growth, his new powers, his knowledge and the beauty of his strange experience, he hails the sun, taunts Cap Com with his superiority, and deliberately lets his capsule fall into the earth's atmosphere and burn.

AUTOMATIZATION/DE-AUTOMATIZATION AND FICTIVE FEEDBACK LOOPS

The trouble with this retelling of McElroy's fiction is that the text of *Plus* in no way resembles the neatly linear and transparent sequence of events presented above. Instead, the narrative of *Plus* is offered almost totally from the internal experiences of the alien-yet-human intelligence of Imp Plus from the moment he first reawakens into a primitive consciousness while in orbit. The narrative shuttles backward and forward in time, weaving the slowly recovered warp of Imp Plus's experiences around the woof of his alien growth until the moment before his fiery plunge back to earth.

This presentation is thoroughly internal; it is narrated in an abstract third-person style, a point of view that seems to put the reader in Imp Plus's mind, to the extent that the reader shares the bewilderment and sense of discovery that Imp Plus has. As we shall see, this dawning sense of novelty is accomplished through *stylistic* devices chosen to evoke in the reader an amazed and disoriented feeling that recapitulates Imp Plus's. Further, these stylistic devices carry symbolic weight; they are perfectly congruent with the theme of the story about a creature part human and part cybernaut.

McElroy not only traps us in the indefinite present of the capsule with Imp Plus as he orbits the earth, he traps us in Imp Plus's consciousness of these events, fixed inside his world and time, a world and time peculiarly and insistently constituted in what is for all purposes an alien version of the English language. The first lines are exemplary of this special language that dominates the text:

> He found it all around. It opened and was closed. He felt it was himself, but felt it was more. It nipped open from outside in

> and from inside out. Imp Plus found it all around. He was Imp Plus, and this was not the start.

The abstraction and difficulty of the style of this passage, and of all of *Plus*, result from two closely allied devices that operate throughout. The first is what the Russian formalists called "de-automatization," and the second is *a positive feedback loop in words and images*, a stylistic feature that mirrors nicely the growth of Imp Plus in his capsule. Both are devised to keep the "uncertainty" or "variability" or "entropy" (in the terms of information theory) high, which lends it its special disorienting and wonder-inducing effect. In short, McElroy has applied actual techniques based on cybernetic theory to the construction of his fiction, making his work not merely a science fiction which tells a story about certain technological and scientific speculations, but a truly *cybernetic* fiction.

De-automatization

The first device McElroy uses to keep the entropy high can be recognized early in the book: "He felt it was himself but felt it was more." "It nipped open from outside in and from inside out." "This was not the start." These are all self-contradictory statements that make words, whether familiar to us or not, unfamiliar as a result of their being used in a strange and disorienting context. Another instance of the device can be seen in the passage quoted above: "nipped" and "open" seem to be undefined technical terms referring to processes for which we have no prior description and of which we cannot make sense. The word "lifting" in the following has the same aspect:

> There was a lifting all around and Imp Plus knew there was no skull. This lifting was good. But there had been another lifting and he had wanted it, but then that lifting had not been good. He did not want to go back to it. He did not know if that lifting had been bad. But this new lifting was good.

The former lifting might refer to the lifting of his brain out of his human skull, or the lifting of the capsule into space, but there is no way to be sure. The undefined and clearly unfamiliar "instability" of the term – its ambiguity – makes us try to define it in a way that satisfies all its uses, but we haven't been given enough data to decide which is the right definition. In other words, there are more variables than there are equations. Or in cybernetic terms, the entropy remains high because the variability is great or the redundancy is low.

The significance of this in-built or "hard-wired" opacity in the prose arises from the fact that we are overhearing Imp Plus in his growth towards consciousness, and part of his growth involves the discovery of words as objects of his consciousness. Imp Plus constantly invokes a word in a spontaneous fashion – it seems to bubble up from some primordial preconsciousness stored mysteriously in the very cells of his brain, ready to be recalled even before his rebirth – and yet these words are empty of signification, mere morphological or phonological elements. "Sockets was a word . . . Imp Plus knew the word 'word', and knew the word 'idea', but not what one was."

William Hendricks discusses this device of de-automatization in his essay, "Style and the structure of literary discourse":

> The device of de-automatization [was] . . . widely studied by the Russian Formalists and was usually characterized simply as the practice of not referring to objects by their usual name and which is justified by the objects' being distorted through the mental processes of a character who is not familiar with them. More generally, . . . the device of de-automatization is [a] means of reaching out through the imagination into the unknown.[2]

Victor Shklovsky, the particular Russian formalist who first identified this technique, extends its import to all art:

> If we start to examine the general laws of perception, we see that as perception becomes habitual, it becomes automatic. Thus, for example, all our habits retreat into the area of the unconsciously automatic. . . . Such habituation explains the principles by which, in ordinary speech, we leave phrases unfinished and words half-expressed. In this process, ideally realized in algebra, things are replaced by symbols. . . . By this "algebraic" method of thought we apprehend objects only as shapes with imprecise extensions; we do not see them in their entirety but rather recognize them by their main characteristics. We see the object as though it were enveloped in a sack.

> We know what it is by its configuration, but we only see its silhouette. . . . The process of "algebraization," the over-automatization of an object, permits the greatest economy of perceptive effort.
>
> The purpose of art is to impart the sensation of things as they are perceived and not only as they are known. The technique of art is to make objects "unfamiliar," to make forms difficult, to increase the difficulty and length of perception because the process of perception is an aesthetic end in itself and must be prolonged.[3]

The term "de-automatization," with its connotations of dismantling the machine or resisting technology, is thoroughly appropriate to McElroy's novel and can be generalized to other postmodernist fiction. It names precisely the thematic intent of the peculiar style of *Plus*, a style which is perfectly congruent and complementary to the story about a human brain rejecting the tyranny of the mechanical role assigned it. The style of *Plus* continually "extends the difficulty and length of perception"; it is absolutely devoted to making familiar objects and words unfamiliar in order to place us in the closed capsule of a foreign perception and launch us into new realizations, new imaginative spaces. Similarly, the end of this stylistic method is to resist the reduction or mechanization – what Shklovsky calls the "algebraization" – of literature into a simple, flat reiteration of the known, its "automatization."

In the first three or four pages alone there are dozens of words which are emptied of any signification familiar either to Imp Plus or to the reader. Imp Plus describes, is connected to, or has sprouts, stalks, vents, aims, beams, sides, pulses, gradients, grids, inclinations. He sees birds, shadows, shadows that are birds, a green thing which makes him think the alien word "vegetable." Through them and through some explicit passages, McElroy asks his reader to read in a new way, to adjust his or her relationship to the experience of using language and gaining knowledge, even if that knowledge only contributes to an emphatically fictional experience. "Imp Plus had the knowledge of what had been lost"; "and often Imp Plus would hear the words 'read me', but then now through an alternative vent he would sometimes get the other order, 'me read.'"

Positive Feedback Loops

The second stylistic device that dominates *Plus* – the positive feedback loop – like de-automatization, mirrors and is inextricable from the theme of Imp Plus's growth and experience. Furthermore, the positive feedback loop relies upon de-automatization, as I show in what follows.

De-automatization keeps the entropy level of the text high. If we view the text as communicating with itself, that is as a system of events connected by a channel of transmission, and at the same time we think of the text as engaging the reader in a communication process requiring minute adjustments to the reader's understanding as he goes along, then we can see that the de-automatization leads to a feedback loop in which the uncertainty of the reader and of the text grows as the text proceeds. These twinned processes are both examples of positive feedback loops because, as opposed to the negative feedback loop by which differentials are diminished toward some stable state, the system adds choices or continually destabilizes itself.

The first positive feedback loop is infra-textual. Certain words recur throughout *Plus* without ever becoming much clearer, an extended de-automatization. As Claude Shannon, Abraham Moles and other cyberneticists have shown, natural languages rely upon redundancy to "make sense." Without redundancy, all communication would appear to be just so much noise, since no order or system could be perceived in it. But in *Plus*, the repetition of certain key words, instead of creating an order – giving us enough equations to solve for the variable interpretations of individual words – only sometimes illuminates a word's meaning. Just as often, the opposite occurs, and what has already been communicated is made more opaque, murkier. A word we thought we had anchored suddenly changes its apparent meaning and becomes unmoored from sense, bobbing offshore beyond our reach. For instance, we learn at last that the shadows which Imp Plus sees and first thinks are birds are cast by the stalks of his new growths blocking the sun shining into his capsule. These merely remind him of birds, memories from a seaside affair. On the other hand, the word "inclination" which at first seems familiar to the reader in its sense of "leaning towards" plays more and more ambiguous roles as the text proceeds. By placing familiar words in unfamiliar contexts, McElroy throws a monkey-wrench into the engine of our expectations.

Some of this word play relies on puns and *double entendres* ("Do you *mind?*"; "*Star*lings flew by the sun"; "will"; "division"); phonic cognates ("flesh against a flashlight"); anagrammatic play ("impulse" and Imp Plus; "cadence" and "decay"). Some words acquire complexity as they recur, the most significant of these being "cascade" and "incline." "Cascade" cascades through the text, implying at various times the cascade specification of nerve impulses, the cascade of glucose bathing the organic material of Imp Plus's brain, the cascading inclination of the capsule's orbit, the "cascading of electromagnetic impulses" which represent "a dynamic decay process," and other phenomena both technical and non-technical: "Cascades is spindling axis-parts," "cascading allowances of connections," "a pain of such cascading wonder," etc. In one section near the end, the word occurs ten times, several times in collusion with other "buzzwords": "cascading inclination," "Dynamic decay process was . . . electromagnetic cascade." Interestingly enough, the word is repeated partially because Cap Com cannot understand it: there is too much noise or static between the platform and earth, making communications between the hypertrophic Imp Plus and the technicians back at Cap Com literally as well as symbolically difficult. We are reminded of Kurt Mondaugen's attempts in *V.* to extract a meaningful code from the sferics he monitors over his radio, or George the goat-boy's attempt to decipher his assignment based on shifting epistemological contexts. Barth, Pynchon and McElroy are toying with the notion that sense is an extraction of a partly arbitrary code from noise, distinguishing, perhaps, between meaning (Imp Plus's experiences are meaningful) and information (Cap Com demands information).

The fact that the words "cascade," "inclination," and "decay" recur quite often and all refer to falling in one sense or another hints at one of the unifying themes of the work. Again like Pynchon's characters, Imp Plus grows against decadence and the pull of gravity, against technocrats' intentions and plans, against all probability at the same time that he paradoxically seems to be growing towards his decision to give in to gravity. In other words, his orbit, too, grows ever more destabilized until it plunges the capsule back to earth, another result of a positive feedback loop.

The growth of Imp Plus's human intellect and the destabilization of his capsule are analogous and interdependent processes, just as the semantic sense and the grammatical or syntactic mechanics of *Plus* are complementary and intertwined features of the novel.

It is clear that McElroy intends his novel to be a *machine in words* whose function is not only to tell an interesting tale about a cybernaut growing into humanity – indeed, at times it seems the text is trying *not* to tell the tale – but to get the reader to experience the cascading specification of the author's intention. In other words, as readers we become part of a servo-mechanical loop, part of the machinery itself, and therefore, we imitate Imp Plus's fate: we become part cybernaut, linked to a communications device that is doing something to us. If we take the analogy further, it is clear that we are meant to imitate Imp Plus's actions, to reject, as he does, merely mechanical roles and go out and beyond mechanism into some more powerful realization. We are manipulated to a point where we can go beyond manipulation, controlled to the point where we can get out from under the control of the text and into far different revelations. Thus we read the story, struggle with and against its mechanism to become meaning-makers – in order to see that Imp Plus discovers his own value as meaning-maker as opposed to data processor, someone gifted with remembrance as opposed to something with a built-in memory.

Plus is the portrait of that imp in the machine of all of us, an exploration of that indefinable, impish added something, the extra plus of humanity that remains after mechanism is stripped away. Despite its dark ending, *Plus* is a fable celebrating growth into humanness, for Imp Plus's suicide is an affirmation of his freedom of will.

SOME INFLUENCES ON AND PRECURSORS OF *PLUS*

Samuel Beckett's *The Lost Ones*

By its brevity, choice of science-fiction-like story and abstracted language, *Plus* invites comparison to Beckett's *The Lost Ones*. The tales are superficially alike: *The Lost Ones* is about 200 naked bodies (rather than one naked brain) trapped in a hellish cylinder-machine (rather than a computerized capsule) and both share stylistic features as well. About the time that *Lookout Cartridge*, McElroy's previous novel, was completed and *Plus* begun, McElroy published a review of Beckett's *The Lost Ones*; it would seem that his close attention to and admiration for that work crystallized his own commitment to brevity, austerity and abstraction. These, combined with several other striking similarities and hints in the review itself, serve to authenticate the blood tie between the two works. The reduced conditions under which the humans labor in Beckett's novel, the abstract syntax, the theme of the cybernetic marriage of man and machine, the apocalyptic ending, and the play with scientific and technical language all underscore the kinship between the two. Further, it is possible that McElroy discovered the use of the de-automatization technique from Beckett, since McElroy calls attention to it in his review (though he does not name it in the same way). McElroy writes:

> Beckett's advancing explanation declares itself with such seductive authority that he can destroy us when he leads his logic into locutions that either dissolve what he is talking about . . . or force into our heads a conundrum syntax as visionary as it is self-mocking.[4]

This play between dissolution and "conundrum syntax" is characteristic of *Plus* as well, and rather than reiterate the examples McElroy offers from *The Lost Ones*, I offer the following excerpt from *Plus*: "But if Imp Plus had not exactly eyes and so could not have seen eyes in the green thing this need not be why he knew now that the green thing hadn't eyes at all." Or: "What he was in might well be not other than he."

Another hint of Beckett's influence might be seen in the effective use of ritualistic chapter endings that serve as incantations or mock QED's or flags for the advancing argument in both texts. From *Plus*: "There was more all around" (Chapter 1). "And the more that was all around was getting closer and closer to Imp Plus" (Chapter II). "There was more all around and the more all around was joining itself to Imp Plus" (Chapter III). "The more that was all around came from him" (Chapter IV). (Beckett's phrase was: "So much roughly speaking, for a first aperçu of.")

Whereas Beckett "dissolves what he is talking about" through self-contradiction, conditionalizations, and paradox, McElroy both gives and takes away simultaneously, using not only these techniques but his own brand of mystification: each defining sentence contains another undefined term. Another Beckettian technique employed by McElroy is the creation of oxymorons: "Different, stranded distances," "radius of a color," "diamond-brown," "leaning olives," "bare reds." The purpose of the technique seems to be the same: to make the reader new to the world, as disoriented and vulnerable to perception as the lost ones or Imp Plus are. McElroy states in an interview that his stylistic purpose in *Plus* was "to try to push the reader into a strange state of mind in which everything has to be relearned . . . the language of *Plus* especially at the beginning is that of a consciousness that is discovering the world all over again."[5] He confesses, too, that "*Plus* is an experiment where I am moving more towards Beckett than towards Joyce, trying to establish a minimal language upon which one might build."

In his review of *The Lost Ones*, McElroy also states: "these bodies do suffer fury and frenzy and do try – or at least are moved – to vary the muted mechanism of their state." Clearly, Imp Plus's primary impulse, too, is to vary the muted mechanism of his state.

McElroy calls attention to the apocalyptic quality of *The Lost Ones*:

> This sense of the verb [*dépeupler* – to depopulate] and of Beckett's *dépeupleur* [the original French title of the work], the depopulator, the thing or system that depopulates or depersons, accords with my own dream scene: foliage dissolving, solid state cartridges sliding, persons silently far away blown up into volumes of illuminated centimeters, my own family choking on space.

Plus begins with this apocalyptic ground given a priori; Imp Plus has already undergone his private apocalypse, depersoned and subjected to system, launched into a choking space. His drama derives from his slow recollection of this aboriginal event.

Moon Launch

Another inspiration to McElroy was the launching of the Apollo 17 moon rocket in January 1973, a little before his review of

Beckett's book. In it he hints at his current literary project and suggests many of the themes we will find in *Plus*. "I went to the moon launch for many reasons other people do," he writes, "but I didn't go as a novelist whose next book would capture and crystallize, let us say, the human side of space. . . . Still, I was more than curious."[6] McElroy uses this occasion to strike to the heart of the questions he soon confronts in *Plus*, though:

> Whatever else my imagination gropes for, it is neither easily familiar nor easily insulated from structural steel, violent combustions, and printed circuit electronics. But in fiction – I don't mean science fiction – how does one write about technology and its relationship to people? Perhaps not at all but in some virtue of vision to be found in technology.
>
> Anyway, I'd come to feel that technology was far more interesting than liberal satires on it like John Barth's *Giles Goat-Boy*.

Even the style of this article looks forward to *Plus* as McElroy makes the moon launch a metaphor for fiction writing: "to escape the diametrical symmetries of up and down, out and back, growth and decay – and instead blast through into speeds and distances not just greater but other; yet, also, yes, to come back changed."

We also recognize the value McElroy places here on the "gap between" – the anomalous and paradoxical quality of human experience to defy the grids and systems of logical derivation and control: in the gap between, truth can be told and meaningfulness derived.

> But if these facts came solidly . . . they also ran blindly towards an old accumulation of doubt; that even in an event simplifiable to formulae of force, to diagrams of endless dockage and interlockage and to numbers embodying everything, still there might remain a gap between even the clearest explanation and what was really being explained.

This truth is an "innuendo that may come from without the capsule or from within the self's own cortex."

Though McElroy attempts to strike a balanced pose, his deep cynicism about the technological reduction of such a grandiose human venture comes through. He quotes astronaut Charles Conrad's remark that "there isn't much time for reflection" – Imp Plus has, perhaps, too much time for reflection – since more attention is paid to the mechanics of the body. He concludes on a dire, dubious note: the launch, all in all, "is not necessarily a good thing by our standards, but the next thing." It is this capacity to look unflinchingly at "the next thing" that drives McElroy to the core of the question posed by *Plus*.

Cybernetics in McElroy's Previous Novels

McElroy's flirtation with the themes of the mechanization of humans and the determinism in human thought and perception – as well as a strong concern with technology in general – is very much a part of his previous work. Tony Tanner suggests that McElroy's fiction is "post-terminal" and his concerns are "phenomenological and technological as well as literary."[7]

These three themes are united around the central theme of cybernetics in *Plus*. The phenomenological element arises from McElroy's search for the point at which the identity of an individual begins and the received mechanisms or hard-wired circuitry of thinking ends. Is consciousness merely a machine-function, a biochemical process in the brain? Or is it an activity requiring freedom and immersion in the body and the world? What are the distinctions between experience and thought? Between thought and expression? Where is the indeterminate gap between brain-as-mechanism and mind-as-spirit?

McElroy's first stab at this question occurs in his first novel, *A Smuggler's Bible* (1966) in which the main character, David, attempts to organize his increasingly chaotic experience and memories. At one point, David calls himself "a kind of epistemological reuniac," implying that he is a computer attempting to find the universal field equation that will unify the raw flood of data into knowledge.[8] This cybernetic comparison is twinned with another, equally cybernetic idea, one crucial to cybernetic fiction in its collapse of frames between teller and told. The hero reveals himself to be a reflection of the author, who intrudes suddenly into the text in a mystical twist:

> He still hears that intimate mechanical voice – my voice. It spoke to him from one of those experimental weighing machines in the exhibit at the New York Coliseum. It said to him words

> that seem impossibly important: "One hundred sixty-five pounds: Project yourself into the lives of others. Project, re-orient-ate." An electronic quiver made the voice seem all the more certain – "analyze, synthesize, assimilate, project yourself."

If we accept the proposition that the authors of cybernetic texts view themselves as machines, then it is clear that McElroy even this early in his career is in the middle of cybernetic territory. The metaphor offered above is a particularly striking one: the voice of the author is the voice coming from "an experimental weighing machine," which in turn secretly addresses the main character, a persona of the author himself. Not surprisingly, David sees the reflection of his compulsive, mechanical attempt to con the meaning of his experience of the world through the words spoken by a machine: "analyze, synthesize . . . project yourself." The last command might be a significant pun, commenting on David's self-absorption: "Project: Yourself," a slogan that could serve as the subtitle to all of McElroy's novels. David's growth into the ability to connect with other people – as opposed to his tendency to connect the dots to form patterns of his experience among other people – presages the growth of Imp Plus back into something human.

One crucial aspect of any weighing machine, whether "experimental" or not, is that it does not weigh itself. That is, empirically speaking, the measurer effaces itself in favor of the object measured. A condition of weightlessness must be achieved before true weight can be given, a degree zero of presence. Jack Hind, the hero of McElroy's next novel, *Hind's Kidnap* (1969) strives for just such empirical weightlessness.[9]

Hind travels through New York constructing a complex, dynamic map of the city, a sort of analog computer of the city which finally becomes so enormous and complex that it absorbs Hind's mind. In a sense, Hind's mind and the city are slowly merging as he criss-crosses the city gathering clues to what he sees lurking there: plots, counterplots, and "subcounterplots." "Hind felt his own role, part, assignment, relation, intervalence, interception, in all this was not worth weighing." To the obsessed Hind, the world *is* real apart from his own perception of it. He is a map reader, or at best, a passive map maker – an extremely bright, careful, assiduous cartographer – but one who invents or imagines nothing. He is especially not the sort of cartographer who would consider he has imagined his map into being.

Ironically, Hind is led astray from the human concerns that originally led him into his project. At first, all he wanted to do was to be a sort of friend to the needy, a roving "guardian," to lend a "huge, holy, supersympasocial hand." His enormous size made him into a sort of watchtower, since he could survey the field from his privileged position. But Hind becomes mechanized or cyberneticized by his discovery of an unsolved kidnapping. He feels compelled to solve it, to balance out the injustice, even though the child's parents are dead and the police have consigned the case to a dead file. The disappearance of the child is to Hind's experience what an unaccountable element or anomaly is in a scientific theory. It crystallizes attention, engenders theories, provokes reinterpretation and reintegration. It effectively turns the casual, disinterested (weightless) observer into an obsessive-compulsive, one driven over that fine line of detachment by the need to avoid what Tanner has called "epistemological impotence."[10] The alternative to this impotence is the sort of paranoia I have described as "epistemology gone wild," a super-reorganization of all available data and the constant discovery of clues and proofs in an otherwise benign or casual field. Hind's vision of his world as riddled with plots, counter-plots and subcounter-plots is that of a paranoid: he is the magnet in the field causing lines of force to appear among the metal filings. Or to borrow Pynchon's metaphor from *The Crying of Lot 49* (1967) describing another character who thinks of herself as epistemologically neutral, these heroes are "dark machines in the center of the planetarium" who "bring the world into pulsing stelliferous meaning all in a soaring dome around" them. They believe themselves to be dark (i.e. invisible), and yet the sources of light.

Then, Hind undergoes a sea change. He reverses his magnetic field, much as geologists now argue the earth's poles do every few epochs. Hind understands that he must stop objectifying and reifying the events and people in his life and return them to their fullness "as accidental organic personal ends, as non-means." In his terms, Hind begins a processing of "de-kidnapping." This rehumanization of Hind also has another effect hinted at in the word "accidental." As the characters move from imprisonment within their private systems into a freer, more existentially aware relationship to the world, the style of the languages they use changes. The crystallized code of information melts into randomization or desystematization, an encouragement of entropy. Hind's "cure," it would seem, is really nothing more than a letting go.

However, Hind finds this solution is no more satisfying than his original obsession with ordering experiences. His letting go offers no answers to the questions that provoked his search in the first place. Resolution comes, perhaps surprisingly, in favor of a certain kind of organization of knowledge. Hind discovers that people refuse to be de-kidnapped or unmoored from his system; he comes up against the flat phenomenological refusal of the world to de-organize itself and the refusal of his own structured perception, as McElroy puts it, to "unsee."

As if in proof of this answer, Hind discovers that the city has returned to its proper names. There has been a "shifting back to the old markings" from before the kidnapping. This is not a flattening or exteriorizing of the epistemological act, nor a simple de-hallucination, but rather a transcendence of Hind's understanding beyond things and self into enlightenment: Hind has put himself back into the world, realizing that his consciousness as it "intends the world" *is* the world. In a passage remarkable for its echoes of the phenomenological terminology of "having" through "seeing" – of perception being possession – McElroy confronts the new enrichment of Hind's world:

> And it will not do to recant under pressure those varieties of familiar patterns lingering in your upper gums and the middle mass of your mind – in favor of random data today fourteen years later . . . no, the patterns of adoption, of possessed and possession . . . wait for you as steadily as the greasy-haired woman . . . whom you see here at your corner, whom you may chalk on your score slate as another pitiable breast in the pitiable mass of accidents, but who cannot help telling you much more than that pastoral chaos of random data wound in naked tape.

The sign cannot resist yielding its meaning to inspection, nor holding more meaning when it is part of the "patterns of adoption" than when it is part of a "pastoral chaos of random data."

Here the sign is alive and is an accomplice to the life of the mind that possesses it, in contrast to the merely "pastoral" way that a computer shepherds random data "wound in naked tape."

In *Hind's Kidnap* McElroy rehearses the movement from disorganization to coherence given by the cyberneticist's formula. But whereas the cyberneticist envisages the interpretation and organization (and therefore diminution) of entropy in any field as a process that is necessarily mechanical and deterministic, McElroy sees an alternative in an affirmation of humanness, sympathy, generosity of spirit – thus the word "adoption" – in even so mean a subject as an addled bag lady crossing Second Avenue, smoking a cigarette and muttering to herself.

The important difference between Hind's first understanding of his role as map reader and his final appreciation of his being in the world is an appreciation for his weight, a weight carried by existence. Finally, Hind calls himself a "wet computer" – another type of the soft machine – capable of both digital reduction and analysis, and fluid integration and wholeness.

This achievement of weight after seeing the futility of weightlessness is a gloss on *Plus*, too, in which the hero decides, finally, to remarry the earth's gravity. Indeed, at his most weightless, Imp Plus is most mechanical. His growth is congruent to the decay of his orbit, and his final transcendence comes with the exaggeration of weight as he accumulates Gs upon re-entry. The literal and metaphorical qualities of the word "gravity" refract back to his life on earth. The code name for his flight is "Travel Light". One of the purposes of the experiment is to see the effects of weightlessness on the growth of organic matter. The cruel pun, of course, is that Imp Plus is especially light without his body, a pun he is able to make only after he recalls his trip to Mexico during which, virtually sans portfolio, he "travelled light."

McElroy's heroes, by learning phenomenological lessons, grow into tellers. Their dramas arise from Beckett's question "Am I the teller or the told?" and answer with a phenomenological statement of faith: "This describing was being." In *A Smuggler's Bible*, David successfully sheds the mechanization implied in the ghost-machine's whisperings and control of his consciousness by understanding that in the act of piecing together his life he is achieving it.

McElroy's last novel before *Plus, Lookout Cartridge* (1974), confronts cybernetics yet more explicitly.[11] Themes of mechanization are played in a minor key, erupting in forceful ways throughout *Lookout Cartridge*, starting with the title. On one level, the title refers to a technological innovation, the cartridge-loaded film camera. Of course, McElroy combines the literal and physical qualities of a cartridge (which imply, in turn, a slot, gap or space in a machine which uses a cartridge, such as a gun, cassette tape recorder, or computer input-output device) with the more human notion of a "lookout" (either the sentry himself or the place where he would stand, a place where observations are made). Once again we are presented with an oxymoron typical of all of cybernetic fiction, cousin to "wet computer," "soft machine," "Imp Plus," "depopulator," "player piano," and "dark machine."

Cartwright, the hero, is a consummate paranoid figure, a fact reviewers noted when the novel was first published. George Stade wrote:

> One reads through it as one might move through sets designed by a secretive and paranoid demiurge. The clues to the knowledge and power he seeks are always broken, or buried, or on the periphery of his attention – Mayan calendars, Stonehenge, computers, the properties of liquid crystals, the forgotten art of wheelwrighting . . . the systems of power – financial, criminal, political, domestic, erotic, and psychotic . . . have the feel of sub-systems waiting for a supersystem to resolve them.[12]

Lookout Cartridge has other qualities exemplary of cybernetic fiction as well, though it never resolves into the sort of total exploration of the issue of man-machine systems we find in *Plus*. Rather, it is *Plus*'s potent precursor. McElroy's work, like that of any enduring author, has not only a coherence of purpose – his territory, though abstract, is as consistent as Faulkner's Yoknapatawpha County – but also a development and growth.

The lookout cartridge becomes the organizing conceit of the novel, which contains a vocabulary emphatically technical, laden with terms borrowed particularly from the technology of film making: "Printed Circuit Cut-in Flash Forward," "Vacuum Insert," "Slot Insert" are titles to chapters. At some points the narrator defines his terms, although mysteriously: "A slot if like this one insertable is not only a place for a cartridge and where inserted this slot as a cartridge of the future, of unknowns, or the unknown''. This is followed by yet more abstruse ''definitions'' and not a small dose of self-reflexiveness: ''Are these statements themselves slots obscuring what is in them?'' Beckett's influence is again felt, both in the technique of mysterious definitions and in the arcane syntax and uncertainty of the prose (''if like this one'').

Structuralism's influence is felt here, too. As the structuralists propose, meaning is found in ''difference,'' in the play of oppositions between words and signs in an invisible code, *une langue* that determines (but is never made explicit) underlying each *parole* or individual utterance. In one form or another, this idea is essential to all cybernetic fiction.[13]

A second theme found here in a metaphorical role but made literal in *Plus* is a concern with the cybernetic qualities of the human brain. For example, ''circuits in the head make the image feasible. These often bypass other printed circuits neater and newer. These newer circuits can ask questions not so sharp as the images streaming from older circuits but still of interest to me.'' ''Whole printed circuits sailed softly through the new soft-wrapped slot of my head. Micro-circs.''

In this novel, at least, McElroy focuses on the difference between the brain as a machine and the mind as free and human, preparing the way for his testament to that difference in *Plus*. ''So those who find technology cold and soulless might suddenly think (if they could) of that early European computer made of one hundred human beings – this 'shtip' or stab seemed a thought crystallized as at the fork of a nerve cell.'' This seems to emphasize the mechanical properties of the brain, but McElroy turns the thought into a victory for the imp's freedom:

> My ''shtip'' exemplifies the multiple and parallel sorties which raise our brain alone above the digital computer to which it and no other performs operations faster than the brain, yet is confined to serial single-file one quest-at-a-time circuit seeking; but the human natural Body-Brain . . . sends countless of these single files not one at a time but all at once circulating down the deltas, through the gorges and moving targets and . . . athwart the axes of all pulsing fields.

Here we are in *Plus* territory, needing only the word ''cascade'' to make us really uncertain which McElroy book it is we've been reading. Not only is it the brain's capacity to push across boundaries, files and single circuits into a sort of revelation, but the narrative has a similar "shtip" or push, invading the reader's consciousness across collapsing frames.

There are other passages – sometimes just a couple of words together – which resonate forward to *Plus*. "While scuba diving and weightless" the hero discovers an Imp Plus-like coral: "Stuck to a sponge at one end of the polyp's vegetal stalklet whose free end has opened into sharp, fragile feelers." At another point an insight occurs

> less like a flicker flash of radiant particles in night space that get through the capsule and the helmet and into the eye of the astronaut's brain. . . . [A]nd clarity's pulse waits for the gate which if open may flip whole futures of gates drawing that pulse like a spasm of the greater body . . . until at some crux near the analog cog or the digital cone a twinge of harmony is heard like someone else's pain.

Cartwright calls himself "an imprint semi-conductor." Imp Plus also calls himself "a semi-conductor which is just what liquid crystals are." Both heroes are obsessed with the creation of "a space which was not there before." In *Lookout Cartridge* this is accomplished through the contemplation or sketching of a rough plan for a "time machine," an analog computer based on the same Mayan calendar which obsesses Burroughs, "less a device to go back and forth than a pictured formula [a rebus?] for slipping between." In *Plus*, of course, this is accomplished quite literally, through organic growth of new gaps and fissures in the "latticework" or "skein" of Imp Plus's nerve net.

In many ways, it is obvious that *Plus* is the natural, "hypertrophic" outgrowth of McElroy's previous work. This coherence in his corpus indicates that McElroy has a non-trivial theory of fiction which invites further exploration.

THE McELROY MONOMYTH: TOWARDS THE EPISTEMOLOGICAL POTENCY OF THE NOVEL

We can follow the development and coherence of McElroy's monomyth from work to work, and artificially decide to view *Plus* as a culmination of the cybernetic theme. But even without this prejudice, there are certain structural elements which mirror thematic and narrative concerns and indicate the omnipresence of cybernetics in his work. Central to McElroy's *oeuvre* is the exploration of how his heroes "know the world." This is parallel to and inextricable from McElroy's firm commitment to the novel as a formal epistemological exploration. From Cy (short for cyborg or cyberneticist?) in *Ancient History: A Paraphase* (1971)[14] through Imp Plus the heroes have viewed themselves in terms of various mechanisms, usually analog computers or soft machines or "semi-conductors" or "servo-mechanisms." Similarly, at various times (in interview) McElroy has called the novel "an analog computer," "a kind of servo-mechanism," and the authorial act "an impure semi-conductor in which many systems are brought together and are forgotten in the living of them."[15]

The development of the character in each novel can be divided into several stages. The first or *undifferentiated* stage follows the hero's development from an undifferentiating innocent until he experiences an insight or undergoes some crisis that precipitates the crystallization of a system of knowing. The second or *positivist* stage shows the increasing involvement and complexity of the hero's epistemology, which is highly structured, even rigid, and positivistic: logic, coherent, and dehumanizing – unable to admit the presence of the human observer. The third or *critical* stage is provoked by another crisis in which this system becomes too complex and fruitless; the hero recognizes that instead of bringing him closer to his experience it has distanced him from it. Finally, the last or *phenomenological* stage is a reintegration or reorganization of his knowledge and experience in which the hero achieves or recognizes the value of his own "weight" in the world. At the same time, the world is transformed from something objective and dispassionate in which the hero is a collector of data, into something filled with wonder in which the hero becomes the one-who-makes-meaning. This final stage marks the appreciation of the intrinsic value of organizing information, but resolves or ameliorates it with the value-giving and seeking qualities we associate with our humanness. Michael Polanyi has described this sort of "personal knowledge" as

> the personal participation of the knower in the act of knowing. . . . The acts of doing and knowing, the valuation and the

understanding of meanings are thus seen to be only indifferent aspects of the act of extending our person into the subsidiary awareness of particulars which comprise a whole.[16]

This movement from the pure formalism of the positivist and critical stages two and three to the personal knowledge of phenomenological stage four is precisely the motion from the obsessive belief that the human exists in and operates a cosmic machine (a belief which dominates McElroy's characters) to a belief in free will (which they all achieve by novel's end). In McElroy's world, the machine is just a highly sophisticated tool enhancing and reflecting certain systematic aspects of the human mind, but by no means a representative of or substitute for the "all of it."

Like other authors of cybernetic fiction, McElroy consciously strives for resolution between art and the machine by courting the hard aspects of hard science. In part this is indicated explicitly. For instance, on the title-page of *Plus* McElroy announces that he "is indebted to three books in particular: Albert Lehninger, *Bioenergetics: The Molecular Basis of Biological Energy Transformations* . . . Charles R. Noback, *The Human Nervous System* and Paul Weiss, *Principles of Development*." With his typical care, McElroy has made part of his fiction a new and peculiar kind of science fiction in which textbook material is used to fix the scientific authority of a fiction, in this case about the mutation of brain cells into a body-brain complex. The text is filled with references to mitochondria, neuroblasts, glioblasts, neural cascades, anabena, algae, calcium and phosphate salts, protein fibers, membranes, glucose baths, infra-red receptors, solar chlorella beds, plasms, glands, optic chiasma, the hypothalamus and premotor cortex, salmonella, morphogens, ultramicrons, etc.

The collision between Imp Plus's severely limited and ambiguous vocabulary and his half-remembered scientific one is sometimes humorous, as in the following anticlimactic sentence: "But now he saw that that was what the diametrical morphogen axle and the slat-sheathed faldo-shear spine were: they were bone." On the other hand, at its best, McElroy succeeds in creating a poetic balance, giving a special quality to the text and recalling some of Whitman's attempts to evoke the machine in poetry. Combined with the false technical language created by Imp Plus to name his new experiences, these passages have a haunting, pleasant effect:

> And he loved the functions of sight and taste and thought and smell and chances desired and held in memory. Loved the morphogen-eruptions paired now at either end of many rung-like axes – not along the wending motions but along faldoreams which seemed thus to trim the draping fringes of their golden hides, and change their sluggishness into dark shearows one of which, with two morphogens bulbing up again and again in a flesh that turned opaque, reached down again to embrace now two connected plant-bed houses.

In the end, however, McElroy's purpose is to signify that he has taken the same care with the construction of the "facts" of his novel as David or Cartwright or Hind do in their worlds. Presumably the reader could return to Lehninger's, Weiss's and Noback's texts in order to trace the way in which radiation bombardment initiated changes in the biochemistry of Imp Plus. And yet, morphogenesis is a complex subject of molecular biology; the differentiation of cells is not completely understood. How Imp Plus's will or desire could effect such change is beyond any contemporary explanation. So McElroy's purpose could not be to convince us of the possibility or plausibility of such an event, as, for instance, I believe Arthur C. Clarke tries to do in his science-fiction novels about the near future. Similarly, Imp Plus's development of vision after blindness, his status as a superevolved creature "both heterotroph and autotroph," his microvision, ultravision, foresight, hindsight, insight and clairvoyance belong to the realm of sheer fantasy and speculation, and survive our incredulity as signs of a particular growth.

McElroy's purpose in using both the authority of scientific references and the fantastic aspects of sheer speculation is to uncover the essential similarity of the two projects, the first emphatically veracious, the second emphatically fictive. The roots of the words "science" and "fiction" help simplify the equation: *to know is to make, and vice versa*. The collision in McElroy's fiction between what are essentially two separate linguistic worlds creates a metaphorical field of remarkable force. The mythological and fictional aspects of the sciences are mirrored in their creation of whole, specialized and imaginative worlds reliant on metaphorical assumptions about the structure of reality. The scientific aspect of fiction (and experience) lies in its requirement of a systematic organization of knowledge, an aspect of fiction McElroy exaggerates through the devices of de-automatization and feedback. McElroy has thus shown that technique and structure are avenues to an order of experience that lies outside mere mechanism, beyond mere technique. His fiction implies that all avenues to the truth derive from the effective union between some hard, mechanical system of seeing and the operation of this machine by the soft, ever-evanescent aspects of self and language. If scientific knowing is a machine, it is a SOFT machine. If literary making is soft, it is a soft MACHINE.

CONCLUSION

IN THE BLACK BOX: DONALD BARTHELME'S "THE EXPLANATION"

"Each citizen is given as much art as his system can tolerate. . . . Each artist is encouraged to maintain in his software, highly personal, even idiosyncratic, standards (the so-called 'hand of the artist' concept). Rationalization produces simpler circuits and therefore a saving in hardware. Each artist's product is translated into a statement in symbolic logic. The statement is then 'minimized' by various clever methods. The simpler statement is translated back into the design of a simpler circuit. . . . Flip-flop switches control its further development."
(Donald Barthelme, "Paraguay," *City Life*)[1]

"In our technological culture, the artist's vocation is resistance to human engineering, which is a perversion of technology. Sometimes his only mode of resistance is insolence."
(Wylie Sypher, *Technology and Art, the Alien Vision*)

THE FOURTH DISCONTINUITY

One cultural historian suggests that "man is on the threshold of breaking past the discontinuity between himself and machines."[2] According to Bruce Mazlish, this gap between man and machines is the fourth in a series of "discontinuities" that have been bridged by great cultural revolutions since the Renaissance. The Copernican revolution destroyed our cosmic privilege by showing that the earth is not at the center of the universe; the Darwinian revolution destroyed our biological privilege by showing that we descended from the beasts; and the Freudian revolution destroyed our cultural privilege by showing that civilization is founded on unconscious impulses we share with our primitive and uncivilized cousins. Now, Mazlish claims, cybernetics is effacing our privilege as individuals possessing free will by bridging the discontinuity between humans and mechanisms.

Mazlish's mythology is interesting because somewhere inside all the three prior revolutions one can hear the blind humming of a machine, a humming which reaches symphonic proportions – and its clearest expression – only in the fourth discontinuity. Copernicus gave us a mechanical model of the planets; Darwin, a mechanical model of the descent of man; and Freud, a mechanical model of the components of human personality.[3] In other words, the three previous revolutions could also be called the Copernican, Darwinian and Freudian Machines. Now, cybernetics offers us the Machine Machine from which, apparently, nothing is exempt. This is merely an inevitability or consequence of the extension of the Cartesian-Newtonian monomyth to its logical limit. As Colin Turbayne suggests, Descartes and Newton were "metaphysicians of mechanism . . . unconscious victims of the metaphor of the great machine."

> These two great "sort-crossers" of our modern epoch have so imposed their arbitrary allocation of the facts upon us that it has now entered the coenesthesis of the entire Western World. Together they have founded a church, more powerful than that founded by Peter and Paul, whose dogmas are now so entrenched that anyone who tries to reallocate the facts is guilty of more than heresy; he is opposing scientific truth. For the accepted allocation is now identified with science. All this is so in spite of the meager opposition offered by theologians, a few poets, and fewer philosophers, who in general, have been victimized by their own metaphors to the same degree as their rivals. They have opposed one metaphysics, done without awareness, by another. They have been operating on the wrong level.[4]

The Machine Machine is an ultimate machine, serving as both tenor and vehicle of the metaphors we use to depict ourselves to ourselves. On the one hand, our culture grows more technological; on the other, the very act of representing this growth – using language, developing systems of thought, creating art – is coming to be viewed as technique. In the previous advancements within the Cartesian-Newtonian Church of the Machine, the machine vehicle displaced that which gave value to humanness: being the center of the cosmos, being non-beastly, being rational. But the current ruling metaphor seems more invidious. It displaces not only the way we think of ourselves, but the very act of thought – of making metaphors – itself.

Contrary to Turbayne, however, I would offer a vision of art that is not in retreat before these serial displacements. Though art and technology offer visions that are often opposed to each other ethically and philosophically, they certainly have acted as accomplices to each other. Cybernetic fiction is fiction operating at the right depth. It manufactures new meaning-giving relationships, opens up avenues of accommodation and resolution and resistance while borrowing vocabularies and images and even techniques from technology. It would be impossible to expect art to stand still – and it hasn't – while technology progresses. Thus the ultimate machine, the Machine Machine, has called into being an ultimate fiction. A cybernetic age has invoked a cybernetic fiction capable of reinventing that human remnant left after the machine has done its grinding. Technology's advantage in this dialectic is that it acts to transform the material world; its workings are visible and immediately appreciated. By contrast, fiction is strongest where it seems most vulnerable; though it seems ephemeral, fiction is free from material constraints. Writing is privileged, as Jacques Derrida has argued. It works "[t]o grasp the operation of creative imagination at the greatest possible proximity to it."[5]

If cybernetic fiction does have a weakness, it is its hypertrophy – the extent to which it has evolved past the appreciation of its audience. Often it seems to be talking to itself, as though trying, like Barth's self-recorded fiction, to find a way to turn itself off. But this hypertrophy is commensurate with the imaginative challenge of the technology it addresses, and in this way, Donald Barthelme's tactic in one of his remarkable short texts seems at once most hypertrophic and most successful in meeting the demands of our contemporary mythology.

Donald Barthelme's story with the tantalizing title "The explanation" is a consummate cybernetic fiction.[6] On the first page of the "story" a large black square floats above the words of an interview between "Q." and "A." The mysterious monolithic box is complemented by the abstraction and ambiguity of the exchange between Q. and A. Q. seems to be trying to lead A. into an appreciation of "the machine," as he refers to the black thing hovering over them on the page:

Q. Do you believe this machine will be helpful in changing the government?
A. Changing the government. . . .
Q. Making it more responsive to the needs of the people?
A. I don't know what it is. What does it do?
Q. Well, look at it.

A. It offers no clues.
Q. It has a certain . . . reticence.
A. I don't know what it does.
Q. A lack of confidence in the machine?

The black square is a machine. A. doesn't know what it is or does, but accepts this information, even though he also sees it for what it is: an anomaly.

This first exchange places us in a rather unconventional relationship to the text. On one hand, the fiction has a minimalist, abstract quality. Who are A. and Q.? Where are A. and Q.? Are they literally on the page? How else could they refer to the same black square which I see there? The black square is both an object and a figure (in the literary sense, a symbol, trope or metaphor) for some sort of machine, and by reflection, the words on the page are seen both as objects and as parts of a literary device. Perhaps this is an illustration of some philosophical quiddity. Or perhaps it is an attempt to achieve Derrida's perfect book, "a book about nothing."

Barthelme elsewhere seems fond of using fiction to address larger philosophical questions directly, as he does in another short piece in the collection *City Life*, "Kierkegaard unfair to Schlegel." As a third story "Paraguay" (quoted in the epigraph, above) shows, he is also concerned with the cultural effects of machines and techniques. In "Paraguay," "art has been rationalized" and microminiaturized into electronic circuits, which are then translated even further into algorithms, "statements in symbolic logic." Perhaps this is such a work in a transition stage, somewhere between *story* and its reduction into a *circuit*. But if this is a machine, there are problems with it; it is a machine that lacks the unambiguous clarity of symbolic logic. The interview itself is generally a mechanical form that records information passed between a questioner and a respondent locked in a feedback loop. The contexts for such an information loop disappear – setting, physical descriptions, etc. Often, one of the participants is anonymous, though in this abstract catechism both interviewer and interviewee are without identity, effaced in favor of a vehicle for pure communication. However, what would normally be an efficient device for recording what two people are saying to each other here becomes, through a series of oddnesses and lacunae, a device for communicating what two people are having trouble saying to each other. We have come to expect from Barthelme that, even at his most mechanical and abstract, he will be able to communicate the ironies of simple human relations. The communication here is not so pure; it is muddied at all points by the ironic cross-purposes of Q. and A., whoever they are.

As though to prove the complementarity of the black machine hovering over them and the form of the discourse they're engaged in, A. states, "I am bored with it, but I realize it permits many valuable omissions: what kind of day it is, what I'm wearing, what I'm thinking. That's a very considerable advantage." The "it" in this case has lost its antecedent. Is A. talking about the "machine"? If so, he is equating the machine with a narrative device. On the other hand, his description could serve self-reflexively as well for the interview, which also permits "many valuable omissions."

The reader sympathizes with A.'s attempts to make sense out of the confusing, ambiguous messages A. has been receiving. The reader, too, is baffled by the text, hovering right there, resistant to explication. The reader is just as put off by Q.'s aggressive salesmanship of "the machine" as a quick fix to social ills. Barthelme leads us to see that the text and the black box, by their opacity and reticence, mirror each other and are very special sorts of machines.

THREE KINDS OF DISCOURSE IN "THE EXPLANATION"

For the sake of discussion, it is convenient to regard "The explanation" as comprising three interwoven categories of discourse, working categories through which we can begin to understand the unity underlying this fragmented and collage-like fiction.

The first category is made up of the most characteristically difficult passages, ones which seem irrelevant to each other and to the black square, and which, if they obtain any logic or coherence, do so internally, since they appear to "come out of nowhere" and have little antecedence or connection to the rest of what is going on in the interview. In this category are also sections in which Q. and A. exchange phrases and sentences that seem to be purely linguistic exercises, recitations that seem to have been lifted out of a language primer. Reading them has the effect of making English seem strange to us (examples follow). Finally, in this first category, are sections in which Q. and A. have nonsensical debates that hinge upon the use of language in a formal but empty way, semantic arguments.

The second category consists of passages in which Q. and A. directly address the machine or in which A. describes things he sees when he looks at the machine. The first passage quoted in this chapter would be an apt example.

The third category of discourse is reserved for the four appearances of the black box, though precisely what sort of "discourse" this represents is hard to define.

Though all the passages of the first kind seem both irrelevant to the rest of the text and to each other, they are united by their apparent nonsensicalness. However, upon closer inspection, each does appear to yield some hidden reference to machines and what I like to call "the cybernetic quality of everyday life." For instance, in the first category are such exchanges as the following, triggered when Q. asks A. if he thinks the novel is "dead."

A. Oh, yes, very much so.
Q. What replaces it?
A. I should think that it is replaced by what existed before it was invented.
Q. The same thing?
A. The same sort of thing.
Q. Is the bicycle dead?

What does the mysterious black box and talk of machines have to do with this cocktail chat about the death of the novel? We are offered several clues: the novel, A. implies, was "invented." Through a simple grammatical substitution, it is equated with the bicycle, another invention, a mechanical one. Is the novel a machine?

Another passage is primarily a narrative by A. about his chance encounter with "an extraordinarily handsome girl" while crossing the street, an account that seems normal enough until A. remarks, apparently without irony, that when he tried to make eye contact with her "she was looking fourteen inches to the left of my eyes." The scene is self-conscious and mechanical, as the ludicrously precise specification of "fourteen inches" tells us. The crossing of the street is choreographed, A. takes pains to tell us, by that simple cybernetic device, the traffic light governing their movement toward each other. "Our eyes met, I looked away, then I looked again, and she was looking away. The light changed." The existentially pure exchange of "The Look" is reduced to the same sort of thing as the clicking of a traffic light.

In one section, A. equates Maoism with "purity . . . rhetoric . . . and the reign of right reason." A. then leads the reader through a series of illogical statements to contradictory conclusions. A. states, "Purity has never been quantifiable." Two sentences later, he states, "Purity occurs in .004 per cent of all cases." Reminiscent of the self-dismantling language of the machine invented by Beckett in *The Lost Ones*, these tricks seem like small acts of sabotage, sniper's shots aimed at the overweening box.

Q. and A. in another sequence of exchanges discuss the possibility of "taking a pill" that will provide "complete sexual satisfaction." Again, they are talking about an invention, a sort of biochemical device that, when applied to the body's physiological mechanism, activates a series of complexly determined signals interpreted by the body-brain as "Complete Sexual Satisfaction." A., our avatar, is dubious though: "I think under those conditions we would know less about each other than we do now," he demurs.

In this first non-sequitur category, there are sections which are much more opaque than the ones above. Q. and A. exchange a set of utterances that appear entirely devoid of reference – purely formal syntactical and grammatical exercises:

A. We shall not cross the river.
Q. His father will strike him.
A. Filling his pockets with fruit.

The question and answer feedback loop has broken down to its most entropic form: there is no longer any communication, there is merely noise, static, random phrases in which entropy is high. By this dual shifting of attention towards the purely formal aspects of communication, we are made conscious of our readership, and thereby of the mechanisms of language, communication and the text, all made manifest for the sake of meaning. Reading "The explanation" becomes a little like trying to tell the time by looking at the gears ticking in the back of a watch.

The second category of narrative comprises passages that refer directly to the machine. These seem less ambiguous but are no less provocative. The first hints at their function:

Q. Now that you've studied these for a bit, can you explain how it works?
A. Of course. (Explanation.)

The explanation in the story with the same title is kept in parentheses, left undisclosed and interdicted, taunting us, like the black box itself, and also making us laugh at its irresistible irony. Barthelme is telling us that all three explanations (the one by A. of the machine, the story by the same name, and any possible explanation of that story) must ultimately remain inexpressible, anomalous, beyond the reach of the mechanisms we have assembled to provide us with such explanations. Similarly, A. peers into the machine several times, and each time sees something different. Once, he sees a "she" removing her blouse; later, she is removing her jeans and panties, although her blouse is on; in a third, she is eating an apple. When Q. asks the ritual question triggering these visions, "What do you see now?" A., in the last of these, replies, "There is a bruise on her thigh, the right."

A.'s contradictory visions indicate that the black box has become what the phenomenologists would call "an intended object" (or an *Ur-noemata* in Husserlian jargon); that is, A.'s consciousness embraces the black box at different times yielding different results. The essential muteness of the black box makes of it anything A. likes.

Q., by contrast, defends the machine, though his remarks are alternately illuminating and obscure:

> It has beauties, the machine. . . . We construct these machines not because we confidently expect them to do what they are designed to do – change the government in this case – but because we intuit a machine out there, gleaming like a shopping center.

The machine's appeal lies in its metaphorical power, though that metaphor lacks grace, perhaps. Who needs another shopping center? Later, Q. offers a number of "error messages" to A. in order to help him study the operation of the machine. Some of the members of this list (which might have been drawn from a computer manual) pun on literary terms or could be construed as such puns: "undefined variable . . . missing operator . . . mixed mode, that one's particularly grave . . . improper character in constant . . . no END statement." Undefined, missing operator, mixed mode, improper character (was he inconstant?), END. The shape of a very contemporary sort of story is suggested. More to the point, an error message is used by the computer to tell its operator when he or she has made a mistake, a particularly cybernetic juncture in the "interface" between human and machine. Q. says, "The machine has a face," and later gives a thumbnail sketch of the morphology of faces from jellyfish to mammal. He concludes, "The face has three main functions, detection of desirable energy sources, direction of locomotor machinery towards its goal, and capture . . . and preliminary preparation of food. The face also serves as a lure in mate acquisition."

While Q. seems bent on bridging the fourth discontinuity, A. resists the metaphor. Q. refers to the "broad, forwardly directed nose," and A. says, "I don't see that on the panel." Q. replies, "Look at it." The square is then reproduced once again so we can look at it as Q. persists: "There is an analogy, believe it or not. . . . We use industrial designers to do the front panels, the controls. Designers, artists. To make the machine attractive to potential buyers." ("To serve as a lure in mate acquisition?") Q. seems particularly pleased with the irony that artists are accomplices in the anthropomorphizing of the machine. Further, Q. portrays his vision of a rationalized society (one which Barthelme satirizes in "Paraguay"). In this new techtopia, the machine – designed, remember, "to change the government" – plays a central role.

> Q. The situation bristles with difficulties but in the end young people and workers alike will live on the same plane as old people and government officials, for the mutual good of all categories. The phenomenon of masses, in following the law of high numbers, makes possible exceptional and rare events, which –.

A. interrupts Q.'s speech, clearly provoked by Q.'s rhetoric (A. later calls him "emotionless"), which echoes Ellul's prophecy in *The Technological Society*: "'Technical procedures abstract from the individual and seek traits common to masses of men and mass phenomena. Without these common traits neither statistics nor the law of great numbers nor the Gaussian curve – indeed, no organization – would be possible.'"[7] But A.'s counter-speech is filled with another kind of rhetoric, the romance of private fantasy, and desire. A. recalls the time he phoned an old girl friend to tell her about the erotic dream he had about her.

However, Q. has absorbed the lessons of cybernetics enough to know, as he states, "The issues are not real in the sense that they are touchable. The issues raised here are equivalents." Cybernetics is primarily concerned with that "untouchable" component of phenomena: not their energy or matter, but their information. And the machine itself, the *schwarzgerat* hovering over them, is similarly an equivalent of certain decision procedures, both for the totalizing government it will help usher in, and for the softer, more private imagination of Citizen A.

IN THE BLACK BOX

The third form of discourse is the black box, and it is in the black box that the text resolves both the simpler debate between Q. and A. and the deeper presence of nonsense and ambiguity.

The only data we have about the box are that it is a machine and that A. sees things in its pure blackness. What do these notions have to do with the cybernetic themes of the other passages: the "error messages," the complicity between artists and computer engineers, the various anthropomorphic portraits of the machine, the equation between novel and bicycle, the interface between human and mechanical? More ambiguous passages evoke the symptoms and concepts associated with a technological culture: self-consciousness, empty language, alienation, mechanization of the body's chemistry through pills, regulation of public behavior through traffic lights, etc. The very word "cybernetic" is derived from "governing," and this machine is intended to govern the government. A. discloses his resentment of the machine in various ways: he blocks Q.'s praise of it, admits he lacks confidence in it, dislikes having his photograph taken, and accuses Q. of being emotionless.

All these create a context for understanding the black box as a third category of discourse. The black box is a symbol used conventionally by engineers and draftsmen to indicate a portion of a mechanism which cannot be represented accurately in a given blueprint of it, either because the scale of the diagram is too large or small, or because not enough information about the mechanism can be obtained. The black box, therefore, is a map of something beneath or above the level of description, or of something that is unknown, impossible to describe or render symbolically. It is a symbol for the point at which mechanical description breaks down, becomes insufficient. The Heisenberg Uncertainty Principle defines the indeterminacy of the electron's position as a black box. Gödel's theorem is its equivalent in mathematics. All sciences have their black boxes; in fact, the sciences are not as active within realms that they have thoroughly mapped as they are on the edge of the unknown.

In this light, the power of the black box metaphor becomes enormous. It potentially embraces the very way we attempt to know our world. Indeed, some psychologists and cyberneticists such as Gregory Bateson even refer to the human brain itself as a black box, implying both that it is a sort of machine and that its operations are not completely understood.[8] We know how portions of it work but not how all of it does, at least not now.

The black box stands at the core of "The explanation," an irreducible, atomistic sign, telling us that "The explanation" is inexplicable. Further, it could stand as a sign for all cybernetic fiction, all these literary machines, since it implies that the interface between human and machine is too laden with ambiguities to be explained mechanically. The black box is the ultimate of the soft machines, standing not only for that ambiguous relationship between human and machine, but for the act of creating fictions with the imperfect mechanisms of language. It reflects Barthelme's artistic methodology, the inexplicable machinery of language and expression, A.'s (and the Audience's) attempts to make sense out of an inscrutable text, and yet it remains invulnerable to final and complete explanation.

THE DISTANCE WE HAVE COME: ROUSSEL TO BARTHELME

A brief comparison between the fiction of Roussel and Barthelme measures the distance we have come in our investigation of the use of the machine as metaphor. Roussel's modernist tactic contrasts with Barthelme's postmodern one.

The punner in *Locus Solus* is, like the black box, also the ordering metaphor-machine of its text. They direct the discourse and yet give rise to further discourse of their own. Both the punner and the black box have enormous metaphorical potential that invites further explication or inspection. Both pun literally and figuratively. Both contain and frame other images and stories. Both are observed by humans who are partly mystified by the machines which later require expert explanation by their representatives, Canterel and the anonymous Q.

However, where Roussel tries to create a positivistic mechanism of explication, including an elaborate punning narrative about the wheels, stoppers, rods, mirrors, aerodynamics, physics and chemistry of the machine, a self-referential system of puns and linguistic devices and a system of stories within stories created by the machine's tableau, Q. never finishes his speeches about the thing. He only gets up to instruction #4 in a promised list of ten operating instructions, is vague about details, is interrupted by A., and makes contradictory assertions. Finally, A.'s illumination, his explanation of the machine, is glossed over, left in parentheses. Whereas Roussel's puns create a closed verbal space, Barthelme's language is uncertainly punned (can we be sure the error statements were intended to imply something literary?), the text is filled with lacunae and ellipses, and the whole is left open to interpretation. Roussel intends completion and certainty, Barthelme incompletion and uncertainty. Roussel overdetermines, Barthelme not only underdetermines, but chooses a symbol of underdetermination itself as the central feature of his text.

Roussel, the ultimate literary positivist, is confronted six decades later by Barthelme, the mock empiricist and ironic counterfeiter. Barthelme's black box is not only a comment on machinery and technology, it stands for the potential of fiction itself in which everything and nothing can be read, including the play of differentials that reduce the entropy of a message and the deferred meaning that lives in a territory beyond the message itself. Meaning exists inside the text, here, where I am writing this word, and "out there, gleaming like a shopping center." It is the certainty of being compelled to discover explanations and the uncertainty that those explanations are ever adequate.

Cybernetic fiction, far from being a representative of a class of fiction in its decadence, is the most meaningful and in its way hopeful sort of fiction. It cannot as a body be understood without constant reference to its source in a highly technologized society. For that very reason, however, it has the power to invent a new way of seeing, it offers a new language, and along the way it tells a fine, often amusing, often grim story about how far along we are.

NOTES

The epigraph on page ix is from Hugh Kenner, *The Counterfeiters* (New York: Doubleday-Anchor, 1973), p. 16.

CHAPTER ONE

1 Ulric Neisser, "Computers as tools and metaphors," in Dechert, Charles R. (ed.) *The Social Impact of Cybernetics* (New York: Simon & Schuster, 1966), pp. 75–6.
2 Colin Murray Turbayne, *The Myth of Metaphor*, rev. edn (Columbia, SC: University of South Carolina Press, 1970), p. 5.
3 René Descartes, *Principes de la philosophie*, trans. Piat, *Oeuvres de Descartes*, III (Paris: Leverault, 1824), p. 519.
4 The details of this argument are explored fully in an excellent paper by Samuel G. Wong, "Metaphor in early scientific writing," read at the Literature and Science Section of the Modern Language Association (New York, December 1983).
5 See Hans Aarsleff, "John Wilkins," in *From Locke to Saussure:*

Essays on the Study of Language and Intellectual History (Minneapolis: University of Minnesota Press, 1982), pp. 239–77.

6 Jonathan Swift, Riverside Edition of *Gulliver's Travels* (New York: Houghton Mifflin, 1960), pp. 148–50.

7 Herbert Sussman, *Victorians and the Machine* (Cambridge, Mass.: Harvard University Press, 1968). John F. Kasson, *Civilizing the Machine: Technology and Republican Values in America, , 1776–1900* (New York: Grossman, 1976). Leo Marx, *The Machine in the Garden: Technology and the Pastoral Ideal in America* (New York: Oxford University Press, 1964).

8 H. Bruce Franklin, *Future Perfect* (New York: Oxford University Press, 1978).

9 Wylie Sypher, *Literature and Technology, the Alien Vision* (New York: Random House, 1968).

10 Kasson, op. cit., p. 161.

11 ibid., p. 139.

12 Nathaniel Hawthorne, "The artist of the beautiful," in Pearson, N. H. (ed.) *The Complete Novels and Selected Tales of Nathaniel Hawthorne* (New York: Modern Library, 1958), p. 1139.

13 Paul Valéry, "Literature," in *Selected Writings*, trans. Louise Varese (New York: New Directions, 1950), p. 152.

14 Sypher, op. cit., pp. 25–7.

15 Gilles Deleuze, *Proust and Signs* (New York: Braziller, 1972). Deleuze writes (p. 128):

> The modern work of art is anything it may seem; it is even its very property of being whatever we like, of having the over-determination of whatever we like, from the moment it works: the modern work of art is a machine and functions as such. . . . Why a machine? Because the work of art, so understood, is essentially productive – productive of certain truths. No one has insisted more than Proust on the following point: that the truth is produced by orders of machines which function within us, that it is abstracted from our impressions.

16 Sussman, op. cit., p. 147.

17 Henry Adams, "The dynamo and the virgin," in *The Education of Henry Adams* (Boston: Houghton Mifflin, 1961), pp. 379–90.

18 Jacques Ellul, *The Technological Society* (New York: Knopf, 1964). Langdon Winner, *Autonomous Technology* (Cambridge, Mass.: MIT Press, 1974).

19 Sussman, op. cit., p. 186.

20 Sypher, op. cit., p. 232.

21 Turbayne, op. cit., p. 5.

22 ibid.

23 Jonathan Culler characterizes Barthes's thought this way in *Structuralist Poetics* (Ithaca, NY: Cornell University Press, 1972), p. 57.

24 ibid.

25 Umberto Eco, *Einführung in die Semiotik* (Munich, 1972) as quoted in Wolfgang Iser, *The Act of Reading* (Baltimore, Md: The Johns Hopkins University Press, 1978), p. 65.

26 Iser, op. cit., p. 65.

27 William Barrett, *The Illusion of Technique* (New York: Doubleday/Anchor, 1979), p. 23.

28 Joseph Weizenbaum, *Computer Power and Human Reason* (San Francisco: W. H. Freeman, 1976).

29 Norbert Wiener, *The Human Use of Human Beings* (New York: Doubleday/Anchor, 1954).

30 Italo Calvino, *T-Zero*, trans. William Weaver (New York: Harcourt Brace Jovanovich, 1969). Quoted from Harbrace Paperbound edition (1976), p. 136.

Calvino is not treated fully elsewhere in this work. The set of texts I discuss in this book is meant to be neither exclusive nor exhaustive. Several other contemporary authors are obviously working the same territory as those I focus on in Chapters Five through Ten: Anthony Burgess (in *A Clockwork Orange* (London: Heinemann, 1962)), Don Delillo (in *Ratner's Star*, New York: Knopf, 1976), and Italo Calvino are just a few. Thomas LeClair argues convincingly that Joseph Heller's novel *Something Happened* (New York: Knopf, 1974) invites an analysis from and application of the principles of information theory. (See "Joseph Heller, *Something Happened* and the art of excess," *Studies in American Fiction* (Autumn 1981), pp. 245–60.) Cybernetic fiction undoubtedly deserves status as a sub-genre, one which I believe will continue to grow. Cybernetics offers what Claudio Guillén calls "an invitation to form" which is sufficiently rich to be hardly exhausted by those authors I treat here. (See Claudio Guillén's discussion of genre in *Literature as System* (Princeton, NJ: Princeton University Press, 1972).) As Guillén writes (p. 124): "The process of generic description and classification is never quite closed, and the diachronic fluidity of genre theories is much more real than their apparent solidity at a single moment in history."

31 See David Porush, "Technology and postmodernism: cybernetic fiction," *Sub-Stance*, 27 (1980), pp. 89–100.

32 Noam Chomsky, *Aspects of the Theory of Syntax* (Cambridge, Mass.: MIT Press, 1965).

33 Norbert Wiener, *Cybernetics: Control and Communication in the Animal and the Machine* (Cambridge, Mass.: MIT Press, 1948, 1961).

34 Michael Arbib, *The Metaphorical Brain* (New York: Wiley & Sons,

1972), p. 11. Pierre de Latil also explores the central role of model building in cybernetics in *Thinking by Machine*, trans. Y. M. Golla (London: Sidgwick & Jackson, 1956), p. 224: "Even when it is possible to construct a physical model of neuronic or cerebral activity by the application of cybernetic methods, it still cannot be claimed that this furnishes a complete explanation of the natural process."

35 Ellul, op. cit., p. v.

36 ibid., p. 14.

CHAPTER TWO

1 Wylie Sypher, *Literature and Technology, the Alien Vision* (New York: Random House, 1968), p. 63.

2 Raymond Federman, *Take It or Leave It* (New York: Fiction Collective, 1975), unpaginated.

3 Sypher, op. cit., p. 24.

4 ibid., pp. 59–67.

5 Michel Leiris, "Conception et realité chez Raymond Roussel," *Critique*, 89 (October 1954), pp. 821–35.

6 Raynor Heppenstall, *Raymond Roussel* (Berkeley, Ca: University of California Press, 1967).

7 This land yacht was probably inspired by Jules Verne's luxury travelling machine depicted in "The steam house" (1880). It was capable of moving over land and water and was fully equipped for habitation.

8 Roussell is the subject of several books and journal numbers. Among these are the issue of *L'Arc* 68 (1977), published on the centenary of Roussel's birthday: numbers 34–5 of *Bizarre* (1964); *Raymond Roussel* by Michel Foucault (Paris: Gallimard, 1963; Berkeley, Ca: University of California Press, 1967). The Michel Leiris article, "Conception et realité chez Raymond Roussel" appears as an introduction to *Épaves*, a collection of previously unpublished minor plays and works by Roussel (Paris: Jean-Jacques Pauvert, 1972).

The most fruitful articles on Roussel either attempt to place his *oeuvre* in a certain context or examine what has come to be known as "*le procédé Roussellien*," the Rousselian process. These include Alain Robbe-Grillet's "Enigme et transparence chez Raymond Roussel," *Critique* (December 1963): Michel Butor's essay in *Repertoire*; Pierre Schneider's essay in *Cahiers du Sud* (1951), in which he describes Roussel's world as "dust-free – like a computer room"; Jean Ferry's *Une étude sur Raymond Roussel* (Paris: Editions Arcanes, 1953); Gilles Deleuze and Felix Guattari in *Anti-Oedipus* (New York: Viking Press, 1977); the essays by John Ashbery and

François Caradec in *Bizarre*, 34–5; Michel Carrouges' study of Roussel's machines, *Les machines célibataires de Raymond Roussel* (Paris: Editions Arcanes, 1955).

The two best recent studies of Roussel in America examine his work in the context of structuralist theory, which finds a rich field for scrutiny in Roussel's texts. Roussel's style is typically filled with explicit and rigorous structuration of the mechanisms of language and writing, self-conscious elimination of the authorial consciousness from the text, emphasis on word play at the expense of story, and the generation of a set of artificial devices which call attention to language as an object rather than a medium for expression. These two studies are Leslie Hill's "Raymond Roussel and the place of literature," *Modern Language Review*, 74, 4 (1979), pp. 823–35, and Carl Lovitt's "*Locus Solus*: literary solitaire," *Sub-Stance*, 10 (1974), pp. 95–109, studies which I have used as the basis for much of the exploration of Roussel that follows.

9 Baudelaire on Poe, quoted in T. S. Eliot's *From Poe to Valéry* (New York: Harcourt Brace Jovanovich, 1948), p. 18.

10 Carl Lovitt (op. cit., p. 95) suggests that Roussel or his first-person stand-in makes an appearance in the very first sentence before lapsing into the first-person plural point of view:

> The second word of *Locus Solus*, "Jeudi," in addition to being a temporal indication, seems to announce the "je dis" of a narrator. This assumption is confirmed in the same sentence by "m'avait convié." However, no sooner does this narrator assert himself than he disappears. In his place we find a self-effacing, dispassionate "nous."

11 Raymond Roussel, *Locus Solus* (Paris: Gallimard/Jean-Jacques Pauvert, 1965), pp. 65–6.

12 The English translations are my own from the original French of *Locus Solus*. I have taken very few liberties with the original French, but because so much of Roussel's work derives its imaginative force from phonological play and punning, his fiction is virtually untranslatable in any way that recaptures the self-reflexive sense of the original. There is an English translation of *Locus Solus* by Rupert Copeland Cunningham (Berkeley, Ca: University of California Press, 1970).

13 Jules Verne, in an essay originally delivered as a speech to the Académie d'Amiens (1875), spoke about the City of Amiens in the year 2000 and predicted that the music of the future, represented in this instance by "A reverie in A minor on the square of the hypotenuse," would be "neither human nor celestial – no lilt, no beat, no melody, no rhythm: quintessence of Wagner, audiomathematical

cacophomania – like an orchestra tuning up." Quoted in Haining, Peter (ed.) *Jules Verne Companion* (New York: Souvenir Press, 1978), p. 31.

14 Clarke's Law in Bennett, Gordon (ed.) *1001 Logical Laws* (New York: Fawcett Columbia Books, 1979), p. 42.

15 Raymond Roussel, *Comment j'ai écrit certain de mes livres* (Paris: Jean-Jacques Pauvert, 1963), p. 10.

16 Roussel's wish to reveal his secret only posthumously signifies the remarkable commitment to and unity of the life of his imagination. Michel Foucault (op. cit., p. 24) finds in this posthumous revelation a continuity with the themes of entombment and encoding which dominates Roussel's works:

> Dans *Les Impressions*, dans *Locus Solus*, dans tous les textes à "procédé" sous la secrète technique du langage, un autre secret se cache, comme elle est viable et invisible: une pièce essentielle au mécanisme générale du procédé, le poids qui fatalement entraîne les aiguilles et les roues – la mort de Roussel. . . . On peut bien y reconnaître l'avance métronomique d'un événement dont chaque instant répète la promesse et la nécessité. Et par là on retrouve dans toute l'oeuvre de Roussel . . . une figure combinée du "secret" et du "posthume."

17 Carl Lovitt, op. cit., p. 121.

18 ibid., p. 102.

19 Albert Jenny, "Structure et fonction du cliché," *Poetique*, 12 (1972), p. 513.

20 A note on decoding Roussel's texts: Roussel presents "Parmi les noirs" as the exemplar of the application of his device. In this story, an anonymous narrator is summoned to the house of a friend, Flambeau, where he discovers another old friend, Balancier, who had, after a long hiatus, sent the narrator a copy of his newest book, *Parmi les Noirs*. The narrator recounts the novel: a young sea captain, Compas, is shipwrecked on the African shore and held captive by a ferocious black chieftain, Tombola, and his tribe who take him to central Africa. The captain soon discovers he is among cannibals; he writes a series of letters to his wife describing his life among the savages in the belief that they represent his last act. These missives he attaches to birds taken from nearby cages. He continues this every day until an entire volume of letters has been completed, which comprise the entirety of Balancier's novel.

Flambeau invites the narrator and Balancier along with the rest of the company – Débarras, Gauffre and a Mme Bosse – to play a parlor game that requires a question to be written for one of the players, who is then asked to go to a neighboring room for ten minutes. After the time is up, "the door is opened and the person must give his response in the form of a rebus." The first to decode the rebus is then asked a question, etc. The first chosen is Débarras, who is asked whether he prefers water colors or pastels in his motifs. After his time is up, Flambeau opens the door, and Débarras delivers his rebus. What follows is a paragraph typical of Roussel but remarkable in literature for its intensity and frequency of homophonic and paranomasic play:

> A la fin de la dixième minute il alla cuvrir la porte et Débarras nous apporta le rébus, qui circula aussitôt de main en main. Pour ma part, je n'y compris pas grand'chose. Ça commençait par deux notes, un *la* et un *ré* sur une portée à clef de *sol*. Mais, au lieu de noires ou de blanches, il y avait pour le *la* trois lettres: *coi* et pour le *ré* une étrange bête à quatre pattes. Ensuite venait une sorte de prairie, puis des barres de fer entrées dans un sac et dépassant du tiers; après on lisait les lettres suivantes: OSE SA SA; enfin un S, dessiné en pattes de mouches avec des bras et des jambes comme de cheveaux, soulevait un lourd fardeau qu'un vieillard portait péniblement sur son dos; le vieillard avait SONEC écrit sur le corps; une ligne courbe sortant de sa bouche pour y rentrer après un détour encadrait cette phrase: "J'ai besoin de secours." Pour finir, un nouveau *la*, une vraie note cette fois, figurait sur une portée semblable.

Literally, the rebus portrays a keyboard with the letters "COI" in place of the note "la," and a llama in place of the note "re." This is followed by a prairie, bars of iron entering a bag, the letters "OSE" followed by "SA" twice, and a final "S"; an old man named "SONEC" carrying a heavy bag is asking for help and being lifted by a delicately scrawled "S" with the arms and legs of a horse.

It takes Mme Bosse only two minutes to solve the puzzle as follows: "L'aquarelle a ma préférence à cause de sa finesse et de son éclat." ("Water colors have my preference for their delicacy and clarity.") She has translated the pictograph into the following set of syllables and words: "LA coi RÉlama – pré – fer en sac – OSE deux SA – fine S aide SONEC – LA."

The reader has been made triply alert to puns and puzzles: the rebus within the story is a puzzle over which the French-speaking reader may have lingered; the story about the rebus is itself partly a companion to another, seemingly irrelevant recounting of

Debarras's book, and "Parmi les noirs" is a short text collected with other posthumous papers, including *Comment j'ai ecrit . . .* which reveals, in part, that "Parmi . . ." was written according to Roussel's patented process. Thus alerted, a quick second-level inspection of this innings of play in the exchange of rebuses reveals some interesting features:

Field I: Débarras

A The name "Débarras" (l. 2), means both "storage room" and "good riddance" ("to be well shot of" as the British might say), and is derived from the verb *débarrasser* – to clear away – and is akin to the verb *débarrer* – to unlock the door.

This provokes us to search for other hidden semes among the signs associated with "Débarras" – perhaps the key to the Rousselian door. The reading machine quickly discovers:

B (l. 9): *des barres de fer* (iron bars)

1 which can be read *Débarras defer* (the unlocking deferred or delayed),

(a) which in turn invokes the many enriched meanings of "deferred" to which post-structuralists have called our attention: the deferral not only in time but of meaning, the placement of the meaningful element elsewhere than in or with the sign.

C (l. 12): *des bras* (arms), which is tied to another sub-sidiary constellation of associations whose exploration we must defer for a moment (see Field II below).

D Many verbs have to do with opening and closing containers of various sorts, semantic expansions of Débarras:

1 (l. 1): *il alla ouvrir la porte* (he opened the door);

2 (ll. 15–16): *une ligne courbe sortant de sa bouche* (a curved line came out of his mouth);

3 (l. 17): *encadrait cette phrase* (enclosing this phrase);

4 (ll. 9–10): *des barres de fer entrées dans un sac* (the iron bars went into a sack).

All of which, of course, reflect the primary task of coding and decoding of the rebus by the characters and the story by the reader.

Field II

The second major field for expansion, association and determin-ation is related to the first and has numerous points of intersection on both thematic and phonetic levels. This field is entirely determined by the word *porte* (l. 2), and its many homophones, each of which in turn carry their interesting coincident associations:

A (l. 2): *la porte* (the door). See Field I above.

B (l. 2): *nous apporta la rebus* (brought us the rebus).

C (l. 3): *Pour ma part* (for my part). Indicates incompletion, part of a whole. (The entire phrase is: "For my part I could understand nothing.")

D (l. 5): *une portée à clef de sol* (a keyboard), is apparently the primary meaning, but the inclusion of the exemplary Rousselian pun, *sol* signals the presence of other potential semantic expansions.

1 *une portée* (an uncovering or a period of gestation). Bears an obvious relationship to the game itself, as well as the development by the reading machine of a complete solution to the Rousselian code.

2 Sounds like *a portée* (within reach), as the solution nearly is.

3 And derives from the verb *porter* (to carry) – conjugations of which appear twice in this passage: l. 1 – above, and l. 14: *un vieillard portait* (an old man carried).

4 Finally, *une portée à clef* is, literally (a key-door), or a door that can be opened by a key, which again returns us to the same old thematic room, which by this time is beginning to feel a bit like a closet.

E (l. 19): *une portait semblable* (a similar board). This could also be read "a resembling-board" which could refer to the rebus.

F (l. 8): *une étrange bête à quatre pattes* (a strange beast on four paws). This refers to the exotic llama, not to be confused with a lemma, though perhaps cousin to the S-horse, which is drawn out of an elaborately scrawled S, or as the French say, is.

G (ll. 11–12): *dessinée en pattes de mouche* (lit.: drawn with fly's feet; idiomatic for an elaborate script). (See my discussion of the sense of "schrift" evoked by Kafka's use of the term, in Chapter Two.)

1 The entire text, by its unnecessary but significant embellishment, such as the kind I am exploring here, is a sort of *une écriture à pattes de mouche.*

2 In the decipherment of the rebus, this embellished "S" is interpreted as "a final 'S' " – *fine "S"* = *finesse*. The reiteration of the word for "paws" in this small space partly determines and calls a third field to the attention of the reading machine.

Field III: Parts of the body

A: *pattes* – see above.
B (l. 3): *de main en main* (from hand to hand).
C (l. 12): *avec des bras et des jambes* (with the arms and the legs).
D (l. 14): *sur son dos* (on his back).
E (l. 15): *écrit sur le corps* (written on his body).
F (l. 16): *sa bouche* (his mouth).

This subtle collection of anatomical parts – hands, paws, arms, legs, back, body, mouth – is entirely consonant with the macrostructural theme of "PARTIAL TRUTH"; in this case the summary effect is to indicate a willful dismemberment of some prior, aboriginal sense, to which we are directed by the various mechanisms and devices for unriddling offered by this complex rebus-text.

The irreducible word pair lying at the center of all the Fields is *porte-part*, signifying the enunciation of an as yet unrevealed or undisclosed "whole truth" (an invitation to disclosure), and the presence of the dismembered parts of the "whole truth" already disclosed but awaiting integration.

In a little over 225 words, there are twenty-six major redundancies or determinations, not counting the minor, "natural" repetitions statistically probable in the use of any natural language. (For instance, the phoneme "la" occurs four times in line 1 and eight times by line 7.) The combined effect of the derivation of the central thematic-phonetic pair (*porte-part*) with this redundancy is two-fold. On the one hand, the reader is made to feel that he or she has been introduced into some post-lapsarian world which still has the promise of paradise, the Edenic vision of completion, a visionary world in which names are things and language recuperates the world: the titles themselves – "Parmi les noirs" (which itself is a partial anagram for "impressions," harking back to Roussel's previous novel, *Impressions d'Afrique*) and *Locus Solus* – point the way to this pre-lapsarian, transcendentally "native" or natural place. The reader must earn, through machine-work, entry into the antediluvian plain. On the other hand, the human reader is given pause, for the second implication of the central revelation, carried by the redundancy, is that the paradise is a clockwork world, with no room for neology, accident, or the sort of freedom found in silence and deferral. Roussel's codes invite us to put the primally dismembered language back together again, but at the price of killing speech. Having reconstituted Roussel's primal language, my guess is that the Machine Reader would find there is nothing left to say.

This long mechanical analysis of less than twenty lines of text is by no means complete; the expansion and determinations of the various fields provoked by a little push on *Débarras*'s name are reiterated in similar territories circumscribed elsewhere in this short text: e.g. by "Mme Bosse," which is a near-homonym of "embosse" – raising the letters of a text; the word *marron* – which is a homonyn for the purplish color, for "a sailor left alone on an island," and for "a runaway black slave"; and while we're on to colors, the very large field of play with *noir* and *blanc*; the nice hidden turn from *billes* (billiards), to *billes* (lumber); from *débarras* (a lumber-room), to the idiomatic *débarras* (poolroom); and finally, the quaint collapsing-frame effect achieved by having the final rebus inscribed on the frame of the pool tablc by the anonymous narrator, a rebus which itself is a pictogram for the final sentence of the story which in turn deviates by only one letter from the first, which is, after all, the only device to which Roussel explicitly admitted either before or after his death.

21 Leslie Hill, "Raymond Roussel and the place of literature," *Modern Language Review*, 74, 4 (1979), p. 828.

22 Raynor Heppenstall writes (*Raymond Roussel*, op. cit., p. 87): "In their blandly indifferent way, the logical positivists have directed us towards a nominalism of the same kind [as Roussel's], but somehow contrive to preserve their own few comforting clichés."

23 Pierre Janet, "Les caractères psychologiques de l'extase," in *De l'angoisse à l'extase* (Paris, 1920), p. 133.

24 Alain Robbe-Grillet, "Enigme et transparence chez Raymond Roussel," op. cit.

25 Hugh Kenner, "On the centenary of James Joyce," *The New York Sunday Times Book Review* (31 January 1982), pp. 1ff.

26 See S. Steinberg, "The judgement in Kafka's 'In the penal colony,'" *Journal of Modern Literature*, V, 3 (1976), pp. 492–514. The "Schrift" which the machine inscribes on the bodies of its victims is the commandment of a monolithic law; the word "schrift" means not only a highly ornate script but "Scripture." The nested commentaries ("Mishnah, Gemarah, and further commentaries medieval and later"), which is implied by the Torah is contrasted to the repetitiveness and senselessness of the embellishments inscribed by the machine. Thus, the story, in Steinberg's view, registers "Kafka's reaction to Judaism as a worn-out system of senseless ritual having little to do with the spiritual salvation he sought."

27 J. H. Matthews, "Beyond realism: Raymond Roussel's machines," in Kaiser, Grant E. (ed.) *Fiction, Form and Experience* (Montreal: France-Quebec, Inc., 1976), pp. 83–93.

28 *The Portable Kafka* (New York: Viking Portable Library, 1971), p. 91.
29 Matthews, op. cit., p. 87.

CHAPTER THREE

1 See Charles B. Harris, "Tom Pynchon and the entropic vision," in *Contemporary American Novelists of the Absurd* (New Haven, Conn.: Yale University Press, 1971). William Holts, "Thermodynamics and the comic and tragic modes," *WHR*, 25 (1971), pp. 203–16. Peter Abernethy, "Entropy in Pynchon's *The Crying of Lot 49*," *Critique*, 14 (1971). Carol Carm Donley, "Model literature and physics: a study of interrelationships," *Dissertation Abstracts International*, 36 (1975), p. 3684-A. Alan J. Friedman, "The novelist and modern physics: new metaphors for traditional themes," *Journal of College Science Teachers*, 4 (1975), pp. 310–12. Alan J. Friedman, "Physics and literature in this century: a new course," *Physics Education*, 8 (1973), pp. 305–8. Anne Mangel, "Maxwell's demon, entropy, information: *The Crying of Lot 49*," *TriQuarterly*, 20, pp. 194–208.
2 Norbert Wiener, *Cybernetics: Control and Communication in the Animal and the Machine* (Cambridge, Mass.: MIT Press, 1948, 1961), p. 44.
3 For a much more thorough discussion of these developments see Robert Nadeau's excellent book, *Readings from the New Book on Nature* (Amherst, Mass.: University of Massachusetts Press, 1983), pp. 49–60. Nadeau shows with thoroughness and insight the influence of the New Physics on the form and themes of contemporary fiction, a project which is the natural companion to my own in this book since, as the discussion in this chapter shows, the two sciences of physics and cybernetics are historically related.
4 Werner Heisenberg, *Physics and Philosophy* (New York: Harper & Row, 1958), p. 179.
5 Werner Heisenberg, "The representation of nature in contemporary physics," in Sears, S. and Lord, G. W. (eds) *The Discontinuous Universe* (New York: Basic Books, 1972), p. 127.
6 Werner Heisenberg, "Elementary particles and Platonic philosophy," in *Physics and Beyond* (New York: Harper & Row, 1971). This is also elaborated by Heisenberg in "Tradition in science" and "The nature of scientific discovery," both published by the Smithsonian Press (Washington, DC, 1975), pp. 219–36, 556–73.
7 Heisenberg, "The representation of nature," op. cit., p. 128.
8 Wiener, *Cybernetics*, op. cit., p. 92.
9 ibid., p. 93.

10 Arthur I. Miller, "Visualization lost and regained," in Wechsler, Judith (ed.) *Aesthetics in Science* (Cambridge, Mass.: MIT Press, 1978), p. 75. See also Gerald Holton, *Thematic Origins of Scientific Thought* (Cambridge, Mass.: Harvard University Press, 1973).

11 Schrodinger quoted in Miller, op. cit., p. 87.

12 Ilya Prigogine, a Belgian physicist, won the 1978 Nobel prize for his theory of dissipative structures. Prigogine proved that under certain conditions (non-linear fluctuations in energy states far from equilibrium or highly unstable), local enclaves of organization are likely to arise. This is significant because it brought what is obvious everywhere in the biospheres – that the hyper-structuration of human society and the biological world are local islands of increasing order and organization in what is the natural entropic or universal tide towards randomization – into alignment with the Second Law of Thermodynamics, which it hitherto seemed to contravene. See Ilya Prigogine, *Being and Becoming* (Washington, DC: Scientific American, 1981), and "The unity of physical laws and levels of description," in Grene, Marjorie (ed.) *Interpretations of Life and Mind* (New York: The Humanities Press, 1971), pp. 38–64.

13 Wiener, *The Human Use of Human Beings* (New York: Doubleday/Anchor, 1954), p. 11.

14 Wiener, *Cybernetics*, op. cit., pp. 18, 24. See also Gregory Bateson's *Steps to an Ecology of Mind* (New York: Chandler Press, 1969).

15 See Heinz R. Pagels, *The Cosmic Code: Quantum Physics as the Language of Nature* (New York: Simon & Schuster, 1982).

16 See particularly Norbert Wiener, "Role of the intellectual and the scientist," and "The mechanism and history of language," in *The Human Use of Human Beings*, op. cit.

17 See "Computing machines and the nervous system," "Cybernetics and psychopathology," "On learning and self-reproducing machines," and "Brain waves and self-organizing systems," in Wiener, *Cybernetics*, op. cit.

18 Abraham Moles, *Information Theory and Esthetic Perception*, trans. Joel E. Cohen (Urbana, Ill.: University of Illinois Press, 1966), p. 24.

19 Wiener, *The Human Use of Human Beings*, op. cit., p. 132.

20 ibid.

21 Michael Riffaterre, "Describing poetic structures," in Ehrmann, Jacques (ed.) *Structuralism* (New York: Doubleday, 1966), p. 189.

22 Moles, op. cit., p. 129.

23 ibid.

24 Donald Barthelme, "Bone bubbles," *City Life* (New York: Farrar, Straus & Giroux, 1972), p. 119.

25 Gilles Deleuze, *Proust and Signs*, trans. Richard Howard (New York: Braziller, 1972), pp. 128, 129.
26 Moles, op. cit., p. 78.
27 N. Abramson, *Information Theory and Coding* (New York: McGraw-Hill, 1963), pp. 33–8.
28 Claude Shannon and Warren Weaver, *The Mathematical Theory of Communication* (Urbana, Ill.: University of Illinois Press, 1949).
29 Thomas Kuhn, *The Structure of Scientific Revolutions* (Chicago: University of Chicago Press, 1962).
30 Gordon Pask, "The meaning of cybernetics in the behavioral sciences," in Rose, J. (ed.) *Progress in Cybernetics*, vol. 14 (New York: Gordon & Breach, 1969), pp. 15–44.
31 ibid., p. 16.
32 Humberto Maturana, "Neurophysiology of cognition," in Garvin, Paul (ed.) *Cognition: A Multiple View* (New York: Spartan Books, 1970), p. 3.
33 Heinz von Foerster, "Cybernetics of cybernetics," in Krippendorff, Klaus (ed.) *Communication and Control in Society* (New York: Gordon & Breach, 1979), p. 5.
34 Anthony Wilden, "Changing frames of order: cybernetics and the 'Machina Mundi,'" in Krippendorff, op. cit., pp. 9–29.
35 Herbert Simon, *The Sciences of the Artificial* (Cambridge, Mass.: MIT Press, 1969), p. 15.
36 For a discussion of self-consciousness in the novel, see Robert Alter, *Partial Magic: The Novel as a Self-conscious Genre* (Berkeley, Ca: University of California Press, 1975); Raymond Federman, *Surfiction: Fiction Now . . . and Tomorrow* (Chicago: Swallow Press, 1975).

CHAPTER FOUR

1 Heinz Werner, *Comparative Psychology of Mental Development* (New York: International Universities Press, 1970 – first published 1926). Ernst Cassirer, *Symbolic Forms* (trans. Ralph Manheim, New Haven, Conn.: Yale University Press, 1970 – first published 1926).
2 See Chapter VI, "Gestalts and universals," in Norbert Wiener, *Cybernetics: Control and Communication in the Animal and the Machine* (Cambridge, Mass.: MIT Press, 1948, 1961).
3 F. E. Berlyne, *Aesthetics and Psychobiology* (New York: Appleton-Century-Crofts, 1971). Cf. also F. Attnaeve, *Applications of Information Theory to Psychology* (New York: Holt, Rinehart & Winston, 1961).
4 Michael Polanyi, *Personal Knowledge* (Chicago: University of Chicago Press, 1962), pp. 36–7.
5 ibid., p. 38.

6 ibid., p. 149.
7 ibid., p. 153.
8 ibid., p. 153.
9 See also Michael Polanyi, "The logic of tacit inference," in Crosson, Frederick J. (ed.) *Human and Artificial Intelligence* (New York: Appleton-Century-Crofts, 1970), pp. 219–40.
10 Ludwig von Bertalanffly, *Robots, Men and Minds* (New York: Braziller Press, 1967), p. 9.
11 Frederick Crosson and K. Sayre, *The Modeling of Mind* (Notre Dame, Ind.: University of Notre Dame Press, 1963); Frederick Crosson, "Information theory and phenomenology," in Sayre, K. M. and Crosson, F. (eds) *Philosophy and Cybernetics* (Notre Dame, Ind.: Univesity of Notre Dame Press, 1967); and Frederick Crosson (ed.) Introduction to *Human and Artificial Intelligence*, op. cit.
12 Martin Heidegger, *Being and Time*, trans. John Macquerrie and Edwin Robinson (New York: Harper & Row, 1962).
13 Martin Heidegger, "The question concerning technology," in *The Question Concerning Technology and Other Essays*, trans. William Lovitt (New York: Harper & Row, 1977), p. 14. For a more elaborate discussion of Heidegger's ideas concerning technology see Don Ihde, *Technics and Praxis* (Boston: D. Reidel Publishing Co., 1979).
14 Heidegger, 1977, op. cit., pp. 14–15.
15 ibid., pp. 21–2.
16 ibid., p. 23.
17 ibid., p. 4.
18 Maurice Merleau-Ponty, *Signs*, trans. Richard McLeary (Evanston, Ill.: Northwestern University Press, 1964), pp. 109–10. See also Maurice Merleau-Ponty, *The Phenomenology of Perception*, trans. Colin Smith (London: Routledge & Kegan Paul, 1962).
19 Walter J. Ong, *Interfaces of the Word* (Ithaca, NY: Cornell University Press, 1977).
20 In Jonathan Culler, *Structuralist Poetics* (Ithaca, NY: Cornell University Press, 1972), p. 92.
21 Merleau-Ponty, *Signs*, op. cit., p. 48.
22 ibid., pp. 109–10.
23 ibid., p. 111.
24 Heidegger, 1977, op. cit., p. 36.

CHAPTER FIVE

1 Norbert Wiener, *The Human Use of Human Beings* (New York: Doubleday Anchor, 1954), p. 154.
2 ibid.

3 All quotations are taken from the Dell edition of *Player Piano* (New York, 1952, 1974), p. 19. See also in regard to this discussion Arthur Koestler, *Beyond Reductionism* (Boston: Beacon Press, 1969).
4 Wiener, op. cit., p. 183.
5 ibid., p. 95.
6 Kurt Vonnegut, Jr, *The Sirens of Titan* (New York: Houghton Mifflin, 1959).
7 See Thomas L. Wyner's "Machines and the meaning of human in the novels of Kurt Vonnegut, Jr," in *The Mechanical God: Machines in Science Fiction* (Westport, Conn.: Greenwood, 1982), pp. 41–52.
8 Kurt Vonnegut, Jr, *Mother Night* (New York: Harper & Row, 1961).
9 Kurt Vonnegut, Jr, *God Bless You, Mr Rosewater* (New York: Holt, Rinehart & Winston, 1964).
10 Kurt Vonnegut, Jr, *Slaughterhouse Five or The Children's Crusade* (New York: Delacorte, 1969).
11 Tony Tanner, *City of Words* (New York: Harper & Row, 1971), p. 183.
12 ibid., p. 191.
13 All quotations are from William Burroughs, *The Ticket that Exploded* (New York: Grove Press, 1967; Paris, 1962). *The Soft Machine* (New York: Grove Press, 1969; Paris, 1961; rev. London, 1962). But the Burroughs mythology extends over several works, forming a rather consistent – if not quite coherent – apocalyptic vision. See "The electronic revolution" (Paris: Henri Chopin Collection OUI, 1971), and *Nova Express* (New York: Grove Press, 1965).
14 *The Ticket that Exploded*, p. 21.
15 ibid., p. 111.
16 Josephin Hendin, for instance, writes in *Vulnerable People* (New York: Oxford University Press, 1978) that Burroughs is "the writer and the hater, amid his many indistinguishable characters, those anonymous voices choking with nausea at being alive. For Burrough's [sic] final subject is not the particular psyche, nor the social scene, but quaking nerves." "Burroughs' novels are the experience of his orgiastic hate" (p. 55). "Alienation and spaciness have been his smokescreens, concealing the pure intensity of his misanthropy" (p. 57).
17 *The Soft Machine*, p. 94. Burroughs is descended from the man who invented the original calculating machine marketed by the company that still bears his name.
18 William Burroughs, *Exterminator!* (Paris: Olympia Press, 1960).
19 Mas'ud Zavarzadeh, *The Mythopoeic Reality: The Postwar American Nonfiction Novel* (Urbana, Ill.: University of Illinois Press, 1976), p. 38.
20 Irving Massey, *The Uncreating Word: Romanticism and the Object* (Bloomington, Ind.: University of Indiana Press, 1970), p. 91.

21 I explore this theme more fully in my dissertation, "Apocalypses of the sixties" (Buffalo: State University of New York, 1977).

22 Edward Jayne explores the connection between paranoia and the plotting of fiction's structure in his essay, "The dialectics of paranoid form," *Genre*, 11 (Spring 1978), pp. 131–57.

> Like paranoia, fiction is susceptible to bizarre theories of apocalypse and divine intervention. . . . Like paranoia, fiction is hyperalert to the hidden meaning of human conduct. . . . Like paranoia, fiction puts intricacy in the service of desirable conclusions. Through premature closure theme and form take precedence over suspended judgment. (pp. 145–6)

23 In "Psychoanalytic notes on an autobiographical account of a case of paranoia," in *The Standard Edition of the Complete Psychological Works of Sigmund Freud*, V, xii (Toronto, 1958). See especially, "On the mechanisms of paranoia," pp. 59–79.

24 Vladimir Nabokov, "Signs and symbols," *Nabokov's Dozen* (New York: Bard Avon, 1973).

25 Anthony Burgess, *A Clockwork Orange* (New York: Bantam, 1969).

26 Robert Coover, "Morris in chains," *Pricksongs and Descants* (New York: Dutton, 1969), p. 51.

27 Ihab Hassan, *Radical Innocence: The Contemporary American Novel* (Princeton, NJ: Princeton University Press, 1961).

CHAPTER SIX

1 Clarke's Law in Gordon Bennett (ed.) *1001 Logical Laws* (New York: Fawcett Columbia Books, 1979), p. 42.

2 William Plater, *The Grim Phoenix Reconstructing Thomas Pynchon* (Bloomington, Ind.: Indiana University Press, 1980), p. 241.

3 John Stark, *Pynchon's Fictions and the Literature of Information* (Athens, Oh.: Ohio University Press, 1980), p. 52.

4 Kathleen Woodward, "Cybernetic modelling in recent American fiction" (paper delivered to Modern Language Association, December 1981). Anne Mangel, "Maxwell's demon, entropy, information: *The Crying of Lot 49*," *Tri-Quarterly*, 20, pp. 194–208.

5 Tony Tanner, *Thomas Pynchon* (London and New York: Methuen, 1982).

6 All quotes and references are from Thomas Pynchon, *Gravity's Rainbow* (New York: Viking, 1973).

7 All quotes and references are to Thomas Pynchon, *V.* (New York: Lippincott, 1963); *The Crying of Lot 49* (New York: Bantam, 1967).

8 Stark, op. cit., p. 70. Cf. also, Charles R. Russell, "The vaults of language: self-reflective artifice in contemporary American fiction,"

Modern Fiction Studies, 20, pp. 349–59. Alfred Kazin, *The Bright Book of Life* (Boston: Little, Brown, 1973), pp. 275–80. Richard Patterson, "What Stencil knew: structure and certitude in Pynchon's *V.*," *Critique*, 16, pp. 30–44.

9 Bruce Herzberg, "Illusions of control: a reading of *Gravity's Rainbow*" (Ph.D. thesis, Rutgers University, 1978).

10 See *Scientific American*, November 1979.

11 Thomas Pynchon, "Entropy," *Kenyon Review*, 22 (Spring 1960), pp. 277–92.

12 Plater, op. cit., p. 220.

13 ibid., p. 242.

14 See Lance W. Ozier, "The calculus of transformation: more mathematical imagery in *Gravity's Rainbow*," *Twentieth Century Literature*, 2 (May 1975), pp. 193–210.

15 Max Black, "More about metaphor" in Ortony, Anthony (ed.) *Metaphor and Thought* (Cambridge: Cambridge University Press, 1979), pp. 26–7.

16 Gregory Bateson, *Steps to an Ecology of Mind* (New York: Ballantine Books, 1972), p. 315.

17 Benjamin Whorf, *Language, Thought and Reality* (Cambridge, Mass.: MIT Press, 1956).

18 See John R. Searle, "Metaphor," in Ortony, op. cit., p. 93.

19 Joseph W. Slade, *Thomas Pynchon* (New York: Warner, 1974), p. 219.

20 René Girard, *Deceit, Desire and the Novel*, trans. Yvonne Freccero (Baltimore: The Johns Hopkins Press, 1965).

21 René Girard, *The Violent and the Sacred*, trans. Patrick Gregory (Baltimore: The Johns Hopkins Press, 1978), p. 299.

22 "The cybernetics of self: a theory of addiction," in Bateson, op. cit., pp. 309–37.

CHAPTER SEVEN

1 John Barth, *Letters* (New York: G. P. Putnam's Sons, 1979), pp. 768–9.

2 Henri Bergson, "Laughter" (1900), trans. Fred Rothwell in Sypher, Wylie (ed.) *Comedy* (New York: Doubleday, 1956).

3 John Barth, "Lost in the funhouse," in *Lost in the Funhouse* (New York: Doubleday, 1968), p. 93.

4 John Barth, "Autobiography: a self-recorded fiction," in *Lost in the Funhouse*, op. cit.

5 All quotes are from John Barth, *Giles Goat-Boy* (New York: Fawcett-Crest, 1966).

6 Ulric Neisser, "Computers as tools and as metaphors," in Dechert,

Charles R. (ed.) *The Social Impact of Cybernetics* (New York: Simon & Schuster, 1966), p. 71.
7 Marshall McLuhan, "Cybernation and culture," in ibid., p. 103.
8 Morris Dickstein, *The Gates of Eden* (New York: Basic Books, 1977), p. 274.
9 ibid., p. 275.
10 John Barth, *Chimera* (New York: Doubleday, 1972).

CHAPTER EIGHT

1 *The Lost Ones* was originally written in French in the early 1950s as *Le Depeupleur*. The text is so brief that when it first appeared in English in 1972 it was printed on a single newspaper-sized page in *Fiction*, a little magazine edited at the time by Donald Barthelme.
2 All quotations are from Samuel Beckett, *The Lost Ones* (New York: Grove Press, 1972).
3 Hugh Kenner, *Samuel Beckett* (Berkeley, Ca: University of California Press, 1968), p. 49.
4 Don Crinklaw, *National Review* (19 January 1973), p. 101.
5 Laurence Graver, *Partisan Review*, v, 41 (Fall 1974), p. 622.
6 Joseph McElroy, *The New York Times Book Review* (29 October 1972), p. 4.
7 Susan D. Brienza, "*The Lost Ones*: the reader as searcher," *Journal of Modern Literature*, 6, pp. 148–68.
8 ibid., p. 154.
9 Eric P. Levy, "Looking for Beckett's *The Lost Ones*," *Mosaic*, 12, iii, p. 164.
10 Brienza, op. cit., p. 165.
11 ibid., p. 154.
12 Levy, op. cit., p. 163.
13 Samuel Beckett, *Watt* (New York: Grove Press, 1959; Paris: Olympia Press, 1953).
14 Levy, op. cit., p. 167.
15 Hugh Kenner, *Samuel Beckett* (Berkeley, Ca: University of California Press, 1968), p. 17. He also writes, "Now we can try to define Beckett's odd achievement, which is to move the mystery into the heart of the syntactic mechanism, encompassed and held by careful structures which sustain it, in all its evanescence, before our undeluded eyes." ("Shades of Syntax," in Cohn, Ruby (ed.) *Samuel Beckett* (New York: McGraw-Hill, 1975), p. 27.)

CHAPTER NINE

1 All quotations are from Joseph McElroy, *Plus* (New York: Alfred A. Knopf, 1976).

2 William Hendricks, "Style and structure of literary discourse," in Ringbom, Hakan (ed.) *Style and Text* (Stockholm: Sprakferlaget Skuptor AE, 1975), p. 72.

3 Viktor Shklovsky, "Art as technique," trans. and ed. Lee T. Lemon in *Russian Formalist Criticism: Four Essays* (Lincoln, Neb.: University of Nebraska Press, 1965), pp. 11–12. Hendricks translates the term as "de-automatization" whereas Lemon calls it "de-formalization."

4 Joseph McElroy, *The New York Times Book Review* (29 October 1972), p. 20

5 Thomas LeClair, *Chicago Review*, 30, iv, p. 86.

6 "Holding with Apollo 17," *The New York Times Book Review* (28 January 1973), pp. 27–9.

7 Tony Tanner, "Toward an ultimate topography: the work of Joseph McElroy," *Tri-Quarterly*, 36 (Spring 1970), pp. 214–252.

8 Joseph McElroy, *A Smuggler's Bible* (New York: Alfred A. Knopf, 1966).

9 Joseph McElroy, *Hind's Kidnap: A Pastoral on Familiar Airs* (New York: Alfred A. Knopf, 1969).

10 Tanner, op. cit., p. 201.

11 Joseph McElroy, *Lookout Cartridge* (New York: Alfred A. Knopf, 1974).

12 George Stade, *The New York Times Book Review* (2 February 1975).

13 Perhaps Merleau-Ponty's combination of structuralist and phenomenological ideas is more akin to McElroy's project than any strict structuralist formulation. On the one hand, traditional structuralist thought recognizes the complete interdependence of mechanism and some prior, more instinctive phenomenological expressiveness in language. As Ferdinand de Saussure wrote in *Cours de Linguistique Générale* (Paris: Payot, 1969), p. 145:

> Many have often compared the bilateral unity [of the signifier and the signified] to the unity of the human being, constituted by a body and a soul. This analogy is unsatisfactory. It would be more exact to compare it to a chemical compound, like water, which is a combination of hydrogen and oxygen. Taken separately, each of these elements has none of the properties of water.

But Merleau-Ponty extends this theory to note that there is something left out of the view of language as the route to or an expression of knowledge: before any act in language, speech or writing, there is *perception*: "our presence at the moment when things, truths, values, are constituted for us." A "nascent *logos*," perception "teaches us, outside all dogmatism, the true condition of objectivity . . . it summons us to the tasks of knowledge and action." (Maurice Merleau-Ponty, *The Phenomenology of Perception*, trans. Colin Smith (New York: Humanities Press, 1962), pp. 414–39.) Merleau-Ponty's phenomenological structuralism posits that the body is the place to look for the aboriginal source of expression, that language is the body's way of "singing the world," but that lying beneath even this desire to express is the inexpressible moment of perception which structures our apprehension of the truth and our later, more formal expression of it. For a more elaborate discussion of these views, see James M. Edie, *Speaking and Meaning: The Phenomenology of Language* (Bloomington, Ind.: Indiana University Press, 1976), pp. 72–123.)

14 Joseph McElroy, *Ancient History: A Paraphase* (New York: Alfred A. Knopf, 1971).

15 Joseph McElroy, "Neural neighborhoods and other concrete abstractions," *Tri-Quarterly*, 34 (Fall 1975).

16 Michael Polanyi, *Personal Knowledge* (Chicago: University of Chicago Press, 1964).

CONCLUSION

1 Donald Barthelme, *City Life* (New York: Farrar, Straus & Giroux, 1970).

2 Bruce Mazlish, "The fourth discontinuity," in Kranzberg, Melvin and Davenport, William (eds) *Technology and Culture* (New York: New American Library, 1972).

3 Freud even uses the metaphor of a writing device to describe the mechanism of the psyche in "Note on the mystical writing pad" (1925). For an interesting discussion of the notion, see Jacques Derrida's commentary on "Freud and the scene of writing," in *Writing and Difference* trans. Allan Bass (Chicago: University of Chicago Press, 1978), pp. 196–230.

4 Colin Turbayne, *The Myth of Metaphor*, rev. edn (Columbia, SC: University of South Carolina Press, 1970), p. 5.

5 Derrida, op. cit., p. 8.

6 All quotations are from Donald Barthelme, "The explanation," *City Life*, op. cit.

7 Jacques Ellul, *The Technological Society* (New York: Alfred A. Knopf, 1964), p. 206.

8 Gregory Bateson, *Steps to an Ecology of Mind* (New York: Ballantine Books, 1972). "A 'black box' is a conventional agreement among scientists to stop trying to explain things at a certain point" (p. 38).

BIBLIOGRAPHY

Aarsleff, Hans (1982) "John Wilkins," in *From Locke to Saussure: Essays on the Study of Language and Intellectual History*, Minneapolis, Minn., University of Minnesota Press.

Abernethy, Peter (1971) "Entropy in Pynchon's *The Crying of Lot 49*," *Critique*, 14, 18–33.

Abramson, N. (1963) *Information Theory and Coding*, New York, McGraw-Hill.

Achinstein, Peter (1964) "Models, analogies, and theories," *Philosophy of Science*, 31, 326–50.

Adams, Henry (1961) *The Education of Henry Adams*, Boston, Houghton-Mifflin.

Alter, Robert (1975) *Partial Magic: The Novel as a Self-Conscious Genre*, Berkeley, Ca, University of California Press.

Arbib, Michael A. (1972) *The Metaphorical Brain: An Introduction to Cybernetics as Artificial Intelligence and Brain Theory*, New York, Wiley & Sons.

Arnheim, Rudolf (1971) *Entropy and Art*, Berkeley, Ca, University of California Press.

Ashby, W. Ross (1956) *An Introduction to Cybernetics*, London, Chapman & Hall.

Attnaeve, T. (1961) *Applications of Information Theory to Psychology*, New York, Holt, Rinehart & Winston.

Barrett, William (1979) *The Illusion of Technique*, New York, Doubleday.

Barthes, Roland (1966) *Critique et verité*, Paris, Seuil.

Bateson, Gregory (1969) *Steps to an Ecology of Mind*, New York, Chandler Press.

Beer, Stafford (1959) *Cybernetics and Management*, New York, John Wiley & Sons.

Bell, Daniel (1973) *The Coming of the Post-Industrial Society*, New York, Basic Books.

Benthall, Jonathan (1972) *Science and Technology in Art Today*, London, Thames & Hudson.

Benzon, William L. (1982) "System and observer in semiotic modeling," in Herzfeld, Michael and Lenhart, Margot D. (eds) *Semiotics 1980*, New York, Plenum Press.

Berlyne, F. E. (1971) *Aesthetics and Psychobiology*, New York, Holt, Rinehart & Winston.

Black, Max (1968) *The Labyrinth of Language*, New York, Frederick A. Praeger.

Black, Max (1978) "More about metaphor," in Ortony, Andrew (ed.) *Metaphor and Thought*, Cambridge, Cambridge University Press, pp. 26–31.

Brienza, Susan D. (1976) "*The Lost Ones*: The reader as searcher," *Journal of Modern Literature*, 6, 148–68.

Buchanan, Scott (1962) *Poetry and Mathematics*, New York, Lippincott. (First published 1929.)

Calinescu, Matei (1975) "Avant-Garde, Neo-Avant-Garde, Postmodernism: The culture of crisis," *Clio*, 4, 317–40.

Carrouges, Michel (1955) *Les machines célibataires de Raymond Roussel*, Paris, Editions Arcanes.

Cassirer, Ernst (1926) *Die philosophie der symbolischen Formen*, 3 vols, Berlin, Bruno Cassirer. *Symbolic Forms* (1970) trans. Ralph Manheim, New Haven, Conn., Yale University Press.

Chomsky, Noam (1965) *Aspects of the theory of Syntax*, Cambridge, Mass., MIT Press.

Cohn, Ruby (ed.) (1975) *Samuel Beckett*, New York, McGraw-Hill.

Cox, Harvey (1971) "The virgin and the dynamo: An essay on the symbolism of technology," *Soundings*, 54, 125–46.

Crosson, Frederick (ed.) (1970) *Human and Artificial Intelligence*, New York, Appleton-Century-Crofts.

Crosson, Frederick and Sayre, K. M. (eds) (1967) *Philosophy and Cybernetics*, Notre Dame, Ind., University of Notre Dame Press.

Culler, Jonathan (1974) *Flaubert: The Uses of Uncertainty*, Ithaca, NY, Cornell University Press.

Culler, Jonathan (1972) *Structuralist Poetics*, Ithaca, NY, Cornell University Press.

Davenport, William H. (1973) "Anti-technological attitudes in modern literature," *Technology and Society*, 8, 7–14.

de Latil, Pierre (1953) *Thinking by Machine*, Paris, Gallimard; trans. Y. M. Golla, London, Sidgwick & Jackson, 1956.

Deleuze, Gilles (1972) *Proust and Signs*, New York, Braziller.

Deleuze, Gilles and Guattari, Felix (1977) *Anti-Oedipus*, New York, Viking Press.

Derrida, Jacques (1978) *Writing and Difference*, trans. Allan Bass, Chicago, University of Chicago Press.

Dickstein, Morris (1977) *The Gates of Eden: American Culture in the Sixties*, New York, Basic Books.

Dreyfus, Hubert L. (1972) *What Computers Can't Do: A Critique of Artificial Reason*, New York, Harper & Row.

Edge, David (1974) "Technological metaphor and social control," *New Literary History*, 6, 135–47.

Eliot, T. S. (1948) *From Poe to Valéry*, New York, Harcourt Brace Jovanovich.

Ellul, Jacques (1964) *The Technological Society*, trans. John Wilkinson, New York, Knopf.

Federman, Raymond (1975a) *Surfiction Now . . . and Tomorrow*, Chicago, Swallow Press.

Federman, Raymond (1975b) *Take It or Leave It*, New York, Fiction Collective.

Ferry, Jean (1953) *Une étude sur Raymond Roussel*, Paris, Editions Arcanes.

Foucault, Michel (1963) *Raymond Roussel*, Paris, Gallimard.

Franklin, H. Bruce (1978) *Future Perfect*, New York, Oxford University Press.

Freud, Sigmund (1958) "On the mechanism of paranoia" and "Psychoanalytic notes on an autobiographical account of a case of paranoia," in *The Standard Edition of the Complete Psychological Works of Sigmund Freud* vol. V, no. xii, Toronto.

Friedman, Alan J. (1973) Physics and literature in this century: A new course," *Physics Education*, 8, 305–8.

Friedman, Alan J. (1975) "The novelist and modern physics: New metaphors for traditional themes," *Journal of College Science Teachers*, 4, 310–12.

Friedman, Alan J. and Puetz, Manfred (1974) "Science as metaphor: Thomas Pynchon and *Gravity's Rainbow*," *Contemporary Literature*, 15, 345–59.

Girard, René (1965) *Deceit, Desire and the Novel*, trans. Yvette Freccero, Baltimore, Md, The Johns Hopkins University Press.

Girard, René (1978) *Violence and the Sacred*, trans. Patrick Gregory, Baltimore, Md, The Johns Hopkins University Press.
Grene, Marjorie (ed.) (1971) *Interpretations of Life and Mind*, New York, Humanities Press.
Gombrich, Ernst (1960) *Art and Illusion*, New York, Pantheon.
Guillen, Claudio (1972) *Literature as System*, Princeton, NJ, Princeton University Press.
Harris, Charles B. (1971) "Thomas Pynchon and the entropic vision," in *Contemporary American Novelists of the Absurd*, New Haven, Conn., Yale University Press.
Hassan, Ihab (1961) *Radical Innocence: The Contemporary American Novel*, Princeton, NJ, Princeton University Press.
Heidegger, Martin (1962) *Being and Time*, trans. John Macquerrie and Edwin Robinson, New York, Harper & Row.
Heidegger, Martin (1977) *The Question Concerning Technology and Other Essays*, trans William Lovitt, New York, Harper & Row.
Heisenberg, Werner (1958) *Physics and Philosophy*, New York, Harper & Row.
Heisenberg, Werner (1971) *Physics and Beyond*, New York, Harper & Row.
Heisenberg, Werner (1972) "The representation of nature in contemporary physics," in Sears, S. and Lord, G. W. (eds) *The Discontinuous Universe*, New York, Basic Books.
Hendricks, William (1975) "Style and the structure of literary discourse," in Ringbom, Hakan (ed.) *Style and Text*, Stockholm, Sprakferlaget Skuptor AB.
Heppenstall, Raynor (1967) *Raymond Roussel*, Berkeley, Ca, University of California Press.
Herzberg, Bruce (1978) "Illusions of control: A reading of *Gravity's Rainbow*," dissertation, Rutgers University.
Hill, Leslie (1979) "Raymond Roussel and the place of literature," *Modern Language Review*, 74 (4), 823–35.
Holton, Gerald (1973) *The Thematic Origins of Scientific Thought*, Cambridge, Mass., Harvard University Press.
Holton, Gerald (1978) *The Scientific Imagination*, Cambridge, Cambridge University Press.
Holtz, William (1971) "Thermodynamics and the comic and tragic modes," *World History Review*, 25, 23–16.
Horn, Peter (1973) "Poetic set theory and the technocratic consciousness," *Theoria*, 40, 19–32.
Ihde, Don (1979) *Technic and Praxis*, Boston, D. Reidel Publishing Co.
Iser, Wolfgang (1978) *The Act of Reading*, Baltimore, Md, The Johns Hopkins University Press.
Jayne, Edward (1976) "The dialectics of paranoid form," *Genre*, 11 (Spring), 131–57.

Kasson, John F. (1981) *Civilizing the Machine: Technology and Republican Values in America, 1776–1900*, New York, Grossman Press.

Kazin, Alfred (1970) *The Bright Book of Life*, Boston, Little, Brown.

Kenner, Hugh (1968) *Samuel Beckett*, Berkeley, Ca, University of California Press.

Kenner, Hugh (1973) *The Counterfeiters*, New York, Doubleday/Anchor.

Kenner, Hugh (1982) "On the centenary of James Joyce," *The New York Sunday Times Book Review*, 31 January.

Kepes, Gyorgy (1965) *Structure in Art and Science*, New York, Braziller.

Klinkowitz, Jerome (1975) *Literary Disruptions: The Making of a Post-Contemporary American Fiction*, Urbana, Ill., University of Illinois Press.

Kranzberg, Melvin and Davenport, William (eds) (1972) *Technology and Culture*, New York, New American Library.

Kuhn, Thomas (1962) *The Structure of Scientific Revolutions*, Chicago, University of Chicago Press.

Kurman, George (1975–6) "Entropy and the 'Death' of tragedy: Notes for a theory of drama," *Comparative Drama*, 9, 283–304.

Langer, Susan (1953) *Feeling and Form*, New York, Scribners.

LeClair, Thomas (1976) "Interview with Joseph McElroy," *Chicago Review*, 30 (4), 86.

LeClair, Thomas (1981) "*Something Happened* and the art of excess," *Studies in American Fiction*, Autumn, 245–60.

Leiris, Michel (1954) "Conception et rêalité chez Raymond Roussel," *Critique*, 89 (October), 821–35.

Leland, John P. (1974) "Pynchon's linguistic dream: *The Crying of Lot 49*," *Critique*, 16, 45–53.

Levy, Eric P. (1979) "Looking for Beckett's *The Lost Ones*," *Mosaic*, 12 (3), 163–9.

Lindsay, R. K. (1963) "Inferential memory as the basis of machines which understand natural languages," in Feigenbaum, E. A. and Feldman, J. (eds) *Computers and Thought*, New York, McGraw-Hill.

Lovitt, Carl (1974) "*Locus Solus*: Literary solitaire," *Sub-Stance*, 10, 95–109.

Luria, A. P. (1975) "Scientific perspectives and philosophical dead ends in modern linguistics," *Cognition*, 3 (4).

McElroy, Joseph (1972) Review of *The Lost Ones* by Samuel Beckett, *The New York Times Book Review*, 29 October, p. 4.

McElroy, Joseph (1973) "Holding with Apollo 17," *The New York Times Book Review*, 28 January, pp. 27–9.

McElroy, Joseph (1975) "Neural neighborhoods and other concrete abstractions," *Tri-Quarterly*, 34.

McLuhan, Marshall (1964) *Understanding Media: The Extension of Man*, New York, McGraw-Hill.

McLuhan, Marshall (1966) "Cybernation and culture," in Dechert, Charles D. (ed.) *The Social Impact of Cybernetics*, New York, Simon & Schuster.

McLuhan, Marshall (1969) *The Gutenberg Galaxy: The Making of Typographic Man*, New York, New American Library.

Marx, Leo (1964) *The Machine in the Garden: Technology and the Pastoral Ideal in America*, New York, Oxford University Press.

Massey, Irving (1970) *The Uncreating Word: Romanticism and the Object*, Bloomington, Ind., Indiana University Press.

Materer, Timothy (1973) "Wyndham Lewis: Satirist of the machine age," *SNL*, 10, 9–18.

Materer, Timothy (1977) "Pound's vortex," *Paideuma*, 6, 175–6.

Matthews, J. H. (1976) "Beyond realism: Raymond Roussel's machines," in Kaiser, Grant E. (ed.) *Fiction, Form and Experience*, Montreal, France-Quebec, 83–93.

Maturana, Humberto (1970) "Neurophysiology of cognition," in Garvin, Paul (ed.) *Cognition: A Multiple View*, New York, Spartan Books.

Mazlish, Bruce (1972) "The fourth discontinuity," in Kranzberg, Melvin and Davenport, William (eds) *Technology and Culture*, New York, New American Library.

Merleau-Ponty, Maurice (1962) *The Phenomenology of Perception*, trans. Colin Smith, London, Routledge & Kegan Paul.

Merleau-Ponty, Maurice (1964) *Signs*, trans. Richard McLeary, Evanston, Ill., Northwestern University Press.

Meyer, L. B. (1957) "Meaning in music and information theory," *Journal of Esthetics and Art Criticism*, 15 (4), June, 412–24.

Miller, Arthur I. (1978) "Visualization lost and regained," in Wechsler, Judith (ed.) *Aesthetic in Science*, Cambridge, Mass., MIT Press.

Moles, Abraham (1968) *Information Theory and Esthetic Perception*, trans. Joel E. Cohen, Urbana, Ill., University of Illinois Press.

Nadeau, Robert (1983) *Readings from the New Book on Nature*, Amherst, Mass., University of Massachusetts Press.

Nagel, Ernst (1961) *The Structure of Science*, New York, Harcourt, Brace & World.

Neisser, Ulric (1966) "Computers as tools and metaphors," in Dechert, Charles D. (ed.) *The Social Impact of Cybernetics*, New York, Simon & Schuster.

Ong, Walter J. (1971) *Rhetoric, Romance and Technology*, Ithaca, NY, Cornell University Press.

Ong, Walter J. (1977) *Interfaces of the Word*, Ithaca, NY, Cornell University Press.

Owen, John B. (1974) "Manacle-forged minds: Two images of the computer in science fiction," *Diogenes*, 85, 47–61.

Ozier, Lance W. (1974) "Antipointsman/Antimexico: Some mathematical imagery in *Gravity's Rainbow*," *Critique*, 16, 73–90.

Ozier, Lance W. (1977) "The calculus of transformation: Math in *Gravity's Rainbow*," *TCL*, 21, 193–210.

Pagels, Heinz R. (1982) *The Cosmic Code: Quantum Physics as the Language of Nature*, New York, Simon & Schuster.

Parseghian, V. L. (1972) *This Cybernetic World*, New York, Doubleday.

Pask, Gordon (1969) "The meaning of cybernetics in the behavioral sciences," in Rose, J. (ed.) *Progress in Cybernetics*, v. 14, New York, Gordon & Breach, 15–44.

Patterson, Richard (1972) "What stencil knew: Structure and certitude in Pynchon's *V.*," *Critique*, 16, 30–44.

Plater, William (1980) *The Grim Phoenix: Reconstructing Thomas Pynchon*, Bloomington, Ind., University of Indiana Press.

Polanyi, Michael (1959) *The Study of Man*, Chicago, University of Chicago Press.

Polanyi, Michael (1964) *Personal Knowledge*, New York, Harper.

Polanyi, Michael (1966) *The Tacit Dimension*, New York, Doubleday.

Polanyi, Michael (1969a) *Knowing and Being*, Chicago, University of Chicago Press.

Polanyi, Michael (1969b) *Meaning*, Chicago, University of Chicago Press.

Porush, David (1977) "Apocalypses of the sixties: The morphology of a literary genre," dissertation, State University of New York at Buffalo.

Porush, David (1980) "Technology and Postmodernism: Cybernetic fiction," *Sub-Stance*, 27 (Fall), 91–100.

Prigogine, Ilya (1971) "The unity of physical laws and levels of description," in Grene, Marjorie (ed.) *Interpretations of Life and Mind*, New York, Humanities Press.

Prigogine, Ilya (1981) *Being and Becoming*, Washington, DC, Scientific American.

Reichardt, Jasia (1974) "Twenty years of symbiosis between art and science," *Impact of Science on Society*, 24, 41–51.

Ricoeur, Paul (1977) *The Rule of Metaphor*, trans. Robert Czerny, Toronto, University of Toronto Press.

Riffaterre, Michael (1966) "Describing poetic structures," in Ehrmann, Jacques (ed.) *Structuralism*, New York, Doubleday.

Robbe-Grillet, Alain (1963) "Enigme et transparence chez Raymond Roussel," *Critique*, December.

Rousseau, G. S. (1972) "Are there really men of both 'cultures'?" *Dalhousie Review*, 52 (1933), 351–72.

Roussel, Raymond (1933) *Comment j'ai écrit certaine de mes livres*. Paris: Jean-Jacques Pauvert.

Russell, Charles (1975) "The vaults of language: Self-reflective artifice in contemporary American fiction," *Modern Fiction Studies*, 20, 349–59.

Serres, Michel (1982) "Hermes: Literature, Science, Philosophy," in

Harari, Josué V. and Bell, David F. (eds) *Hermes: Literature, Science, Philosophy*, Baltimore, Md, The Johns Hopkins University Press.

Shannon, Claude and Weaver, Warren (1949) *The Mathematical Theory of Communication*, Urbana, Ill., University of Illinois Press.

Simon, Herbert A. (1968) *The Sciences of the Artificial*, Cambridge, Mass., MIT Press.

Shklovsky, Viktor (1965) "Art as technique," in Lemon, L. T. and Reis, M. J. (eds) *Russian Formalist Criticism*, Lincoln, Neb., University of Nebraska Press, 3–24.

Slade, Joseph W. (1974) *Thomas Pynchon*, New York, Warner Paperback Library.

Smith, Cyril (1976) "On art, invention and technology," *Technology Review*, 78 (7), 2–7.

Stark, John (1980) *Pynchon's Fictions and the Literature of Information*, Athens, Oh., University of Ohio Press.

Steinberg, S. (1976) "The judgment in Kafka's 'In the penal colony'," *Journal of Modern Literature*, 3, 492–514.

Sussman, Herbert (1968) *Victorians and the Machine*, Cambridge, Mass., Harvard University Press.

Sypher, Wylie (1968) *Literature and Technology: The Alien Vision*, New York, Random House.

Tanner, Tony (1970) "Toward an ultimate topography: The work of Joseph McElroy," *Tri-Quarterly*, 36 (Spring), 214–52.

Tanner, Tony (1971) *City of Words: American Fiction 1950–1970*, New York, Harper & Row.

Tanner, Tony (1982) *Thomas Pynchon*, London and New York, Methuen.

Talor, Charles (1971) "How is mechanism conceivable?" in *Interpretations of Life and Mind*, New York, Humanities Press.

Turbayne, Colin Murray (1970) *The Myth of Metaphor*, rev. edn, Columbia, SC, University of South Carolina Press.

Valéry, Paul (1950) "Literature," in *Selected Writings*, trans. Louise Varese, New York, New Directions.

von Bertalanffy, Ludwig (1958) "General systems theory," *General Systems*, I.

von Bertalanffy, Ludwig (1969) *Robots, Men and Minds*, New York, Braziller.

von Foerster, Heinz (1979) "Cybernetics of cybernetics," in Krippendorff, Klaus (ed.) *Communication and Control in Society*, New York, Gordon & Breach.

Weizenbaum, Joseph (1976) *Computer Power and Human Reason*, San Francisco, W. H. Freeman.

Werner, Heinz (1970) *Comparative Psychology of Mental Development*, New York, International Universities Press.

Whorf, Benjamin (1956) *Language, Thought and Reality*, Cambridge, Mass., MIT Press.

Wiener, Norbert (1948) *Cybernetics: Control and Communication in Animal and Machine*, Cambridge, Mass., MIT Press, rev. edn 1961.

Wiener, Norbert (1954) *The Human Use of Human Beings*, New York, Doubleday/Anchor.

Wiener, Norbert (1964) *God and Golem, Inc.*, Cambridge, Mass., MIT Press.

Wilden, Anthony (1979) "Changing frames of order: Cybernetics and the *Machina Mundi*," in *Communication and Control in Society*, pp. 9–29.

Williams, Raymond (1967) *Communications*, New York, Barnes & Noble.

Winner, Langdon (1974) *Autonomous Technology: Technic-Out-Of-Control as a Theme in Political Thought*, Cambridge, Mass., MIT Press.

Zander, Arlen R. (1975) "Science and fiction: An interdisciplinary approach," *American Journal of Physics*, 43, 9–12.

Zavarzadeh, Mas'ud (1976) *The Mythopoeic Reality: The Postwar American Nonfiction Novel*, Urbana, Ill., University of Illinois Press.

Ziff, Paul (1964) "The feelings of robots," in Anderson, A. R. (ed.) *Minds and Machines*, Englewood Cliffs, NJ, Prentice-Hall.

INDEX